-THE PERSON IN WHOSE
HICLE IS REGISTERED MAY OR
BE THE LEGAL OWNER OF
E. PROSPECTIVE PURCHASERS
ED, THEREFORE, THAT THIS
ON BOOK IS NOT PROOF OF
NERSHIP.

Address of the Person registered
ncil whose Date Stamp is affixed
Person keeping the vehicle, the
which are given on page 8.

MR DENIS STEELS
APITALS) 127 REDHILL AVE
GLASSHOUGHTON
CASTLEFORD
Usual Signature } D Steel

(SEE NOTES 10—14 ON PAGE 2)

ATE OF LEEDS LTD.
APITALS) NEW YORK ROAD
LEEDS

Usual Signature }

(SEE NO

Usual Signa

(SEE

APITALS

4 B... TCE
LEEDS 11

Usual Signature } J A Stephens

Annual	£12 : 10 :	£15 : :	£1 7/0 :
Quarterly	£4 : 12 : [4 MONTHS]		

EXT...
REGISTRAT...

Registration Mark .... 6936 WX

(a) Taxation Class .... Private

(b) Make .... Morris

(c) Colour .... ~~...~~ Blue

(d) Type of Body .... Saloon

(e) Propelled by .... Petrol

(f) MANUFACTURER'S :—

Type or Model .... Minor 2door De Luxe

Chassis, Frame or Car No. } .... MA 253/1000086

Engine No. .... 9MUH . 502652

(g) Rating .... 948 cc

(h) Seating Capacity ....

(i) Unladen Weight

.... tons .... cwt .... lbs.

...under the
Act, 1949,
the above
Penalty

...ROAD, MAKE CERTAIN THAT ...
...US OFFENCE TO DRIVE WITHOUT PROPER INSURANCE.

To my wife, Kim and my two daughters Madeline and Isabelle,
who have supported me in pursuing my passion

To Mum and Dad, Ray and Phil – and all who contributed
with the restoration of the Million and production of this book

.... thanks a Million

National Library of Australia Cataloguing-in-Publication Data

McKellar, Richard, 1965 –

Morris Minor – "One in a Million" / Richard McKellar and Ray Newell

Photography	Richard McKellar, Kim McKellar and John Colley
Edition	1st ed.
ISBN	**978-0-646-53468-8** (hbk.)
Notes	Includes Index
Subjects	Morris Minor Automobile – Conservation and Restoration – Handbooks, Manuals, etc Morris Minor Automobile – History Automobile Rallies – Australia
Other Authors & Contributors	Newell, Ray, 1951 – McKellar, Kim Colley, John
Dewey Number	**629.222094**

Published in November 2010 by Richard McKellar Design
10 Golding Street Canterbury Victoria 3126 Australia
Fax +61 3 9836 4784 Email design@richardmckellardesign.com www.morrisminorgarage.com

Cover photography by Richard McKellar

Page design and layout by Richard McKellar Design

Text composition and editing by Ray Newell

Printed by INKON – 5/81 Denman Avenue Woolooware NSW 2230 Phone +61 2 9527 4628 Email inkonbooks@bigpond.com

www.morrisminorgarage.com

MORRIS MINOR

"One in a Million"

A Father and Son Restoration Adventure

RICHARD MCKELLAR DESIGN

GRAPHIC DESIGN & PUBLISHING

THE PARTS LISTED IN THE FOLLOWING PAGES ARE APPLICABLE ONLY TO THE MINOR 1,000,000 2-DOOR SALOON. ALL OTHER COMPONENTS CAN BE FOUND IN THE MAIN BODY OF THE LIST, PAGES A.1 TO T.5 INCLUSIVE.

THE MORRIS MINOR 1,000,000 2-DOOR SALOON

My Country *(I love a sunburnt country)*
– part 2 – first published 1908

by Dorothea MacKellar

I love a sunburnt country, a land of sweeping plains,
Of ragged mountain ranges, of drought & flooding rains.
I love her far horizons, I love her jewel sea,
Her beauty & her terror – the wide brown land for me.
Australia – for me.

Core of my heart my country, land of the rainbow gold,
For flood & fire & famine, she pays us back three fold.
But when the grey clouds gather and we can bless again,
The drumming of an army, the steady soaking rain.
I love a sunburnt country, a land of sweeping plains,
Of ragged mountain ranges, of drought & flooding rains.
I love her far horizons, I love her jewel sea,
Her beauty & her terror – the wide brown land for me.
Australia – for me.

An opal hearted country, a wilful lavish land.
All you who have not loved her, you will not understand.
Though earth holds many splendours, where ever I may die,
I know to what brave country my homing thoughts will fly,
They will fly –

I love a sunburnt country a land of sweeping plains,
Of ragged mountain ranges, of drought & flooding rains.
I love her far horizons, I love jewel sea,
Her beauty & her terror – the wide brown land for me.
Australia – for me.

PLEASE QUOTE WHEN RE-ORDERING

Confidential until 4th January 1961

MORRIS MINOR MILLION

O.P.S. A FEAT UNIQUE IN THE HISTORY OF BRITISH INDUSTRY

One million vehicles of common design and the greatest British-made selling car in any class. Built as a quality car and never down to the cheapest price, the Morris Minor has sold all over the world and 48 per cent of production has been exported.

A triumph for design genius Alec Issigonis who translated his revolutionary ideas of construction, suspension, engine capacity and passenger accommodation into a popular-priced car, the Morris Minor is a miracle of engineering and commercial achievement.

Copyright Free: Press Office, Morris Motors Ltd., Cowley, Oxford.

96608/9

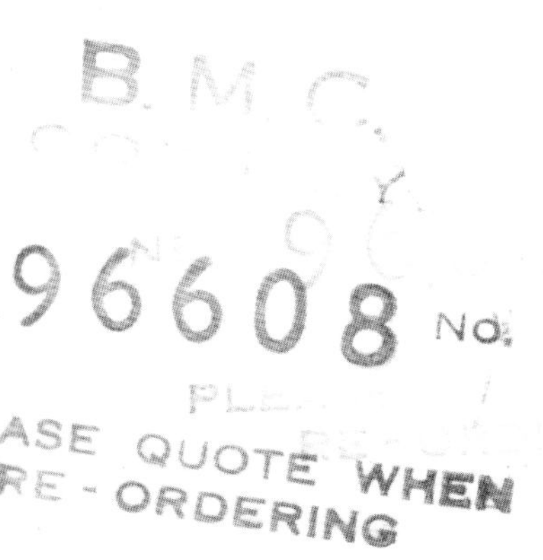

Contents

MINOR 1000 2-DOOR SALOON

"One in a Million"

The Morris Minor was the first British car to sell a million units. As that milestone approached, the British Motor Company (BMC) decided to mark the occasion by producing a limited edition vehicle. Though commonplace today, this was a new concept in 1960. Appropriately named the Minor Million, this unique vehicle was limited to 350 units.

Although standard 948cc Morris Minor 1000 two door saloons were used, the Millions were distinguished by vivid lilac paintwork.

Other external features included chrome wheel rim embellishers and special 1,000,000 badges which were fitted on the sides of the bonnet and on the boot lid.

The interior sported 'white gold' leather seats with black piping and contrasting black carpets.

The actual millionth car rolled off the production line on the 22nd December 1960.

The cars were distributed to all the BMC dealers in the UK, so that every showroom had a Minor Million on display for the official launch date of the 4th January 1961. 30 of the 349 replicas were sent to overseas distributors.

The car which is the subject of this restoration story, car (1,000,086) was built in Cowley, England on the 13th December 1960, and dispatched on the 22nd December 1960 to Appleyard Limited in Leeds, England.

Registered 6936WX, this car spent most of its life in the County of Yorkshire until it was taken off the road in 1978.

The car was advertised in 1993 and was purchased sight unseen. Shipped from Southhampton (UK), it was imported to Melbourne, Australia using a roll-on-roll-off shipping method. For a number of years the car was used to teach the kids to drive before being restored, returning it to its former glory. Restoration was completed in 2010 by Bill and Richard McKellar.

You'll welcome the wonder of brilliant motoring in the MORRIS MINOR 1000

Foreword by Ray Newell

This book charts in detail the restoration of a very special Morris Minor to the highest possible standard. However, it does much, much more than that. It details the trials, tribulations, traumas and triumphs of a father and son working together towards a common goal. What is all the more remarkable is the fact that they undertake the restoration of a much loved British car in a remote location in the Australian Bush.

Richard and Bill McKellar are not professional restorers. However, they are most definitely enthusiastic and dedicated Morris Minor devotees. Bill is a retired Bank Manager and Richard is Creative Director in his own Graphic Design and Advertising Company based in Melbourne. Nevertheless, through sheer hard work and dedication they have overseen the transformation of what Richard engagingly describes as a 'bitser' car, to one that would grace any Concours d'Elegance competition.

Their enthusiasm shines through the text which is written with feeling and contains lots of practical advice gained from first hand experience. Technical manual it is not. However, it is an invaluable guide to the practical aspects of completing the many detailed and often complicated tasks which the home based restorer inevitably has to grapple with. One of the main strengths of the book is the quality of the photographic material. A picture is worth a thousand words is an oft quoted saying and within this book it certainly rings true. What is also significant is that although the vehicle in question is a limited edition model, it is in essence a standard 2 door Morris Minor Saloon. As Richard points out the principles involved are equally applicable to any Morris Minor, though the detail specifications may vary slightly from model to model.

Though modest about their achievements, it is fair to say that the range of the advice, guidance and information provided here is impressive.

Richard and Bill would be thrilled to bits if, through their efforts in completing the restoration and charting their progress, they encouraged other like minded enthusiasts to complete the restoration of their own Morris Minor wherever they are in the world.

With this publication at their side they will be better placed to do so.

Ray Newell.

Ray Newell

Additional contributions to the book by Ray Newell, an acknowledged authority on the Morris Minor, provide an insight into the historical aspect of the Morris Minor Million story and some factual information about some of the other Minor Million survivors. Given the high standard of the restoration undertaken, Ray reviews the Concours scene, and along with Richard adds useful guidance to would be and current competitors including an insight into the rules and regulations governing this prestigious aspect of Classic Car ownership.

All in all a fascinating book with something for everyone with an interest in older vehicles.

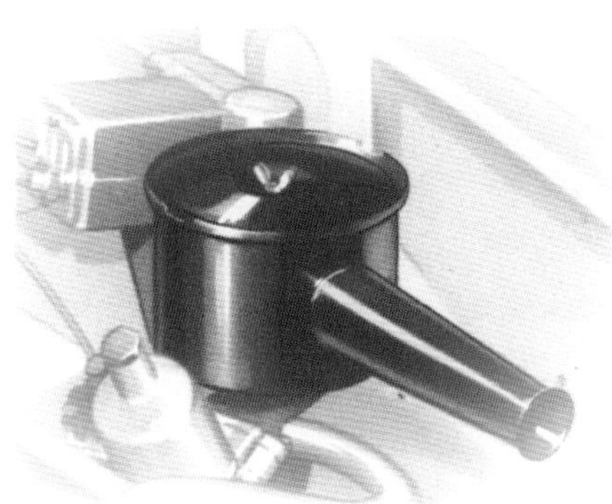

Meet the 'Bitser', the 'Blue Bomb'

above: Madeline at age 13, with my lovely wife Kim, holding on... Another enthusiastic lap around the olive grove, across the drive and into the front paddock, before pulling up just in time with a skid in front of the shed.

right: Isabelle at age 11, doing a few 'Kangaroo hops' as the rear wheels spin, the engine screams and the Minor launches into next year.

Lessons I kept in mind while restoring

Rod Stewart taught me a good lesson in lyrics from the song 'Young Turks' – *"time is a thief when you're undecided* "– my Dad repeats this to me every time I head back to Melbourne – *"time is a thief."*

Nan McKellar also shared a good lesson with me as she was connected to oxygen in her last years... she pulled me aside and said to me *"can you run,"* of which I replied yes... *"well run like the wind while you can,"* because there will come a time when you cannot.

Dad's tip... which he repeats to the waiter every time we go into a restaurant... *"you want a tip, be good to your mother..."*

All these tips came in very handy as I used them along the way, and I kept them in mind and thought about the kind words said of those that have influenced our lives and what we do in the quiet moments of restoring.

'The Blue Bomb' *(where the story really starts)*

A birth right of most Australian kids that grow up on the land, is to learn to drive in an old car, usually a Holden, Ford or Morris Minor. Regardless of the vehicle's origins, it's usually referred to as 'The Paddock Basher' or 'The Bomb'.

'Bashers' sometimes have a white circle with a racing number painted on the side to create the illusion of extra speed and most have a few dints along the front and back where they have been used to open and shut farm gates. Some cars receive particularly rough treatment and are even driven into dams from time to time – just to see what the consequences would be. Inevitably, an old grey 'Fergie' tractor would be pressed into service as a recovery vehicle.

Once other distractions and interests, particularly those in the opposite sex, take priority, interest in the cars wane and they usually end up parked under a tree in the top paddock. The battery is allowed to run down, and the slow "rust in peace process" begins. (and grass starts to grow in places where it would normally not grow... a bit like ear hair!) In Australia this is a common sight on most, if not all, rural properties.

The McKellar family are well acquainted with the above scenario, and although in the case of Madeline and Isabelle, the driving pace was slower, no numbers were painted on the side and no dams were involved, their introduction to driving was by way of what we lovingly called 'The Blue Bomb'. Fortunately that was not the end of the story. Although at times parked under a tree in the paddock, with the battery flat and the tyres deflated, 6936 WX was destined to be revived and returned to its former glory.

'The Blue Bomb' was a 'bitser', even before we purchased it. It had a front section from another Morris Minor, possibly a Roseberry Cream coloured car and four different coloured wheels. It certainly had mechanical components swapped from other Morris Minors, presumably to keep it going in times of strife. However, it did have some redeeming features. It did differ a little to other Minors in the paddock. It had shades of lilac coming through the light blue paint, and as Madeline and Isabelle began to use it less and less, thoughts turned to embarking on another project and returning 'The Blue Bomb' to its original specification... WHAT A STORY THAT WAS DESTINED TO BE.

Death of the Morris Minor

l-r: Percy Scicluna (long time friend and Morris expert) with Bill McKellar, fossicking for a suspension part in the organic Morris Garden, under a large old gum tree in the corner of the property at North Harcourt, Victoria.

Just some of the donated cars which continue to provide a treasure trove of parts for future restorations.

A testament to all the unfinished projects and 'loved to death' Morris Minors.

Loved to Death

Morris Minors in Australia usually have a slow death by literally being loved to pieces.

Back in the days when Morris Minors were still being built, Mum, Dad, Aunty Ethel, or Grandma McKellar would purchase a car, new or second hand. The car would be serviced regularly, kept undercover, and washed and polished religiously. Some owners even kept log books and service records as a testament to their love and commitment to their Minor. Most, if not all cars were given names... like Dot or Amanda Jane. Even regal names like Edward and Elizabeth were used. The Morris Minor was regarded as a family member and treated with the utmost love and respect.
As time went on larger Holdens and Fords found themselves in the driveways of Australian homes, mainly because the larger cars were deemed to be more suitable for covering the vast distances between friends and family members.

The ever resilient Minor found a new lease of life as a respectable second car for mum to do the shopping in and for picking up the kids from school in the wet weather.

By the late 1970's, with many of the cars having provided over twenty five years reliable service, many owners decided to retire their cars to back sheds, cover them up and put them up on wooden blocks.
It seems that they just could not contemplate parting with their now old and outdated family member.

Some were reluctantly sold to students and driven until they were totally worn out.

As a boy it was not an uncommon sight to see Minors in back sheds, or to find a couple of 'utes' tucked away in machinery sheds on local farms. Rural Australians helped my Minor spotting as they tended to park their unused Minors (as well as their more recent outdated cars) under trees in the back paddock for some protection from the elements.

As years passed a new generation of Minor owners emerged – our generation. With renewed interest in older vehicles and the emergence of enthusiast clubs, many new owners began restoring Morris Minors, and as a result, many cars found their way back on to roads.

However, not all the vehicles were completed. Though full of good intentions

A familiar sight. The author lying underneath a donated donor car, harvesting a drive shaft. In Australian terms this car would be considered rusted out and not worthy of repair or restoration. The scenario would be quite different in the UK, where cars with far more deterioration are frequently rebuilt to Concours standard.

Below a rescued 1959 Minor 1000 motor for future use from the above vehicle.

and fired with enthusiasm, many would-be restorers would happily pull a car down, take the doors off, strip out the inside trim, pull the motor out and strip off the paint for a new paint job... but then the project would stall. Enthusiasm would diminish, as thoughts of 'what to do next' would take over. Time would pass and the cars would end up being advertised as 'unfinished projects' in newspapers or club publications.

The cycle would begin again as another enthusiastic person would add the Morris Minor shell and associated component to their existing collection. Interestingly enough, possibly due to the amount of space we have in Australia, it is not uncommon to find enthusiasts who own many unfinished projects. Some have up to twenty or thirty cars. Often these cars remain unfinished projects. Fortunately some become a welcome source of parts. Some useful parts get sold at swap meets or are simply given away to support other projects.

In recent years I have probably been given about eight complete cars, and possibly about as many cars again in pieces.

At one point a good friend Dr. Dave Warren *(inventor of the famous Black Box Flight Recorder, and self confessed Morris Minor fanatic, and founder of the Morris Minor Car Club of Victoria)* had over forty cars complete or in component form in his back and front yard at his home in Melbourne. Much of Dave's collection now resides under my parents' house at their North Harcourt property.

My contacts in the UK advise me that the pattern of unfinished restoration projects is just as prevalent there. If anything it is made worse by the problems associated with rust. Years of being exposed to grit salt on the roads, coupled with a climate which is much wetter than Australia, means that the tin worm bites much harder in UK based cars and adds to the overall restoration costs. Having said that there are many very impressive and stunningly restored UK based Morris Minors which have been resurrected from graveyards of Morris Minors scattered throughout Britain.

Restoration Space

The ideal shed and workspace to restore a Morris Minor in. Clean and dry with plenty of workspace and fresh air. The workspace certainly ticked all the boxes. The only problem was that it was a two hour journey to get there from my home in Melbourne. This created added pressure as activities had to be carefully planned to make most use of the time available. This meant early mornings and late nights as the planned tasks always took much longer than anticipated.

Introducing 'The Shed'

With our restoration, the plan from the outset was to make the whole process as easy and straightforward as possible.

Planning the project from start to finish played a major part in keeping the restoration on track. The first decision was to find a suitable undercover area that would be large enough to accommodate thousands of components, most of which would no longer be bolted together. Having comfortable working surroundings was also high on the list of priorities.

Fortunately I did not have to look very far at all as my father had the perfect facility. In fact, it was almost too good to be true. Many home-based restorers would consider it a place to die for.

'The Shed', as it is affectionately known, is very large, clean, spacious building, equipped with a pot belly (wood burning) stove. In winter this meant that the work area could be pre-heated before work commenced. Another advantage which proved to be a godsend, and improved our comfort no end, was the fact that we were able to carpet the floor area using some second hand carpet which had been kindly donated. Coping with extremes of temperature in Australia is an occupational hazard. Fortunately 'The Shed' was well insulated. This combined with two large roller shutter doors, which could be opened to help air flow, provided some respite from the high summer temperatures which on occasions soared above 45°C (113F). In winter the pot belly stove provided much needed warmth.

'The Shed' is well equipped, and throughout the restoration, we were grateful to have the workbench, complete with vice, as well as a wealth of storage space for the ever expanding list of new and replacement parts.

The only down side for me was the fact that the journey from my home in Canterbury in Melbourne to 'The Shed' took two hours. I spent a lot of hours travelling between Harcourt and Melbourne by car during the course of the restoration! Tiring days indeed!

Safety

Safety can not be taken lightly.
It is very important to keep your work place tidy and always wear appropriate safety equipment.
This photo was taken early on by Bill to demonstrate this point. You really needed to wear ear protection to use this vacuum cleaner it was so loud!

Safety Makes the Top of the List

It goes without saying that working on a car is fraught with danger. Before attempting any activity the first thing to do is to disconnect the earth strap on the battery. Before working under the car, ensure that it is supported by axle stands and that the wheels which are in contact with the ground are chocked so that the vehicle cannot roll off the axle stands. As an extra precaution it is a good idea to place some wheels or tyres underneath the vehicle.

Draining the fuel from the tank, and allowing the fuel tank to dry out is another wise precaution. In our restoration, the petrol tank was removed very early on in the stripping down process, so as to prevent fuel igniting due to a spark from a grinder or electric drill.

Fumes from petrol pose a greater danger than the liquid itself, as the fumes are heavier than air. It is important to remember that brake fluid is also highly flammable and dangerous.

Personal Protection

Eye protection: From experience it is advisable to wear safety glasses for activities around the vehicle and goggles when working underneath.

Ear protection: is often overlooked, but it is important to use ear defenders, particularly when using grinders and power tools.

Gloves and Clothing

Be sure to use gloves and cover up as much as possible particularly when using stripper and acid to remove paint. Make sure you have a bucket of water on hand for neutralizing paint stripper that may accidently splash on to skin and clothes. Always make full use of any appropriate safety clothing.

Keeping the Workspace Area Safe

Cleanliness is next to godliness. Keeping the restoration area as clean as possible is not always a priority when work is in progress. Nevertheless it pays to give this attention as trip and slip hazards can result in personal injury and even damage to the vehicle you are restoring.

Fortunately in our restoration I could rely on my father, (Bill), who was always more aware of the need for tidying up and reducing risks than I was.

He would step in and tidy things as I went... although it did get a bit frustrating at times especially when a screwdriver was put away the second I put it down. However, this really was a small price to pay considering the space, comfort, facilities, company and support he constantly provided. I must admit if I was ever going to trip over, spill or mess things up... it would happen at the end of the day, when perhaps my concentration levels were not at their best... so another safety point could be 'slow down at the end of the day'.

Even though I was very safety conscious at all times, and constantly reminded by my father of possible hazards, I still have a few battle scars following the restoration. In spite of my best endeavours I still slipped up.

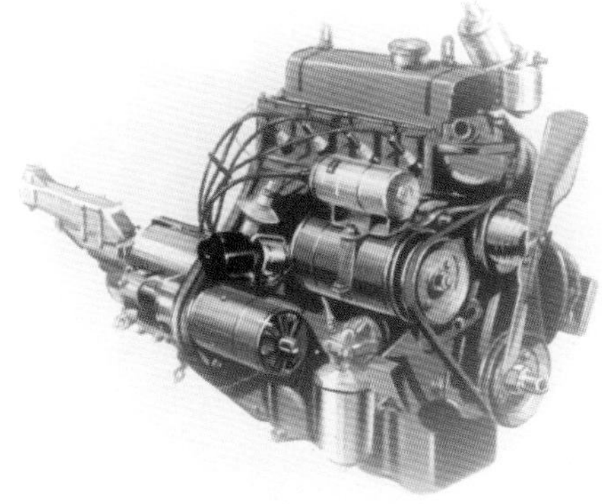

Careful Planning

A Concours Restoration?

When approaching any new project it is important to have a clear idea of what the final outcome is likely to be. Both Bill and I were able to approach the restoration of the 'Blue Bomb' with a fair degree of confidence, having previously restored a number of vehicles together. However, it had been ten years since we restored our last Minor, a 1959 Morris 1000 Traveller. 'Edward' the Woodie was a private import to Australia in the mid 1960's and Travellers were a rare sight on Australian roads. Not many Travellers were imported either, and none were assembled in Australia. 'Edward' had been restored to a very high standard in time for the 'Fifty Years Celebrations' of the Morris Minor in 1998. At the time of the restoration only a limited amount of new or reproduction parts were available, so it was a case of using the best of what was available. The wood kit and other components were purchased from Steve Foreman (ST Foreman Woodies), and imported from the UK. 'Edward' was painted with Acrylic lacquer and fortunately the vehicle has stood the test of time as far as the restoration process is concerned. Fortunately, like childbirth, the pain and expense of 'Edward's' restoration had been long forgotten when attention turned to the new project. Questions remained though.

What type of restoration should this be? What can be afforded both in terms of time and money?

Having been involved with judging Concours cars at the Australian National Rally since 1987 and having been mightily impressed by the standard of UK based Concours cars as featured in Ray Newell's book Original Morris Minor, I was inclined to go for a top notch restoration to recreate a Minor Million just as it would have left the factory back in 1960. Encouragement came from two sources. Dad who was 100 per cent behind me, so much so that he agreed to underwrite the project by 50%, and an unlikely friend in the form of modern technology. The emergence of the worldwide web and eBay in particular, added hope that all the necessary parts to rebuild the car to the highest standard could be obtained, if necessary, from all corners of the world. Another significant decision was then needed.

Was this to be a cheque book restoration?

By this I mean was all the work to be sub contracted to professional restorers? Most definitely not was the consensus view. Where possible this was to be a home based restoration with the vast majority of the work being undertaken by the McKellars.

More than one cheque book might be needed, but this was a necessity to acquire quality parts for what would be a quality restoration of "One in a Million".

above: 1959 Morris Minor awaiting restoration. Rust is a big problem with the English built vehicles.

Lilac was not a popular colour. Like many of the limited edition Millions, this one was painted a light shade of blue, inside and out, early in its life. Note the lilac creeping in through the worn paint on the boot.

Join a Car Club

'Edward', our 1959 Morris Minor 'Woodie' at the "Day of the Morris Minor 60th Year Celebrations" – Caribbean Gardens in Victoria in 2008. One of the many excellent family car club events run by the Morris Minor Car Club of Victoria.

Every two years since 1983, a Morris Minor National Rally has been held in Australia. These rallies are held in major cities. Members of Morris Minor Clubs throughout Australia drive extraordinary distances over many days in their cars to attend such events.

McKellar Tip – Join a local car club before embarking on a restoration.

Advice for Young and Old Players

Possibly the best advice anyone can have when contemplating restoring a Morris Minor, or any car for that matter, is to join a car club. If a single make club exists consider joining that one. The advantages are many, but the main one is that it will open up to you a pool of like minded members willing to pass on their knowledge, often free of charge. They can point you in the right direction in locating specialist services and local contacts. We are members of several local and National Australian car clubs. However, it has been the membership of the Morris Minor Owners Club in the UK that has paid us dividends, particularly through their publication 'Minor Matters'.

This has linked us to the UK, where our restoration car was built. It is important to note that Australian built cars differ somewhat from their English counterparts. Components like fresh air heaters and heating connections, seating patterns and materials, door frames are just a few of the areas of difference.

Local knowledge of these cars abounds in the many Australian Morris Minor Cars Clubs.

The Spending Begins

A Starting Point – Purchase What I Can

After an extensive appraisal of the car and before any dismantling, the decision was taken to purchase as many of the necessary parts as soon as possible.

A very long list of parts which needed to be sourced was compiled and the process began. From the outset it was agreed that where possible we would try to source New Old Stock items (NOS). eBay became increasingly important in our quest. Bidding was fun. Acquiring the parts was exciting but there was the occasional mix-up. On at least two occasions Bill and I discovered we were bidding against each other for the same part.

One eBay purchase of some note was the acquisition of a (NOS) Smith's speedometer still in its original box. It was a 'must have' item which still takes pride of place.

Rubber

The list started with rubber components. In the end this became an extensive list as the decision was taken to replace as many of the rubber components as possible with new. The list read as follows: windscreen, back window, side window, quarter vent window rubbers, all door seals and draught rubbers, boot seal rubber, steering gaiter rubbers, suspension rubbers, gear stick grommet, pedal rubbers, engine firewall grommets. These were mainly purchased locally from Scotts Old Auto Rubber in Melbourne but some were acquired from Bull Motif in the UK.

Tyres

When built at Cowley, 1960/61 Morris Minors were fitted with Dunlop C41 5.00-14 cross ply tyres. Unfortunately this particular brand of tyres has not been in production for many years. After some time consuming research, some similar specification 5.20-14 tyres were sourced in the UK. However, the cost of purchasing and then importing the tyres to Australia so early in the pre-restoration process meant that this option was ruled out. A compromise was needed.

The eagerly awaited new upholstery kit arrives. The leather seat coverings are supplied in kit form ready to assemble to the seat frames. Newton Commercial in the UK took time and care in matching the originals.

The seat frames were stripped clean and welded before being spray painted with black 'Kill Rust' – epoxy resin for extra protection.

A set of cross plys were sourced locally from Antique Tyre Supplies in Melbourne. Fortunately these tyres had a similar tread pattern to the original Dunlops and gave the correct appearance. Five tyres complete with tubes were purchased.

McKellar Tip – If possible, purchase a matching set of five new tyres. When vehicles are judged in Concours competition, points are deducted for a spare tyre that does not match the rest of the tyres fitted. It is surprising how many cars are presented in the Concours arena with non matching tyres.

Glass and Windows

'Wheels and windows are all that matter...' This was a lesson learnt whilst detailing cars as a young boy growing up in Rutherglen (Victoria) from a good friend and car dealer, Gordon MacKinlay. Over the years this has proved particularly true in the preparation of Concours vehicles. Many owners miss this point when presenting their cars and often wonder why the car parked next to them looks in better condition. Glass matters big time. For this reason a new windscreen was purchased and local Castlemaine (Victoria) glazier, Ray Charlten was commissioned to cut and harden new glass for the side windows, quarter vent and rear side windows. The rear window had the remains of the original 'Appleyard of Leeds' dealer transfer adhered to it, and the original BMC glass standard marks were clear to see. For these reasons the decision was taken to keep the rear screen and reuse it. The quarter vent windows also had the glass standard marks, so the newly cut ones were dispensed with, in the interest of maintaining a degree of originality.

Wiring Loom

A reproduction wiring loom was purchased from a local manufacturer. This was produced to the exacting original standards, complete with the correct cloth pattern and red Morris stripe. Unfortunately this worked out to be a very expensive option. Had our research been a bit more thorough we could have purchased a reproduction loom from the UK for half the price. A lesson learnt.

Upholstery and Carpets

The main difference between a Minor 1,000,000 and a standard 1960 Morris Minor is the upholstery and colour scheme. The upholstery was produced to deluxe specification, ie white-gold leather tops and vinyl sides with black piping.

Door cards were plain white vinyl with leather door pulls. These needed to be reproduced as close as possible to the original. Black carpets were also required, as well as the black cloth covered sealing rubbers positioned around the door openings.

A grey headlining and matching new grey sun visors were also required as one original visor was missing and the hood lining was ripped in places.

Original samples of what was left of the upholstery were sent to Heritage approved trim specialists, Newton Commercial, in the UK. They proved they were up to the challenge and were able to provide a very close match. A full kit was purchased from Newton Commercial including new seat squabs (rubber padding) / straps and all associated covers and clips. The standard of service offered by Newton Commercial was impressive.

Chrome Trim and Brightwork

The Minor 1,000,000 has more chrome than the standard 948cc Morris Minor. Wheel embellishers adorn the wheels. Three of these survived from the original car. eBay came to the rescue and four new old stock (NOS) trims were purchased from the UK.

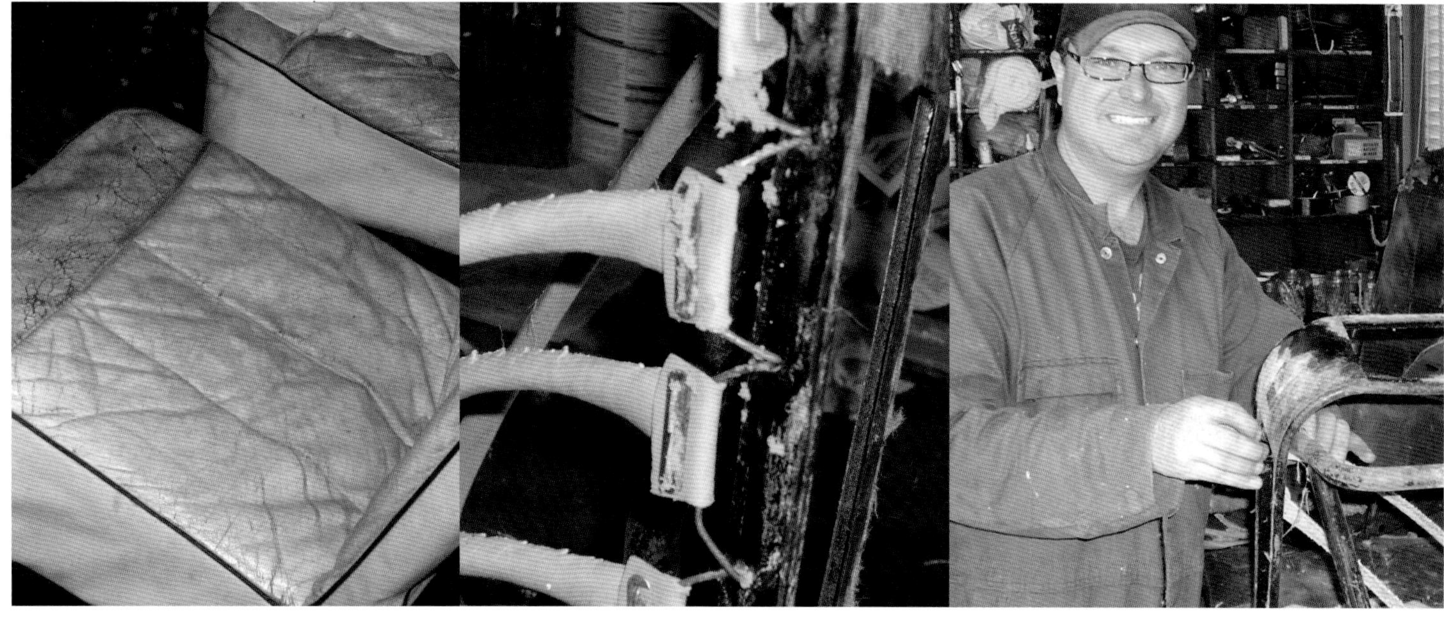

Original Morris Minor 1,000,000 front seats Complete with the black piping.

above right: New straps required. Cleaning up the seat frames in preparation of welding and painting.

below: Morris Minor 1,000,000 rear seat dressed in leather. Door cards and side panels are matching white vinyl. Detailed black piping on back armrests (not pictured).

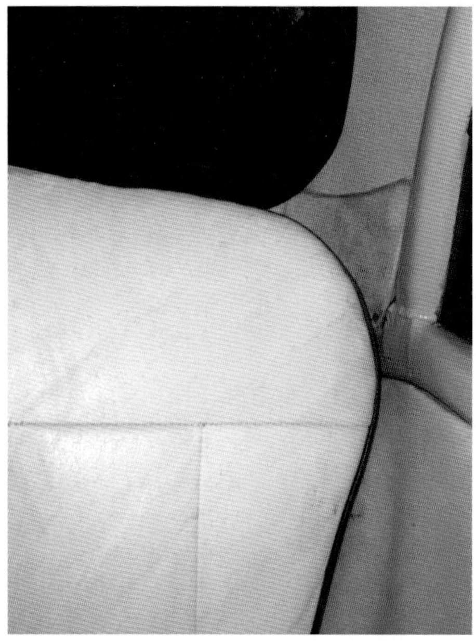

Even though the embellishers were standard on the Minor Millions, they were also available as an optional BMC (British Motor Company) accessory.

Chrome fittings such as the grille top moulding and hockey sticks were badly pitted and required replacing. The bull badge and M-flash on the bonnet were replaced with NOS items found on eBay.

The original 1,000,000 bonnet and boot badges were retained and carefully polished. NOS or reproductions are not available.

Chrome Bumpers and Overriders

The original bumper blades and over-riders needed to be re-chromed. They were carefully removed and expertly panel beaten to remove any signs of battle scars. The hub caps were also removed (and better examples were found). Light bezels (inner and outer) were removed and better ones sourced. All of the above components were taken to a specialist chrome plating company in Melbourne. Unfortunately this worked out to be another very expensive option. Even though the finished products were of a very high standard, it later transpired that the same components could have been purchased as 'off the shelf' items in the UK for half the price. Unfortunately at that time, we were unaware that commercially produced replacement items were available.

Door and Boot Handles

Replacement door and boot handles were sourced using eBay.

Head Lamps

Thorpe, from Morris Minor Australia, in Melbourne stocks boxes of the correct Lucas pre-focus head lamps, still in original boxes. As the lights are very much the eyes of the Minor, a set was a prudent purchase. I could hardly get my money out of my pocket quick enough.

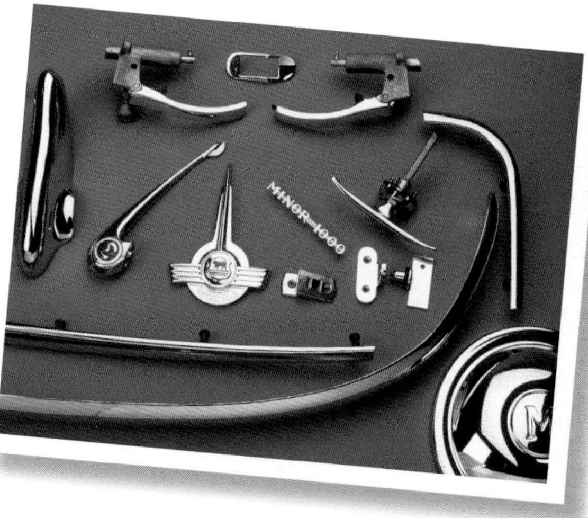

Purchasing the Upholstery

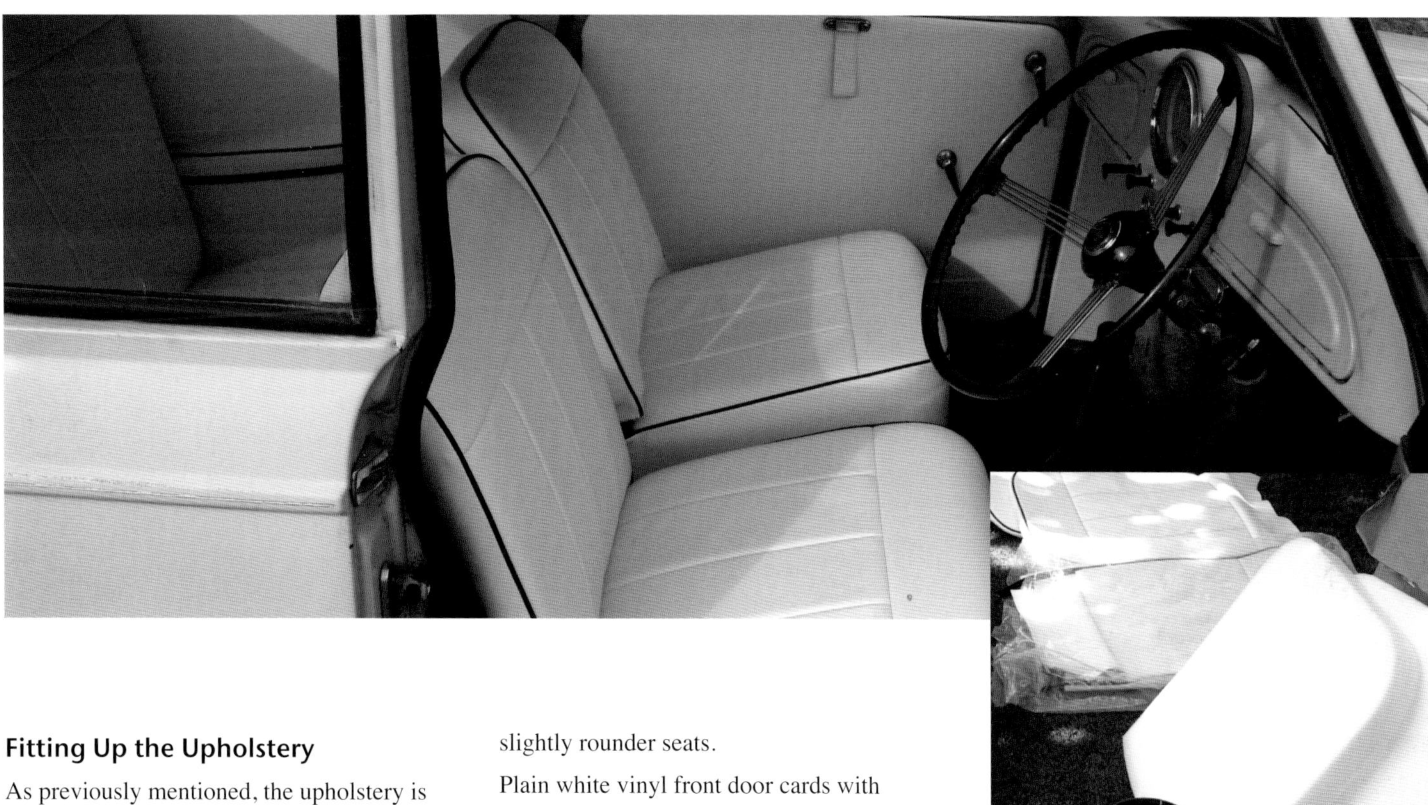

Fitting Up the Upholstery

As previously mentioned, the upholstery is one of the most important and distinctive features of the Minor Million. In order to achieve the best possible results it was decided to outsource the fitting of the seat covers. A local upholsterer, by the name of Charles Sultana was commissioned to undertake the fitting of the new covers to the restored seat frames.

Charlie's initial idea was to 'pimp' the seats up a bit with some extra padding and perhaps add a bit of 'bling'. His enthusiasm was somewhat curbed when shown page 75 of Ray Newell's 'Original Morris Minor' book.

After some polite persuading, Charlie fitted the covers to the seat frames to the original specification. Much care was taken to match perfectly the pleats on the back rest and base seat facings.

The interior trim of the Minor Million adopted the broad-panel style – the second of three trim patterns found on the 948cc between 1959-61. At this time the seat frames were modified to give the back rest and base an updated and more modern, squarer appearance. This stands in marked contrast to most of the Australian cars of this era which retained the fussier five pleated panels with slightly rounder seats.

Plain white vinyl front door cards with a stitched leather door pull were the order of the day. Matching armrests with complementing black trim contrasted well with the black carpets.

above: The newly upholstered seats and trim sitting in position for reference.

right: Laying all the seat components out to determine the degree of difficulty. Opting to outsource the upholstery proved a wise decision. If only a similar decision had been made with the fitting of the headlining.

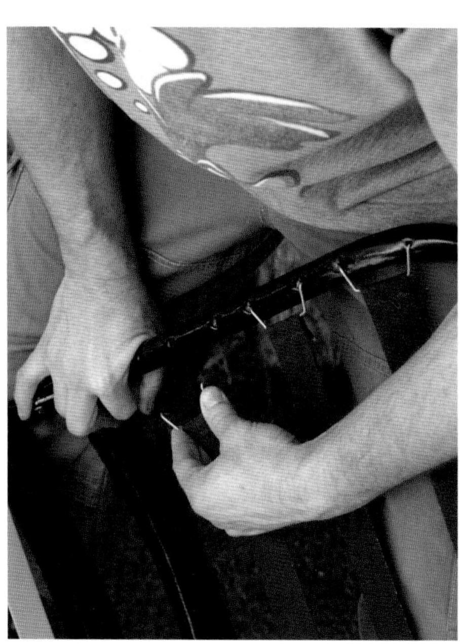

Stretching the Pirelli straps across the seat frames. Working with weights at the gym would have been good preparation for this task!

Stripping the Car

Where it all started. The removal of two Phillips head screws on the strap finisher.

The Point of No Return

With pre-ordered parts arriving, a decision was taken to set aside a room in the house to store the packages until it was time for reassembly. This had the advantage of keeping the work area in 'The Shed', free of clutter and saved the new purchases from getting dirty.

A week or so before stripping the car back to a bare shell, every nut, bolt and screw was sprayed with Inox or WD40, and all the fasteners were tapped with a small hammer. This process was repeated to ensure maximum penetration to assist removal. This paid dividends in most cases.

With the battery disconnected the process began. From the outset a detailed photographic record was kept. In this digital age it is much easier to take and store images. Photographing each item before and after its removal has the advantage of providing a useful visual prompt, particularly when it comes to reassembly. It also creates an 'evidence of industry' record which potential new owners will treasure.

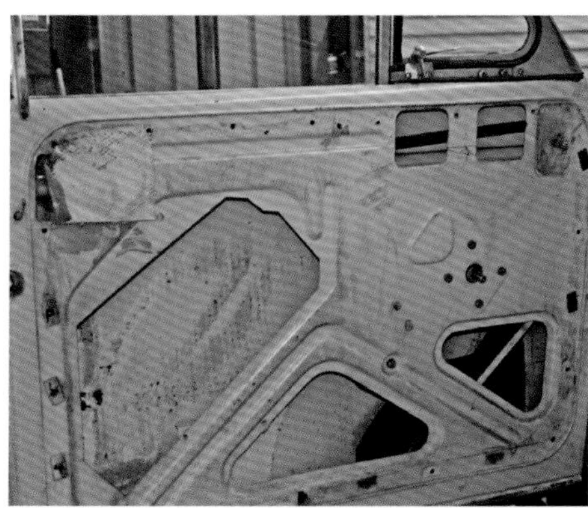

With the window winder, door handle and trim positioning clips removed the door cards were placed in storage.

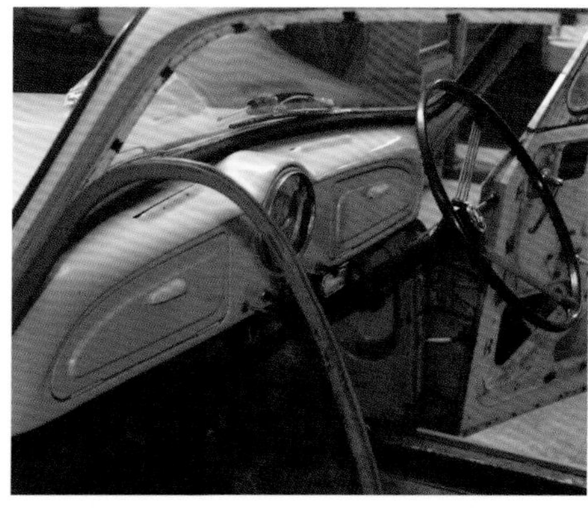

Door to body draught extruder was carefully prized away and the metal holding clips removed. It is important to keep these clips for reassembly.

The soaking of the door bolts in Inox paid off. The bolts were undone carefully with the help of some gentle tapping from a hammer.

Trim Removal

Removing the interior trim is a fairly gentle way to start any restoration process. Immediately progress can be seen. With the trim, seats and the remains of the under felt and carpets removed, a true assessment of the condition of the floor and inner sills can be made. Fortunately in the case of 'The Blue Bomb', the floor was found to be quite sound, possibly due to the amount of protective underseal that had been applied underneath. The boxing plates in the sill area were structurally sound. These were very encouraging signs.

Door Removal

The door stay assembly (housed within the door) was unbolted and a large grommet with washer and nut were removed whilst the doors were on the car.

A job I was not looking forward to was the removal of the door bolts and I must admit that I held my breath every time we attempted to remove any one of the 16 bolts that hold the doors on the car.

When it came to door removal, the restoration gods were on our side. Due to luck and good preparation, the 16 bolts which secure the doors unbolted without a hitch. The doors on a Morris Minor, complete with frames and glass are very heavy. It is certainly advisable to adopt the brace position when lifting or removing them from the car. The door catches, locators and stays were removed next. A hammer driver with a large Phillips head end was used to remove the door stay screws. Surprisingly, these proved to be more of a challenge than the door bolts.

above: Progress at last – with the upholstery, underfelt and carpets removed, the condition of the floors and inner sills could be truly assessed.

Doors removed. A sigh of relief and time for a coffee.

Removal of the door stay screws using a hammer driver (Phillips head) demonstrated by Bill (Dad).

Door locators were unscrewed using a Phillips head screwdriver.

Glass Removal

The front windscreen, stainless steel windscreen trim and finishers had to be carefully removed to avoid distorting them. These were cut out on both sides with a sharp Stanley knife to break the seal and then slid out from the side.

McKellar Tip – Windscreen rubbers on commercial Morris Minors such as vans and utes (pick-ups) do not have the stainless steel insert, so it is important to specify the correct type of rubber seal before purchasing.

Bill exercised great care when removing the windscreen.

A new front windscreen was purchased along with an authentic windscreen rubber.

Note: pictured above... (through the windscreen) is a yellow 1928 Morris Minor which is believed to be the oldest Morris Minor in the Southern Hemisphere, and fourth oldest in the world at the time of writing. It has a fabric body (vinyl) which was fashionable in the late 1920's.

Care must be taken when cutting window rubbers. Keeping the blade close to the glass helps prevent slipping.

These windows were originally fitted from inside. Removing the glass is best done by pushing inwards. Gloves should be used here.

Preparing for the removal of the rear window.

The window rubbers were carefully cut from the car and discarded. This enabled the glass to be carefully removed. The flat glass from the rear side panels was retained and used as a template for the new replacement glass.

While in part it was a personal decision to consider replacing all the glass with new panels, the need to conform to the strict Australian regulations for Certificate of Road Worthiness, meant that in the case of the windscreen at least, there was no option.

Removal of Mudguards

The front and rear mudguards/wings unbolted without too much fuss, due to the preparation with Inox.

The chromed, grille hockey sticks were undone in order to remove the front guards. This was not as straightforward a job as it might have first appeared and the small bolts broke away/sheared (as usual) during this process. When the back guards/wings were unbolted, the electrical wires were cut and left on for future reference.

above left: Introducing Mr Rust, not a Morris Minor's best friend.

above: A well earned coffee and cake break. A good pair of overalls is a must. Even though the car was cleaned before commencing the strip down, I spent weeks covered in dirt and grease... and loving it!

The guards/wings are bolted to the body using captive nuts. Many of these were able to be accessed from both sides and soaked with Inox for easy removal.

Rear guards/wings are attached the same way as the front guards/wings.

Electrical wires were cleanly cut and photographed for future reference.

Removal of the Bumpers

The back bumper bolts on to the bumper irons, which pass though the lower section of the boot. The nuts located underneath the rear valance were badly damaged. The only way forward was to cut the irons with a hack saw. We had replacement items on hand. The bumpers consist of the chrome blade, chrome overriders and a valance covering the strengthening irons.

The number plates were damaged so original type reproduction replacement ones were obtained from Bull Motif in the UK.

Removal of the Radiator

The radiator and cooling system was drained by removing the radiator cap and then opening a small brass tap on the bottom of the radiator. We made sure a dish was underneath to catch as much fluid as possible. The top and bottom hoses were then disconnected by undoing the jubilee clamps and sliding the hoses off.

With the fluid drained, four bolts (two on each side) were unscrewed. The radiator was now able to be pulled out from above. The car had a much earlier domed header tank radiator fitted along the way (probably from a Series ll car). In the interests of originality this was replaced with the correct flat top radiator which was introduced in 1960.

Note the three holes where the guard/wing is attached to the grille via the hockey stick trim.

The front grille assembly and bonnet locking assembly was removed by undoing several nuts and bolts located on the sides and across the bottom edge. It was removed as one complete section.

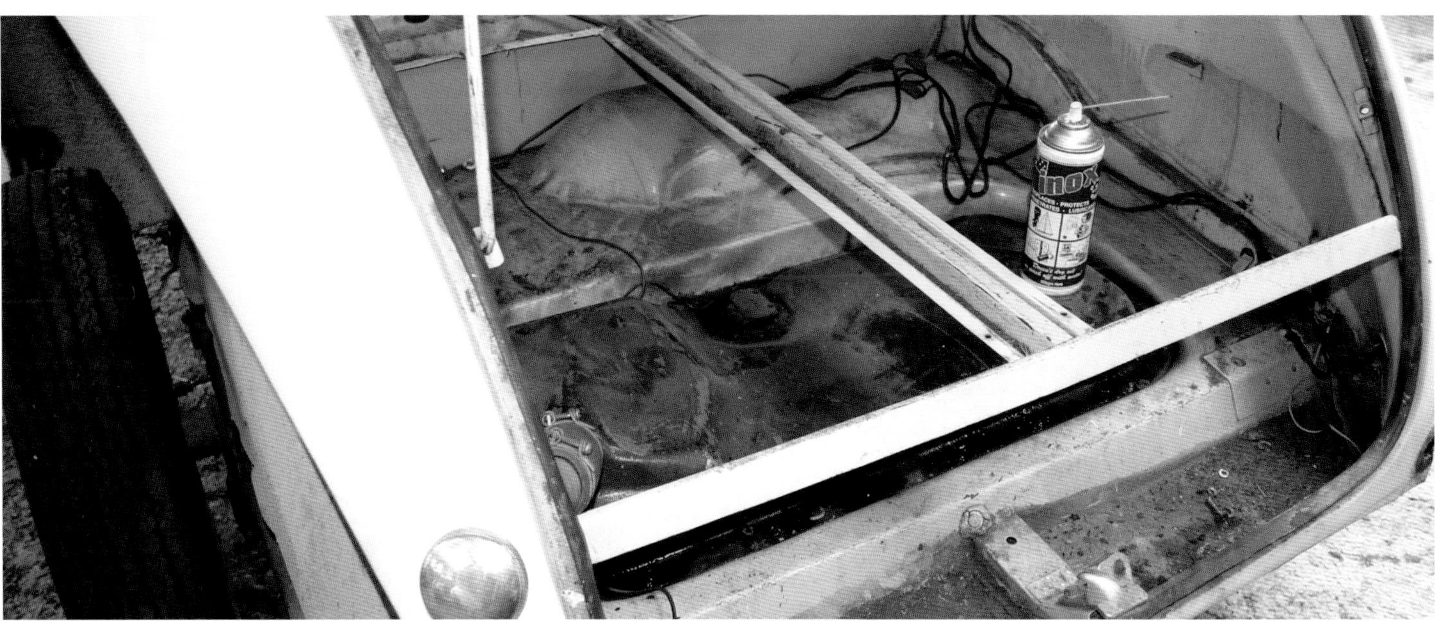

Bonnet and Boot

The bonnet and boot are held on to the body by external hinges. These unbolted without any problems and the panels lifted away easily. The hinges are available in new old stock (NOS) and were ordered complete with new nuts and washers along with other components from Bull Motif in the UK. Care was required when removing the 1,000,000 badges from the bonnet sides. These are held on by pins (which form part of the badge) and retaining clips. In spite of extreme care being taken, one of the pins did break. However, only breaking one was deemed to be a personal achievement.

The 1,000,000 badges are not available as new items (at the present time).

Fuel Tank

The fuel tank was drained by removing a brass drain plug in the bottom of the tank. The filler pipe and hose was also removed to allow any fuel to evaporate. The disassembly of the car was done over the summer months so the fuel evaporated very quickly helped, of course, by high Australian temperatures. The fuel tank was firmly fastened with many rusted self tappers. This presented a small challenge. Planning paid off once again as Inox had been sprayed on the screws over a period of time. With some tapping on the heads the screws released and removal was completed.

The two marine ply floors, held in by small nuts, bolts and self tappers, were removed cleaned, sanded and repainted in fresh black paint.

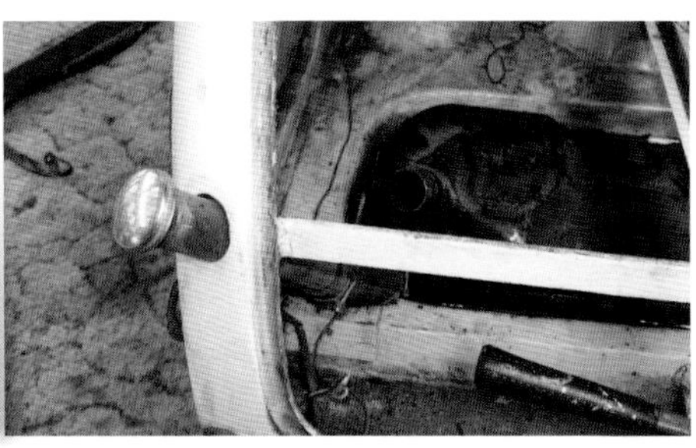

The fuel tank was found to be in really good order. Shortly after the tank was removed it was sealed with tape and stripped back to bare metal. It was later sprayed with black 'Kill Rust', wrapped in bubble wrap, and stored.

The rear guards/wings are attached the same way as the front guards. The bolts were soaked with Inox before undoing.

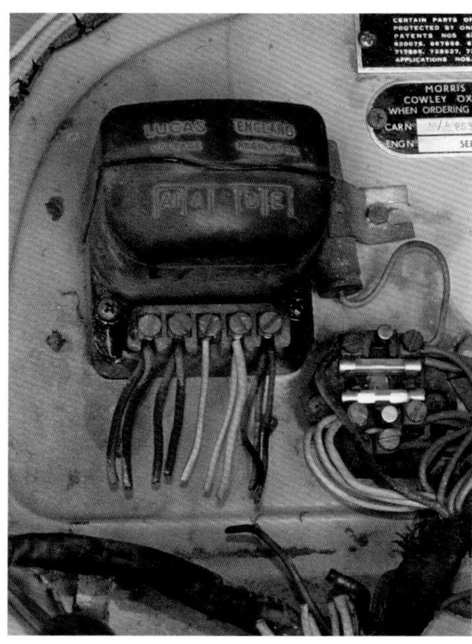

Firewall and Engine Bay

This is one of the areas where digital images are worth their weight in gold come assembly time. All components attached to the firewall were photographed prior to removal and all associated screws placed in labelled freezer bags for safe keeping. The wires on the regulator box were cut and left in position, where possible, for future reference. The fuse box was unscrewed and removed and kept with the wiring loom. The loom was left intact as much as possible.

Heater feed and return hoses were disconnected from the engine and the heater and fresh air intake removed. The cable from the back of the solenoid was released by undoing a screw attachment before the starter solenoid was removed.

The SU fuel pump and associated wiring was marked and the choke and accelerator cables were removed from the carburettor. Attention then switched to removing the engine.

The eight (four on each side) engine support bracket bolts were released which hold the engine to the subframe. This was followed by the engine steady bar which was disconnected. The final task at this stage was to disconnect the oil pressure warning sender.

Small snap lock freezer bags were used for storing all the nuts, bolts and clips.

These were labelled and put away carefully.

This idea, gleaned from previous personal experience, really paid dividends when the assembly process began.

The labelled bags of bolts really saved an enormous amount of time.

Removing components from the firewall.

A close up of the grommet assembly and fuse box.

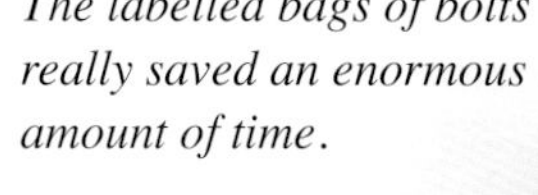

Engine Removal

Removal of Engine and Gearbox

Where the Morris Minor is concerned it is easiest to remove the engine and gearbox as one unit. The first thing to do is to drain the gearbox oil through the central plug into a suitable container. Make sure the gear lever is in neutral, then unscrew the gearshift gaiter plate and the anti–rattle plunger and carefully lift out the gear lever. Then remove the black gearbox cover by undoing what seems like about 100 brass screws.

McKellar Tip – A cordless screwdriver can make light work of this activity. Next, disconnect the speedometer drive. A pair of multi-grips may come in handy here.

Attention should then turn to the removal of the clutch assembly. Disconnect the clutch return spring and remove the two operating rods from the relay lever along the operating rod from the clutch lever. Once this is done the gearbox mounting bracket can be released from the body frame by removing the four set bolts and spring washers. Two are located on each side of the drive shaft tunnel and two underneath it.

The next step is to mark the tail (prop) shaft flange to the rear axle flange with a paint marker, to ensure assembly in the same relative position. After removing the four nuts and bolts holding the flanges together, the tail shaft can be slid rearwards enabling easy removal. Experience has shown that the tail (prop) shaft can only be replaced in two positions.

With the tail (prop) shaft removed and everything unbolted and disconnected, the engine was carefully lifted out with the hydraulic lifter.

above: An engine hoist was borrowed from long time friend Keith White. By using purpose made BMC engine lifting hooks and Keith's hydraulic lifter, the engine and gearbox were removed as a single unit with ease.

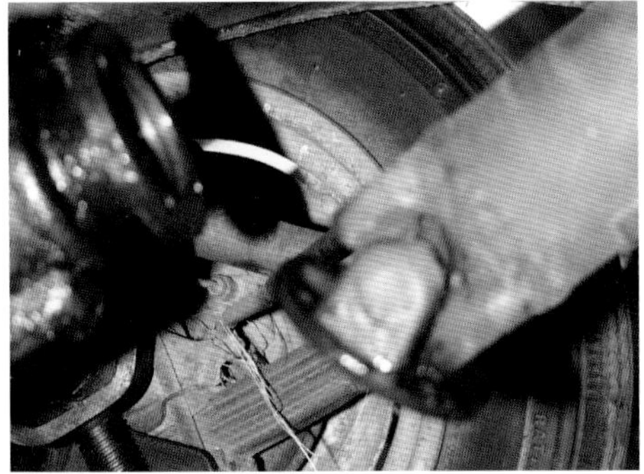

McKellar Tip – Mark the position of the tail (prop) shaft and flange before removing the four bolts and locking nuts. Use new nylon locking nuts when reassembling.

Exercise caution once the gearbox cover has been removed so as to avoid dropping anything into the gearbox. After this photograph was taken the gearshift area was taped over.

Dash Removal

Dash

With all the excitement of removing the engine and gearbox, I neglected to take pictures of removing the dash items. These pictures (above and below) are from two unrestored cars from York in the UK.

The central speedometer is removed by releasing two large Phillips head screws accessed through holes in the left and right glove boxes. A large retaining ring holds the speedometer firmly in place in the dash.

With this carefully prised forward the speedometer can be released. Wires pertaining to the warning lights and dash lights can then be carefully un-clipped from their respective holders. The speedo cable can be unscrewed quite easily at this point.

With the speedo removed, access to the back of the dash is made much easier thus enabling removal of other components.

Glove box doors can be removed by releasing four short screws.

The Millions and other Morris Minors from 1961 have a glove box stay fitted and this must be unscrewed. In order to remove the driver's side glove box cover, the steering wheel has to be lowered by removing the two domed nuts on the steering column bracket.

The cardboard glove box liners can now be removed by folding them inwards thus reducing their size and enabling them to be lifted outwards. The parcel shelf is removed by releasing two large screws fastening it to the sides of the body. Smaller nuts and bolts secure the back edge of the shelf to the firewall. When these are removed and the heater shroud un-clipped from the back of the dash, the parcel shelf can be lowered and removed. Heater vents can be easily unscrewed from the top of the dash particularly with the windscreen removed.

The ignition switch can now be removed by unscrewing two screws from under the dash. Choke and starter cables can be unscrewed from behind. Light and windscreen wiper switches are removed the same way.

Limited access makes removing all the above control switches and cables very difficult. Patience and plenty of time is required to complete this task.

This type of dished 'safety' steering wheel was used in 948cc models from 1956-62.

above: The two toggle switches in the left picture are incorrect aftermarket replacements.

Paint Removal – Back to Bare Metal. The Serious Work Begins

Paint Stripping – A personal Perspective

Right from the outset, the plan was to do as much of the work in restoring the car ourselves. Even on the occasions when specialist help was needed, this was carried out at 'The Shed'. When decision time came regarding whether to strip the car back to bare metal there was only ever going to be one answer. I have my own theory. For me, the best starting point is bare metal. When all paint is removed you can really see what you have to work with. I do not agree with putting good paint over bad, or painting over unknown surfaces. In my experience, acrylic paint does not go over enamel or other paints very well, and in some cases, it reacts very badly indeed. For me, stripping back to bare metal is one of the secrets of a quality restoration. In my opinion, cars that have been stripped back to bare metal always stand out when the rest of the restoration is complete. Having decided that this was going to be a Concours restoration this was the only option. Even though the paint stripping was going to be a time consuming and laborious process, for me it was going to be one of the best stages of the restoration. I could relax, put my mind in neutral and strip paint. Looking back, I'm sure at times I even achieved a some kind of meditational state, but then again that could have been the effect of the fumes!

Some very aggressive automotive paint stripper was purchased from a local company, Perrows Paints in Bendigo (Victoria).

Before starting, we put on goggles, gloves and overalls, and had buckets of clean water and a hose on hand. Much care had to be

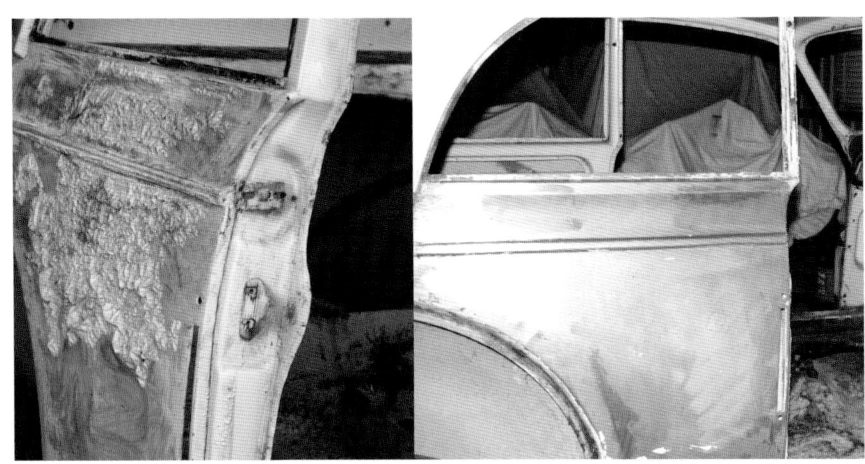

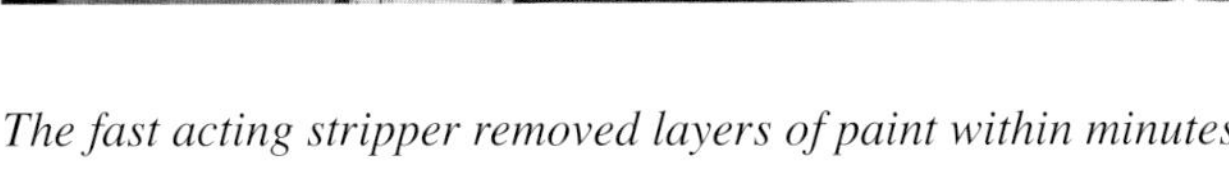

The fast acting stripper removed layers of paint within minutes.

The engine bay minus the paint.

taken whilst opening the container as pressure would build up and the stripper would almost want to leap out over you. The conditions were perfect for using such a product. Paint strippers are stimulated by heat… and at the time it was the middle of an Australian Summer. Before applying the stripper the surface was 'roughed up' with some very coarse sand paper. The stripper was applied by brushing it on in very thick strokes to a depth of approximately 4mm deep. A skin would quickly form on the top layer of the stripper, trapping the gasses underneath. This allowed the chemical reaction to take place. The stripper was very effective and removed many layers of paint in one application.

Starting with the roof, we worked around the sides of the vehicle and down to the engine bay. With so many nooks and crannies, this proved to be the most difficult area to strip. After this was done we moved to the inside of the car and dash area. Within a day or so the upper section on the car was completed.

A vital lesson learnt was the need to neutralise the stripper with lots of water, once a section of the car was complete. We made sure we had buckets of water on hand, as occasionally stripper would splash on to our skin or clothes. A burning sensation would result so it was good to quickly reach for the nearest bucket to neutralise the stripper. Stage two of the metal preparation was to wire brush the metal to clean away any residual paint and provide a good 'keying in' surface for the sealer / rust protector. The best tool for this turned out to be an electric drill with a wire brush in the chuck. Countless wire brushes were used and wads of steel wool were pressed into service for the harder to get at places. This action made the metal glow like the metal on the edge of a knife!

Here I am meditating, or being overcome by stripper fumes as I work on the inside panels.

The shine from the metal was almost blinding… I said almost!

Angus, my 6 year old nephew, giving me the thumbs up for a door well prepared.

The Rollover Frame

An impulse buy, at the 'Bendigo Swap Meeting' – said to be the largest swap meeting in the Southern Hemisphere with approximately 2000 sites, proved invaluable during the restoration.

At the time we purchased the secondhand rollover frame, we had no particular project in mind. However, the price was right and our initial thoughts were that we might hire it out to other Morris Minor owners to recoup our financial outlay. The frame proved to be indispensable and was invaluable in helping achieve the highest possible standard for our restoration. It enabled us to comfortably and safely gain access to the underside of the 1,000,000 for cleaning, welding, painting and repairs.

The frame was easily fitted. With the wheels removed the frame could be bolted onto the front and back hubs. Securing feet were screwed outwards to make contact with the body while holding the car firmly in position. With everything assembled correctly, the car could be safely rolled over by two or three people.

The components of the rollover frame ready for assembly.

With the car on its side, access of hard to get to engine bay areas was made much easier.

Underneath

Top Concours cars always look as good underneath as they do on top. Our car was to be no exception. This was what we were setting out to achieve.

With most restorations the underneath is almost forgotten. An 'out of mind out of sight' approach is usually taken and spraying the underside with gloss or matt black enamel seems to hide all matter of sins. I must admit that it is amazing how good an underside can appear when freshly sprayed with black aerosol paint! The underside of most of my other Morris Minors have been done this way, although not quite as crudely as described. However, this time it was to be different. Inspired, many years ago by a photograph from Ray Newell's book, 'Original Morris Minor'…page 32 if memory recalls, I was determined to remove all the proof paint and top coat paint and start all over again. The picture of the underside of the Series MM in the book which was taken from the rear looking forward was my constant motivation. In my mind this was the benchmark by which I would judge my success. The first step was to remove the build up of dirt, road grime and grease that had been accumulated over years of driving. The layers of underseal proved the most difficult to remove. This had to be dissolved in order to be removed. Using a brush, power kerosene, diesel and petrol were vigorously applied (not all at once) and a pressure washer was then used to blast the underside clean. For ease of operation and to keep my mind on the job, small sections were worked on at a time. This process took ages as it had to be done well to achieve the desired

With the Minor on its side it was time for a cold beer and an opportunity to reflect on progress made in removing some of the underseal.

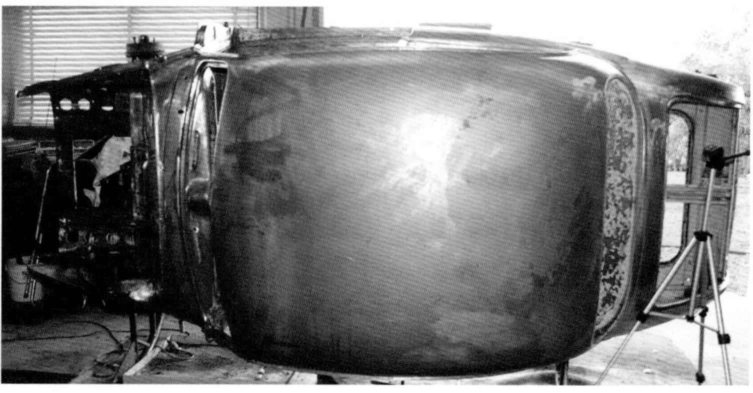

The upper section of the shell was in excellent order for a car built on the 13th of December 1960.

result. An electric drill with wire brushes attached was then employed to remove any residual underseal. With this removed a true assessment could be made of the condition of the spring hangers, the front and rear chassis rails, the cross member, the floor sections and the inner and outer sills.

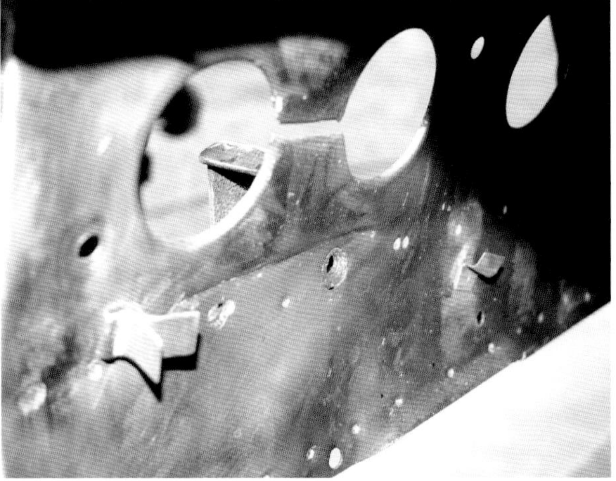

above: The rear spring hangers were found to be in good condition.

left: An interesting battle scar. The car may have been incorrectly towed resulting in damage to the engine floor.

far left: To keep the work area safe and clean, Bill regularly emptied these trays containing the discarded cleaner and underseal.

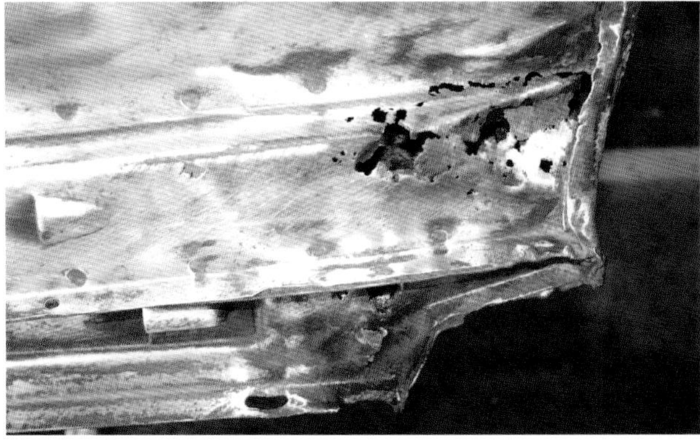

Rust has peppered many sections of the under frame. The holes were unusually localized, with surrounding metal untouched.

Bill felt he had to take this shot. New Year's Eve 2008 at 10.29pm. He was amused by the amount of dirt and underseal that I was covered in.

1948 Morris Minor Series MM Break

above: Be very careful when undoing and removing the hydraulic brake pipes, as you could easily rip the mounting from the front inner wing.

below: The unusual peppered rust holes. Metal either side was untouched by rust.

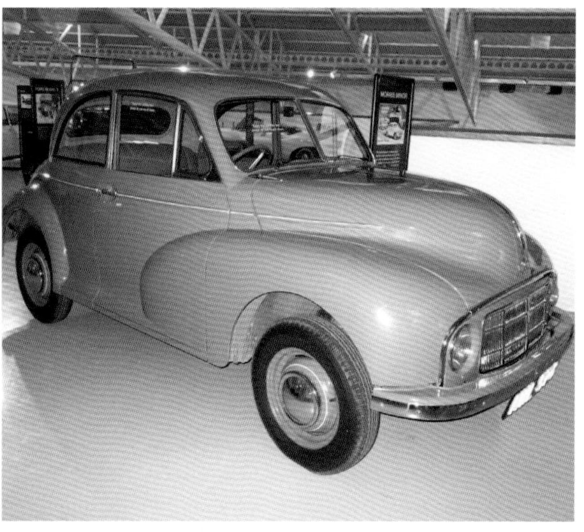

above: (Just to break up the underbody boredom which may be starting to set in). This is a picture of one of the other Morris Minors in the McKellar collection. This is a very early Empire Green low light Morris Minor. Built in late December 1948, it is car number SMM1270, making it the 770th car off the production line at Cowley.

It is very similar to, and shares many unique features with, the first car built, number SMM 501, which resides at the Heritage Motor Industry Museum at Gaydon in the UK (pictured left).

The side valve engine had been performance modified at the time of purchase in Australia. It is fitted with an Australian Monroe inlet manifold with twin SU carburettors along with a specially modified aluminium Klining head to raise the compression ratio. Combined with a high differential ratio, this car is easily able to cope with long journeys, which are common in Australia, in spite of being well over 60 years old.

Peppered rust holes were found along the side rail near the jacking point, as well as in the boot lower floor section.

Suspension Removal

Suspension Removal

Of all the tasks involved in the restoration, the removal of the suspension components was seen as a necessary evil. The motivation to complete the task was as much to do with the prospect of achieving the perfect underside as it was to see the suspension components refurbished. Inspired by the picture in Ray's book the process of removing the various parts began. In preparation all the nuts, bolts and associated components were soaked with Inox and a Whitworth Socket set and spanner were located. Before tackling the main suspension components, the steering wheel, tie rods and steering rack were removed. The tie rods required some tapping with a tie rod splitter but amazingly they came off with ease. The rack was easily removed by undoing four long bolts. It lifted out easily and was put aside for cleaning. Attention then switched to the torsion bars. It is very important when removing the torsion bars that they are marked left and right as they need to be replaced on the same side that they have been removed from or they will fail to operate efficiently. Further consideration of this aspect of the suspension is contained in the section describing the suspension reassembly.

Disassembly began in earnest by firstly removing the large nut on the end of the torsion bar and then the bolt through the lower arm and the two on the lower joint. With the small bolt through the tie bar removed it was possible to separate the tie bar from the lower wishbone. Careful leverage, using a screwdriver, allowed the lower wishbone to be removed. It was then possible to lift the swivel or fulcrum pin out and then remove the nut on the rear lever end of the torsion bar. With all these tasks completed the stub axle assembly and torsion bars were easily removed from the car. With both sides removed it was definitely a case of mission accomplished albeit with less hassle than anticipated. In retrospect the only downside was that it was heavy and awkward to take the suspension off the car when it was on its side on the rollover frame.

The tie rod ends were removed by using a tie rod end separator and a few persuasive taps with a hammer.

Removing the steering rack bolts.

Removing the nut on the end of the tie bar.

Rust Repairs

Rust Panel Replacement

After assessing the condition of the underside, an order was placed for a range of rust repair replacement panels from Bull Motif Spares on-line.

As I do not have the welding skills to be able to replace rusted sections with new metal a local welding expert, friend and neighbour Norm Deumer was approached for some advice. Norm is a member of the Castlemaine Historic Car Club (Victoria) and has many restored vintage and classic cars. He is an excellent welder and fortunately for us, he agreed to take on the welding part of the project. The new panels duly arrived from the UK ready for the big day. However, things took an unexpected turn when Dad and Norm decided they could do a better job by making and folding their own repair panels from a heavier gauge metal than the replacements. This was a throw back to the old Australian way of over engineering things. I actually disagreed with the decision as the quality of the replacements was excellent. However, on this occasion, I was out voted.

Each section was approached systematically. Outer sill sections were cut out with a small angle grinder, new metal sections were folded up and welded into place. This was followed by lower door hinge pillars, inner wing and chassis leg sections. The new metal and welding took about two days to finish. When completed, an angle grinder was used to grind the welds flat. To finish off, a very small amount of body filler was used before etch primer was applied to provide protection over the joins. Additional jobs included cutting out the rusted bottom sections of the doors and replacing them with new metal. Extra holes for aftermarket accessories in the firewall were filled with weld and filed flat.

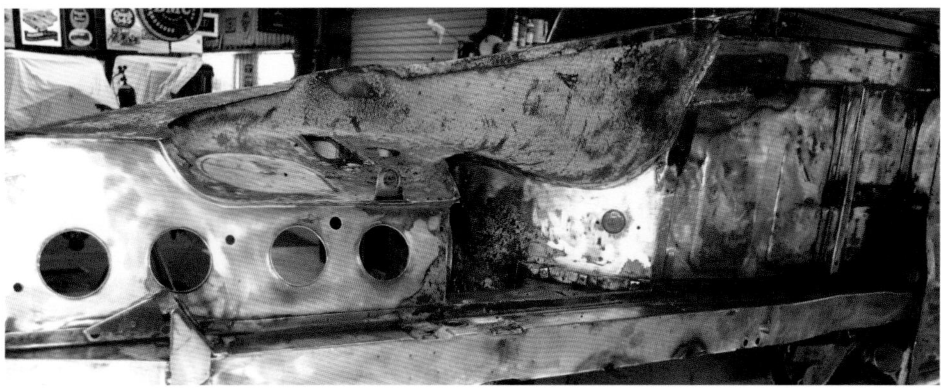

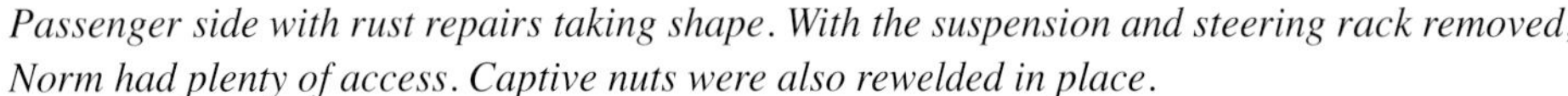

Passenger side with rust repairs taking shape. With the suspension and steering rack removed, Norm had plenty of access. Captive nuts were also rewelded in place.

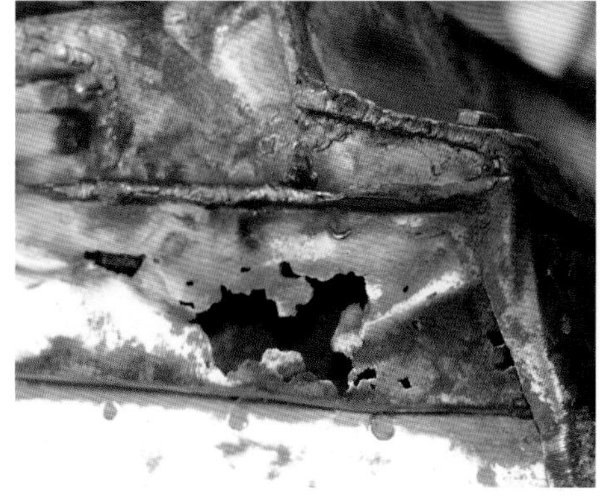

A close up of the driver's side rusted floor edge panel. This section was cut out and replaced.

above: A true master craftsman at work. Norm's experience, professionalism and attention to detail enhanced the quality of the restoration.

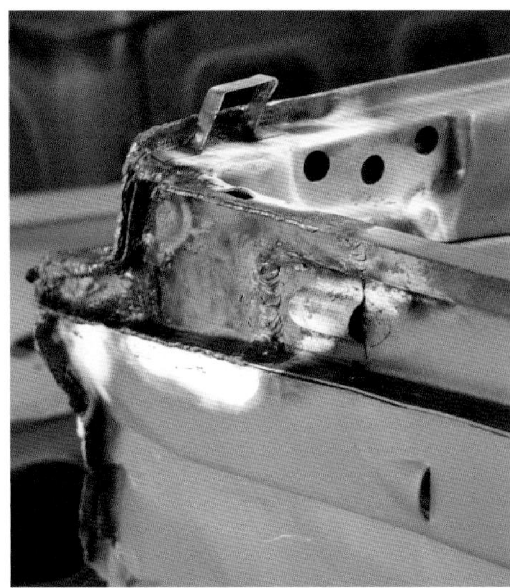

right: Drain holes in the outer door sill and floor edge panel were welded back in place and sealed. Once painted it was almost impossible to work out what areas of the floor had been repaired.

left top: Replacing stripped captive nuts for the cross member.

left: Repairs to the firewall in progress.

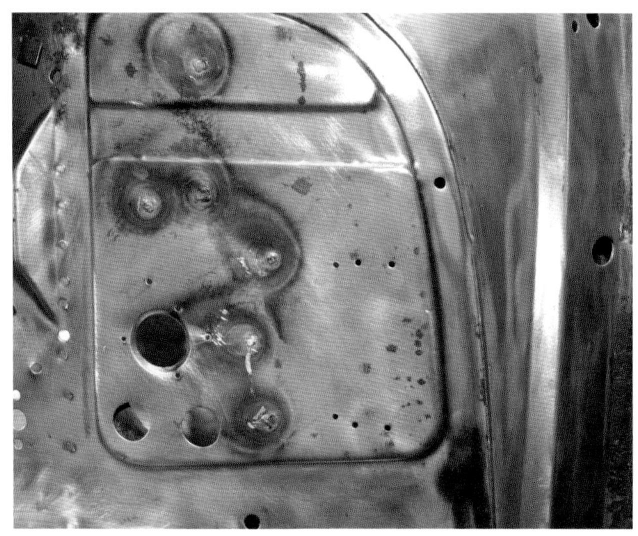

Wheels and Tyres

Wheels

One of the delights of the Minor Million is the colour scheme. Being a designer by profession and considering myself to be a man of great taste and style, I consider the relationship and harmonious contrasts in colour between the Old English White wheels, the Lilac body colour and chrome wheel embellishers to be just perfect. Joking aside, it really is a nice colour combination. Getting the wheels prepared and finished perfectly was of great interest to me. An added bonus was that doing this job was a welcome departure from the welding and the relentless removal of paint and underseal.

The starting point was to get the wheels repaired and made true. Six wheels were sourced from the 'Morris Garden' and sent by courier to Ajax Motor Wheels in Moorabbin, Victoria. Five returned straight and true. One was rejected due to excessive rust. Sandblasting was a definite requirement and Bill organised this to be done in Bendigo, Victoria.

Undercoating the wheels was done using Tetrosyl, an English spray putty/undercoat. This was applied using a low pressure gun. Three generous coats were applied in order to achieve a good thickness for sanding back. The yellow Tetrosyl was allowed to harden for a day and then rubbed down with wet and dry abrasive paper to achieve a smooth finish. The Old English White top coat was applied the next day. Like the lilac top coat, the BASF Spartain Acrylic lacquer paint system was used. This system is ideal for the home restorer to use as it can be applied easily and it dries within minutes.

Home Invention

In order to paint the wheels a special portable wheel painting station was made. This consisted of a 'Work Mate' workbench and a

One of my better inventions – the portable wheel painting station. Trusty bottle of Prepsol on the right.

Acrylic Lacquer works a treat. Gloves and a Respirator were used for safety reasons. It is advisable to spray between $20^0 – 25^0$ C. Any hotter and the paint dries before reaching the surface.

Morris Minor swivel pin and stub axle. With this clamped firmly in the 'Work Mate' workbench, the wheels could be spun as the paint was applied. This home produced invention was a rare stroke of genius, even if I say so myself. It made light work of painting the wheels, and helped ensure that the paint went on thickly and very evenly.

With the Old English White paint in the gun, the opportunity was taken to paint the front grille at the same time. The wheels and grille were allowed to harden for four weeks before any cutting back or polishing was attempted.

Later, tyres and tubes were fitted and the wheels balanced by the local Bendigo garage. Wheel weights were put on the inside of the wheels (they are usually on the outside) in order to give the wheel a cleaner line. This is a good tip for anyone restoring a vehicle especially if they are hoping to enter it in Concours competitions.

One of those brighter restoration moments – viewing for the first time the distinctive contrast of colour for which the 1,000,000 edition is renowned.

The MRF 520 x 14 tyres fitted. A compromise, as the 520 x 14 Dunlop tyres on the wish list were unaffordable, due to freight costs from the UK.

right: The fitted wheel rim embellisher in place with the hub cap on.

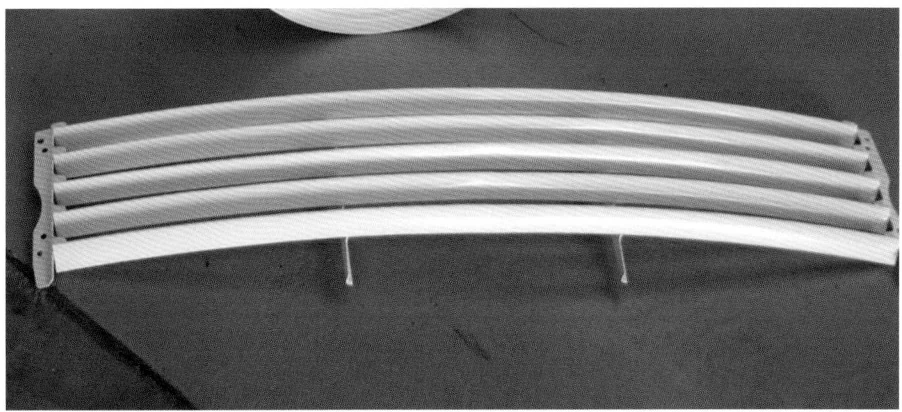

The grille panel was painted in Old English White at the same time as the wheels.

Painting Stage 1 – Etch Primer

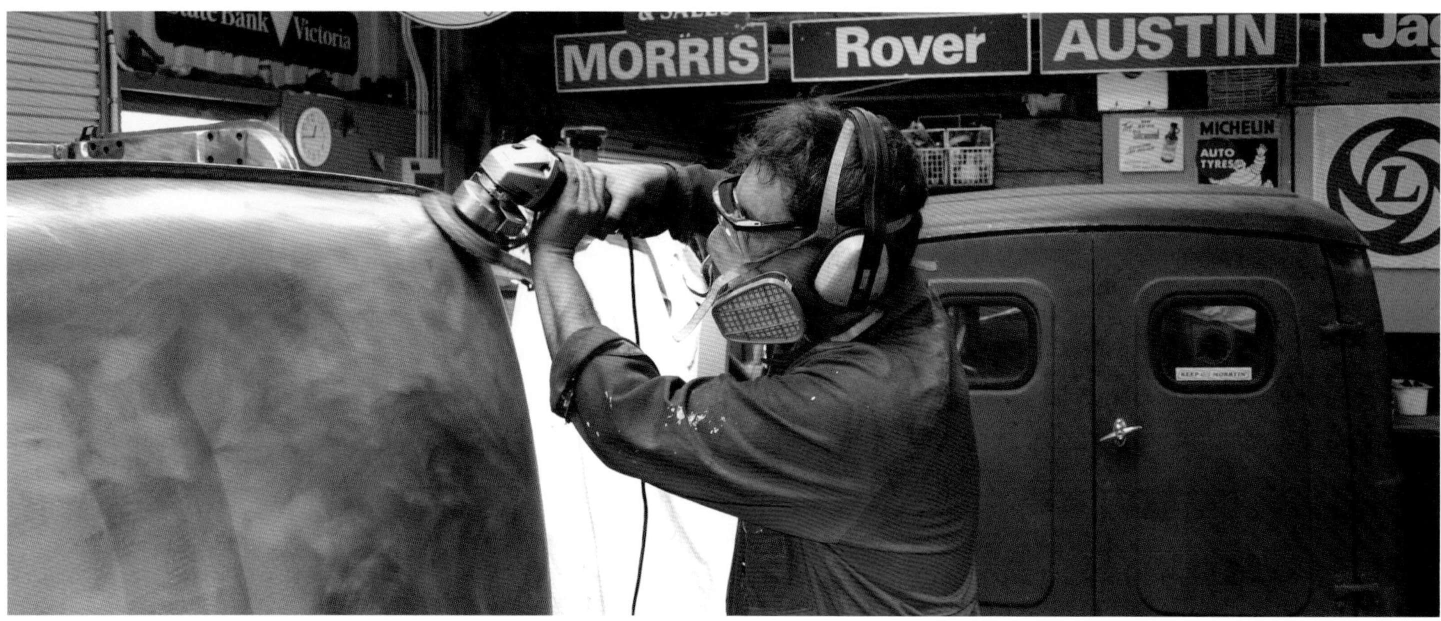

Etch Primer

With the end of the warm weather drawing nearer, metal protection was required sooner rather than later. With the warm climate in Australia and my parent's property being situated well away from the coast, the car could be left in bare metal for months undercover during the summer without fear of surface rust developing. The welding was ninety five percent finished and the metal was as clean as a whistle. The removal of all that underseal was now a distant memory. Before applying any etch primer to the car, one last 'sand' was required. Using an AEG sander with a flat wheel and sanding discs every inch of the car was carefully sanded one last time. Care was taken to remove any marks which may have been made whilst using the paint stripper and the wire brushes.

With a Concours finish constantly in mind, advice was sought from Perrows Paints in Bendigo, Victoria. We were advised to use a new product on the market, Wattyl Industrial Coatings Super Etch, manufactured in Sydney, Australia. This promised to provide excellent results but most importantly of all it would be compatible with the Acrylic paint system we intended to use.

Preparation is, of course, all important and care was taken to wipe the car down with Prepsol to remove any traces of contaminants that might interfere with the bonding process. The etch primer was applied with a low pressure gun and administered by spraying full wet coats. It dried in less than twenty minutes. The car was sprayed inside and out including the engine bay, floor, boot area and the under dash area. The transformation was amazing, and an added bonus was the knowledge that the car could, if necessary, be left for two years without rust setting in. The outer panels – doors, bonnet, boot wings etc. were sprayed at a later stage.

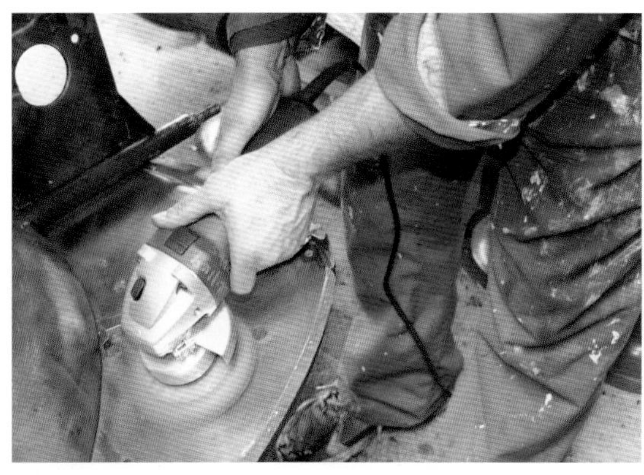

Driver's side front inner wing sanded for the last time.

Hearing protection was required when using the sander.

A contrasting action shot of the application of the etch primer with a low pressure spray gun over the bare metal stripped of underseal and paint. A breathing respirator and gloves were required when handling the metal etch. All bare metal was thoroughly wiped down with Prepsol to remove any oil from hands or other residue that would cause the paint not to etch.

Any previously unseen imperfections with the metal were revealed by the etch primer.

top: Looking from the back of the car through the rear window, which was enlarged to improve rearward visibility as part of the restyled 1000 Morris Minor in 1956.
above: The dash is finely sanded with wet and dry and prepared for undercoat.

Freshly etched primed driver's side, right hand rail and cross member. Note the definitions in the floor pressings.

above: Passenger side rear quarter panel. Note the aperture (middle) right of the door opening for the semaphore direction indicator (trafficator). The Morris Minor Millions were some of the last cars to have this indicator arrangement. From August 1961 direction indicators were incorporated into the front and rear lamps and blanking plates were fitted for a time.

Filler and Seam Sealer

The spraying of the etch primer highlighted a few problem areas, particularly in the engine bay and on the firewall. A small skim of PlastaBond body filler ('Bog' in Australia) was used to fill the offending areas. The filler was able to be sanded flat within a few hours of application. With the edges feathered and cleaned off with Prepsol, each area was given a couple of build up coats with etch primer. During the stripping back to bare metal process, all the seam sealer and proof coat that had been generously slapped-on during production at Cowley was carefully removed from the joints.

The aim was to have the perfect firewall and engine bay. Great care was taken to apply carefully metered designer seam sealer in the required areas to good effect.

The large hole in the back of the battery tray is a legacy of the Rotadip rust-proofing process which ensured the bodyshells received adequate anti-corrosion treatment back at the factory. The condition of the metal of this body, and the fact so many Morris Minors have survived in greater numbers than other vehicles of the same vintage, stands as a testament to the success of the Rotadip process.

top: The seam sealer helped give the engine bay a professionally restored appearance.
above: Applying some high build coats of etch primer over the PlastaBond.

top right: Tidying up the floor spring hanger area with PlastaBond.
above: Filling some low areas on the firewall.

Painting Stage 2 – Undercoating

Undercoating

It was important to wait for the correct conditions before commencing spraying. In an Australian home based environment the temperature is critical and timing crucial. Selecting a time when the temperature was 25⁰C proved just right for spraying Acrylic undercoat. In preparation for painting, the car was lightly sanded with wet and dry and then thoroughly wiped down with Prepsol.

Though reasonably competent at spraying, it was important to gain confidence and develop my spraying technique, as more attention and careful application would be required when it came to applying the top colour coats.

Starting with the underside, I honed my technique before moving on to the engine bay. This was followed by the boot area and then the inside and the dash. Whilst the car was on its side on the rollover frame, it seemed the perfect opportunity to spray the roof. The broad sections on the roof proved much more difficult to spray in order to achieve an even finish. I soon discovered that the spraying strokes needed to be long and overlapping.

Once the paint had been applied to the roof, the car was rolled back onto the wheels and the paint was applied to the rear sides.

The hardest part proved to be avoiding any contact between the bottom of the spray gun and the vehicle, whilst trying to keep the gun close enough to put the paint on wet. If the gun was moved too far away from the panel, the paint would dry mid-air and an unwanted sandy texture would result. Fortunately the Acrylic system is quite forgiving.
Any blemishes can be easily sanded flat and repainted after the paint has hardened. Experience proved that it was all a matter of patience and perseverance. This paid off handsomely when the time came to do the top coat.

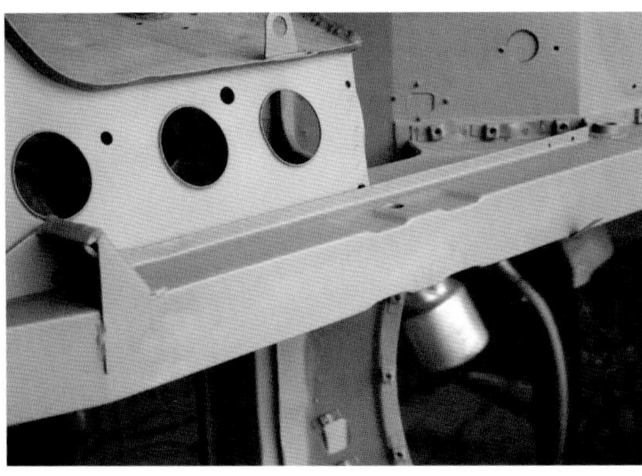

Even at this stage repairs to the rails/chassis legs and engine tie plate were a distant memory.

Repairs to the floor and box sections are barely noticeable. The careful retention of the drain hole cover in the outer undersill gives this repaired section the original factory appearance.

With the shell now back on its wheels, it was time to finish off spraying the rear side panels with undercoat.

The boot lid from the Million. Note the extra holes in the middle of the boot for the pins of the 'Minor 1,000,000' badge.

Filler

With the body now in undercoat, the rubbing back process revealed some problem areas around the back window and trunk panel. Yellow Tetrosyl filler was used to rectify these areas. To minimise the risk of shrinkage, the filler was allowed to harden for a day and then rubbed down with wet and dry abrasive paper to achieve a smooth finish. Any smaller imperfections were eradicated by careful use of red quick stop putty. Final sanding and feathering of the putty provided an extra smooth surface.
Once dry, the surface was wiped clean with Prepsol and painted with the undercoat.

Scheduling the painting process meant that panels like this rear guard/wing and other panels were undercoated in conjunction with the rest of the body.

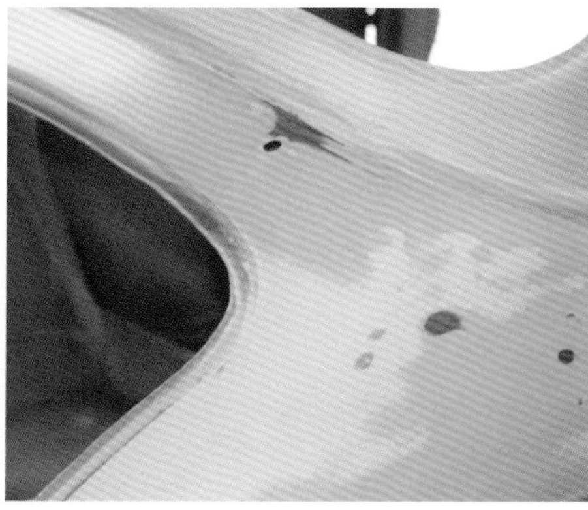

Imperfections in the undercoat were effectively rectified using Tetrosyl and quick stop putty. It is important to 'feather the edges' of the putty. Any slight blemish or high spots will show up in the top coats.

Painting Stage 3 – Colour

Paint Decisions (A Personal Perspective)

One of the most crucial decisions to be made was the choice of paint to use for the respray. The Million would have been finished in cellulose paint originally but this was not an option for my home based restoration.

The choice was between the use of Two Pack (epoxy enamel) paint or Acrylic lacquer.

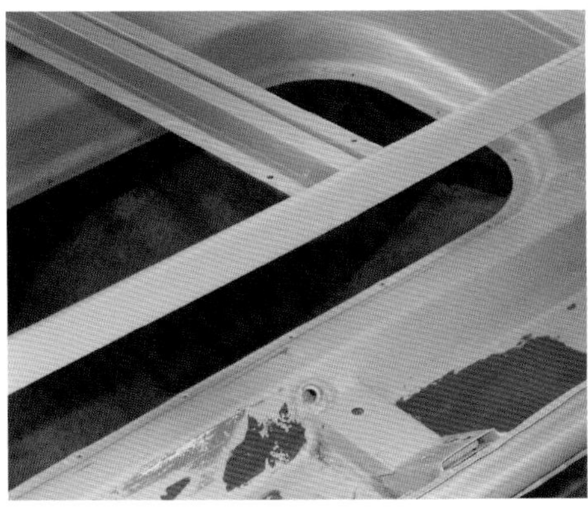

A smooth result was achieved by block sanding the red quick stop putty in the boot area.

The main advantage with Acrylic lacquer is that it is relatively safe to use. I would still advise the use of a respirator and gloves when applying it, but there are no deadly Isocyanates (Cyanide) which are found in the Two Pack enamel paints. The Acrylic can be sprayed in the open air because of the quick drying time. The other advantage is that Acrylic can be reworked/resprayed over and over again until a satisfactory finish is achieved. Runs and blemishes and the odd bug can be removed with wet and dry abrasive paper. Any problem areas can be built up and sanded flat (repeatedly).

The main disadvantage with Acrylic is that it does not provide an 'off the gun' finish. In order to achieve a glowing glass, Concours like shine, it requires an enormous amount of rubbing and buffing. It does provide a more authentic finish which suits a car of the Morris Minor and its contemporaries. I personally find that Morris Minors repainted with the Two Pack finish have a 'toffee apple' glow about them. It does look sensational, and provides a real 'wow factor'.

If a Two Pack painted Minor is put along side an Acrylic painted Minor, the Two Pack will out shine every time. However, from my point of view, if the Two Pack is not dulled down, it looks a little out of place on a Morris Minor.

The advantage with Two Pack spraying is that it is an 'off the gun' finish which requires little or no cutting or buffing to achieve a sensational 'wet glass' like shine. Another big advantage with Two Pack is that, unlike Acrylic, there is little paint shrinkage.

The high ratio of thinners to paint, three to one, means that the Acrylic has a tendency to shrink as the thinners evaporates over time. This is particularly true where the paint is applied over previously repaired areas. However, it is a more forgiving medium and provides more opportunity for reworking if problems do arise.

In spite of the fact that Two Pack is a more user friendly finish once applied, I decided to go with the Acrylic lacquer in conjunction with a Teflon paint protection system.

The Lilac Colour

Adopting the exciting style of the Swinging Sixties, BMC employee Jack Field chose the delicate shade of lilac for the limited edition Millions. Silver was the first choice but paint technology was not advanced enough in 1960 to guarantee a metallic silver finish beyond six months. Nearly half a century on, getting an exact colour match for the distinctive lilac colour was always going to be a challenge.

The starting point was the recognised reference code RD17. Following my quest for the perfect match, I now have a new found understanding and respect for the work of paint technicians.

In order to get as close a match as possible, the plan was to take off the glove box doors/ lids and remove the vinyl covered wooden inserts and get the paint matched in Acrylic from this untouched sample. I supplied a Melbourne company with the RD17 code and the lids and asked them to supply me with two colour pots with their best Acrylic match. Regrettably neither sample was even close to the original shade.

It was clear that another approach to the colour matching process was needed. Perrows Paints in Bendigo came recommended as having the experience and expertise to meet our demanding standards.

above top: The underside had several coats of colour without a single paint run. What a stroke of good fortune!

The Acrylic top coat was applied in small sections at a time. Care was taken to ensure the coats were applied wet with full trigger, without overspraying on to dry paint. This was achieved by starting at the top and carefully working downwards.

Dale West from Perrows mixed up the RD17 Enamel from a formula he got from an old BMC colour matching guide. Bingo! An exact match. With the paint purchased, there was renewed motivation to get the bodyshell in to full colour.

At this stage none of the bolt on panels were painted with colour, so a makeshift spray area was set aside in order to keep the project moving during the winter months.

above top: The off the gun shine soon dulls back as the paint dries, leaving a much flatter finish. Fortunately the expected drips, runs and paint sagging never materialised. Painting conditions were almost perfect, around 23^{0}C. All was right with the world.

Even the music was good. During the restoration a country radio station playing golden oldies from the 60's, 70's and 80's added a real period ambiance to the project.

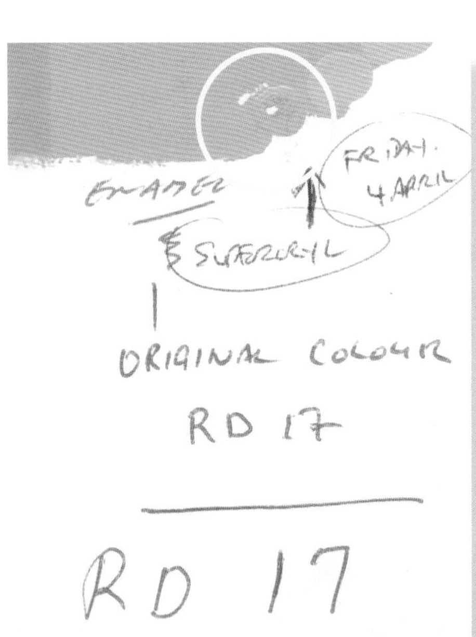

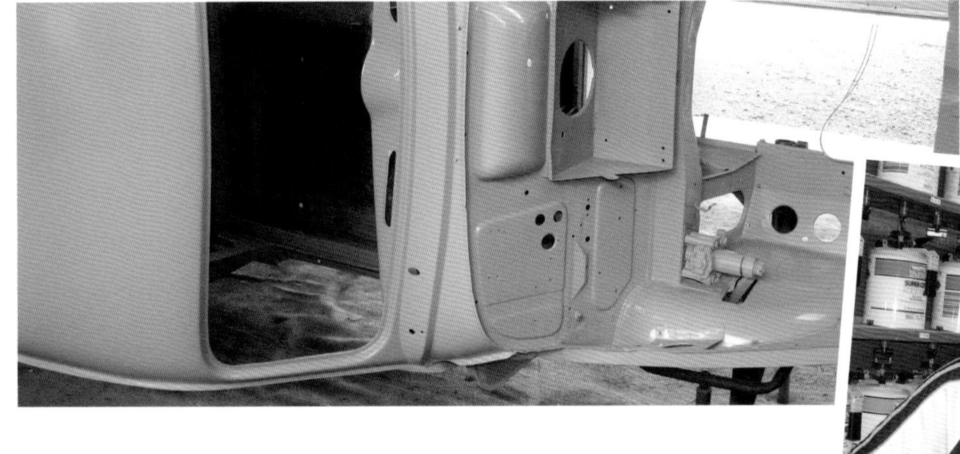

The easy access provided by the rollover frame made the painting of the roof a much easier process.

Dale West from Perrows mixed up the RD17 Enamel from a formula obtained from an old BMC colour matching guide. He then matched the sample with an Acrylic mix.

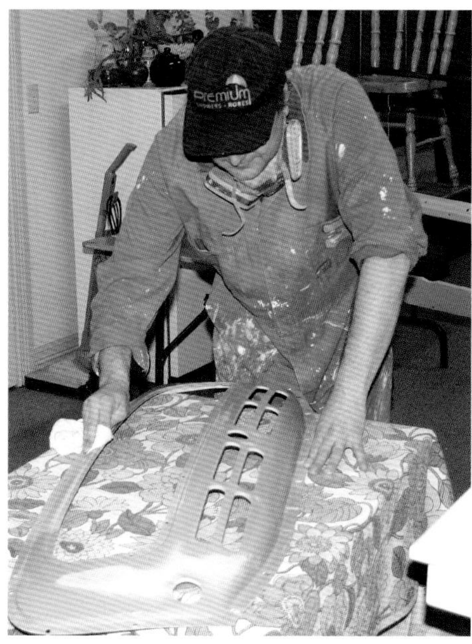

Bolt on Panels

With the body painted in lilac and the weather now too cold to paint outdoors, an indoor spray booth arrangement was a necessity. I am very lucky to have agreeable parents. This time I have to give credit to my mother, Claire McKellar, who kindly offered me the use of her painting studio (water colour & oil, *not automotive*). It was perfect. The space was clean and dry, had plenty of natural light and could be heated. An adjoining carport was converted into a spray painting station. Tarpaulins were used to cover the wall and damping the floor down helped minimise any problems with dust. The arrangement worked a treat. Family members brought panels in and removed them in rotation until all colour work was finished. The only downside was that there was little ventilation in the carport with doors down. I relied heavily on the respirator and got in and out as quickly as I could when applying the Acrylic lilac. Another downside was the mess the overspray made. Like naughty school kids we furiously tidied up before Mother could see the true extent of mess which resulted from the spraying!

Storing the Panels

Storing panels so that they do not get knocked or scratched can be a problem when they are sprayed off the car. One of the quirks of using the Acrylic finish is that the paint can remain soft for up to three weeks after it has been sprayed. Heavy blankets have been known to leave marks in freshly sprayed Acrylic. Consequently care needs to be exercised when storing freshly painted panels. Once again it was a question of calling on the goodwill of the family. A bedroom was allocated as a makeshift storeroom at my parents' house.

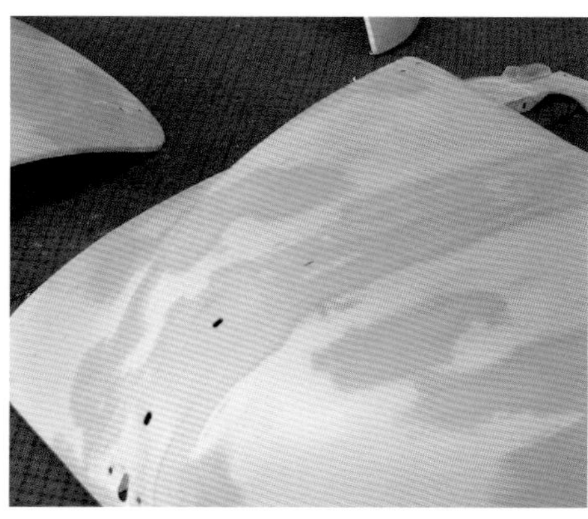

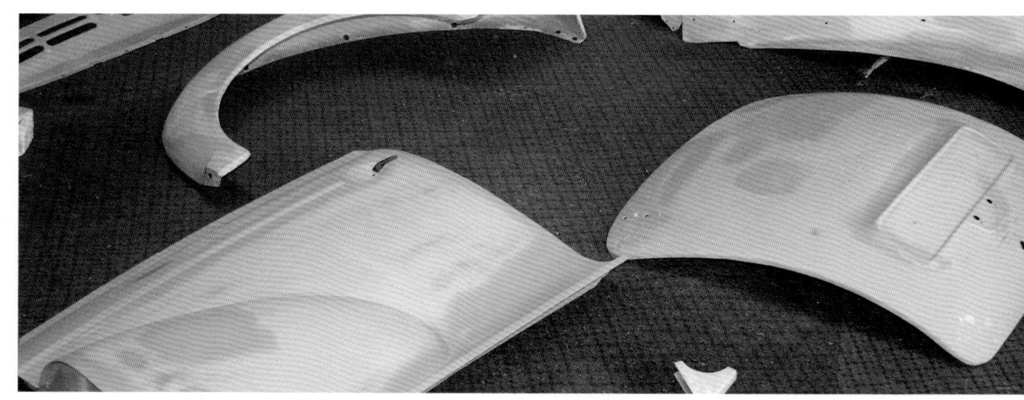

above: Bonnet, doors, boot and all other bolt on parts were rubbed down in readiness for the final undercoat application.
above top: A final wipe over with Prepsol for the front grille panel before applying the lilac top coat. Note: Acrylic lacquer is best left for as long as possible before cutting back to achieve a 'wet look shine.' The paint shop recommended three weeks for the DIY home tradesman.

above: Putting a few finishing strokes of lilac on to the passenger side door. Plenty of paint was applied, as it can easily be rubbed through in the polishing stages.

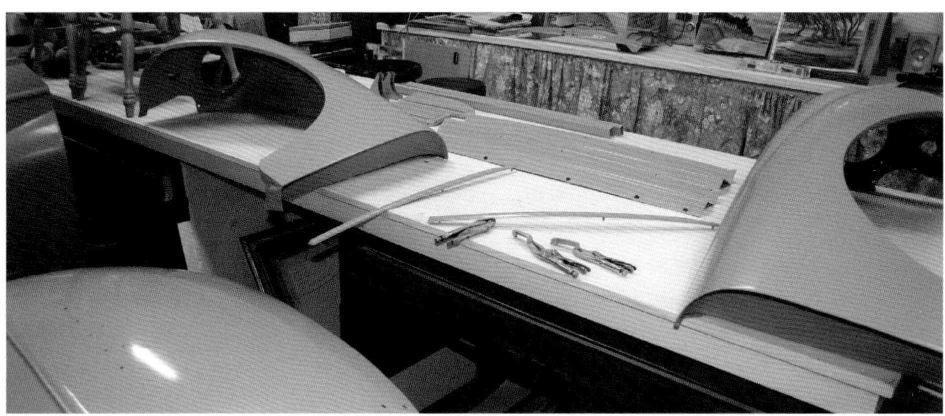

Lilac panels were left overnight in the painting studio with the heater on to cure.

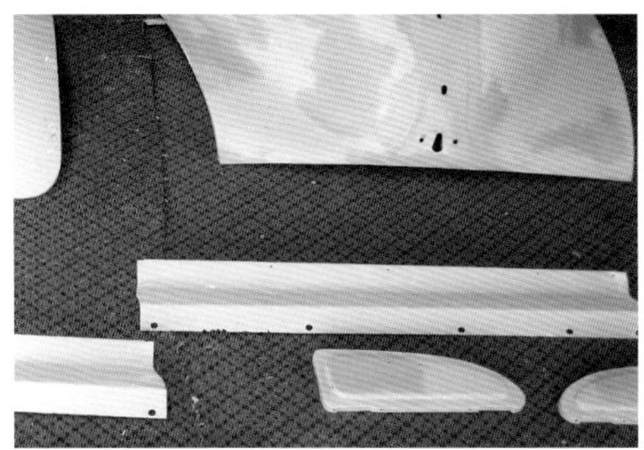

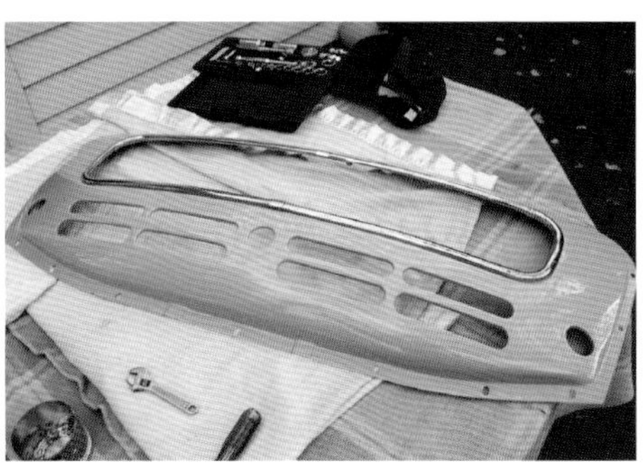

above top: Polishing and assembling the front and grille at home in Canterbury. This was a nice Sunday morning 'feel good' job. I kept the grille at home in the dining room and would look at it often to keep my mind on finishing the 1,000,000. The chrome grille surround was off an earlier car and is chrome plated brass. I had to be careful not to 'bling things up' or over restore at times. The original is constructed from aluminium and is not as presentable.

One of those moments when you can imagine how it is all going to look when assembled.

Headlining

Headlining Removal

Removing the headlining is a very time consuming job, but it is one not to be rushed, as there is much to learn about the way it is constructed and fitted.

For the 1,000,000, a new headlining kit and sun visors were imported from Newton Commercial in the UK. It soon became apparent that the new headlining would require the bows and front tension board from the existing headlining, so this had to be carefully removed. This was done by unscrewing the tensioning wires at the rear of the body (tensioned by Phillips head screws and flat washers). These are located directly under the rear window opening and screwed into the upper rear squab support more commonly referred to as the rear shelf behind the back seat *(pictured)*. Access to this screw is from inside the boot. The lining was then un-clipped from some very aggressive looking teeth around the top of the back window.

Additional tensioning wires needed to be released. Their location was easily found by following the wires towards the front of the car, until the 'B' pillars were reached. Tensioning screws are located half way down each of the 'B' pillars. Towards the front of the car another two tensioning wires are located under the lower sections of the dash (on both sides). Releasing all of the tensioning screws allows the process of removing the headlining to begin.

The final task involves removing the front wooden retaining fillet (tensioning board) which is held in place by two clips on the left and right. This is best achieved by carefully sliding a small steel ruler in between the headlining and the roof reinforcement panel (just above the sun visors). The clips are located about 250mm in from the sides.

By positioning the ruler over these retaining clips and levering upwards they will release. Well, they will if you are incredibly fortunate. I spent a frustrating hour or so with this task alone. I succeeded in the end, although my headlining was unusable due to my lack of patience and inexperience.

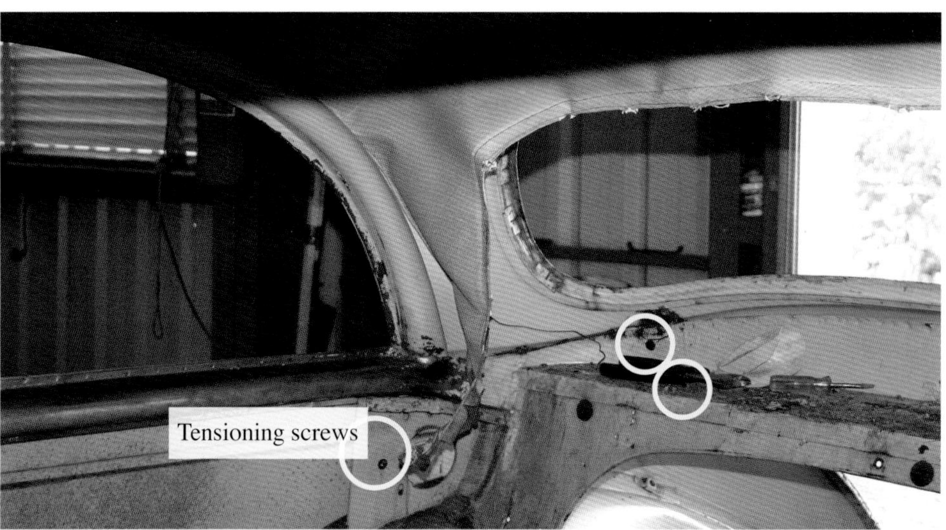

Possibly one of the most difficult tasks in restoring a Morris Minor. I was constantly worried about tearing the recently imported lining and constantly harboured the thought of having to get another if it all went wrong. In fact the lining is made of very strong flexible material and is able to be stretched without fear (This picture was taken early on in the restoration).

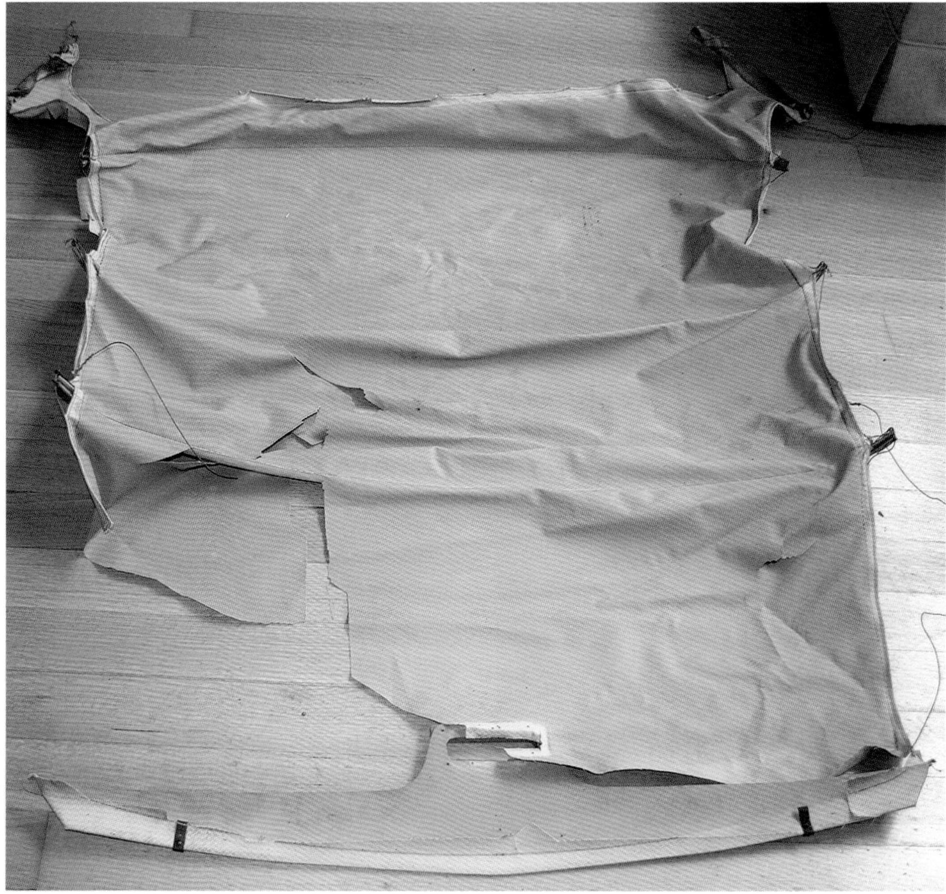

above: If only I had had a picture like this of the headlining out of the car before attempting to replace it. It is important to study how it is fitted, where the clips are located, what tensioning wires are required and where they go. With this knowledge the installation would have been much easier.

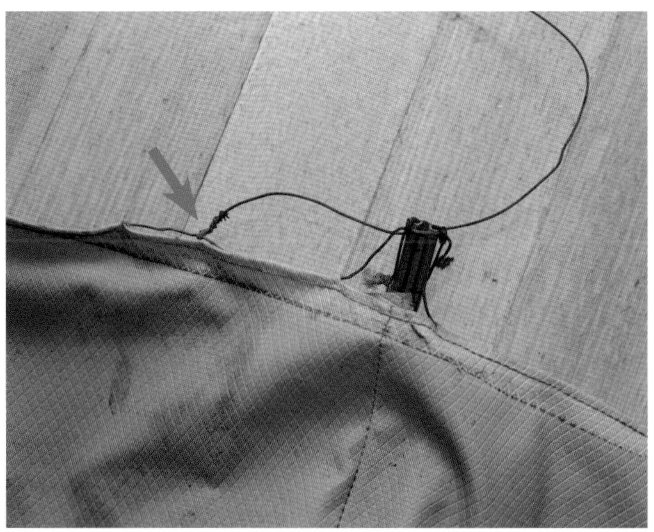

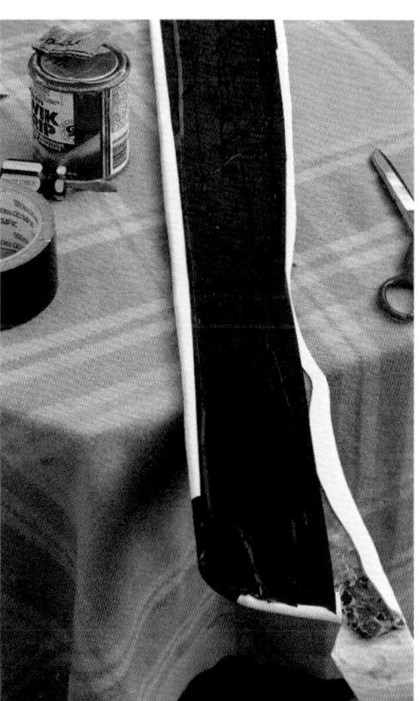

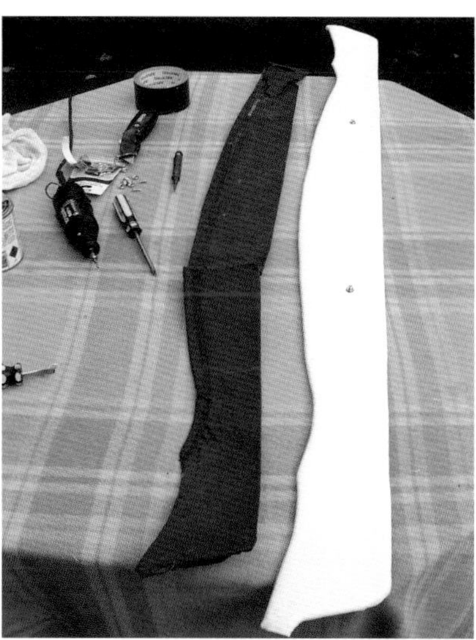

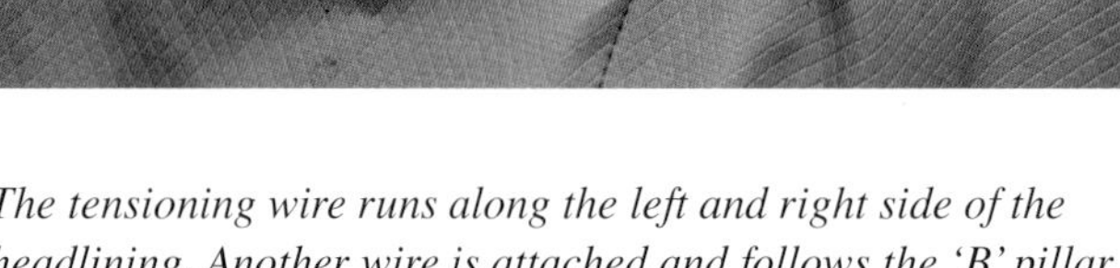

The tensioning wire runs along the left and right side of the headlining. Another wire is attached and follows the 'B' pillar down to a tensioning screw, halfway down the door opening.

The rear finishing board was reconstructed from a piece of tin. Using an original as a template, the tin was cut with some tin snips. Some thin foam padding was glued on with 'Kwik Grip' and covered with some white vinyl.

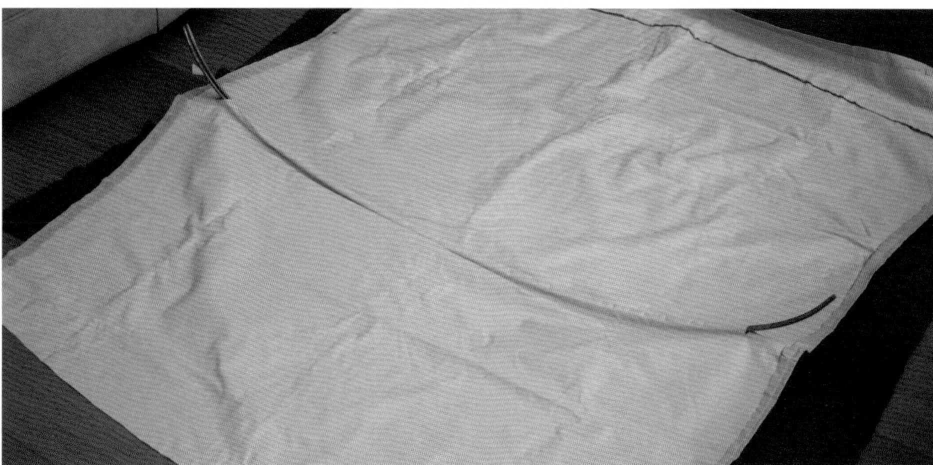

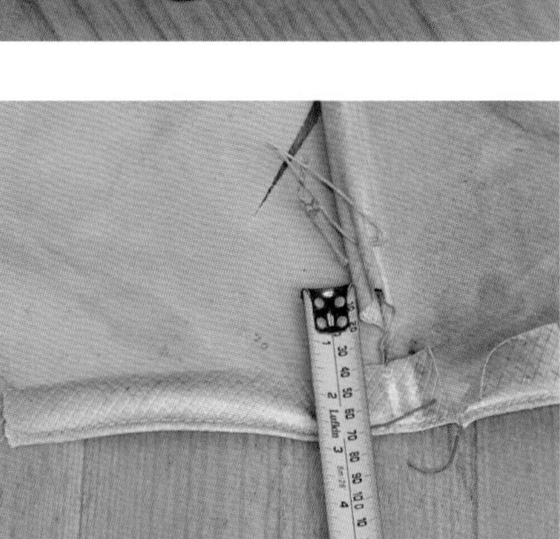

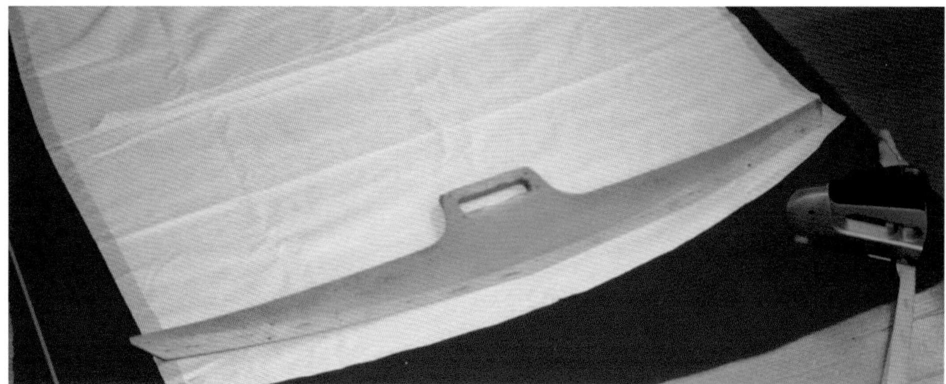

Taking accurate measurements from the existing headlining is imperative.

Laying out the new headlining and transferring the original tensioning hoops and board. Measurements should be taken from the original and the lining stapled to the tensioning board at the correct position.

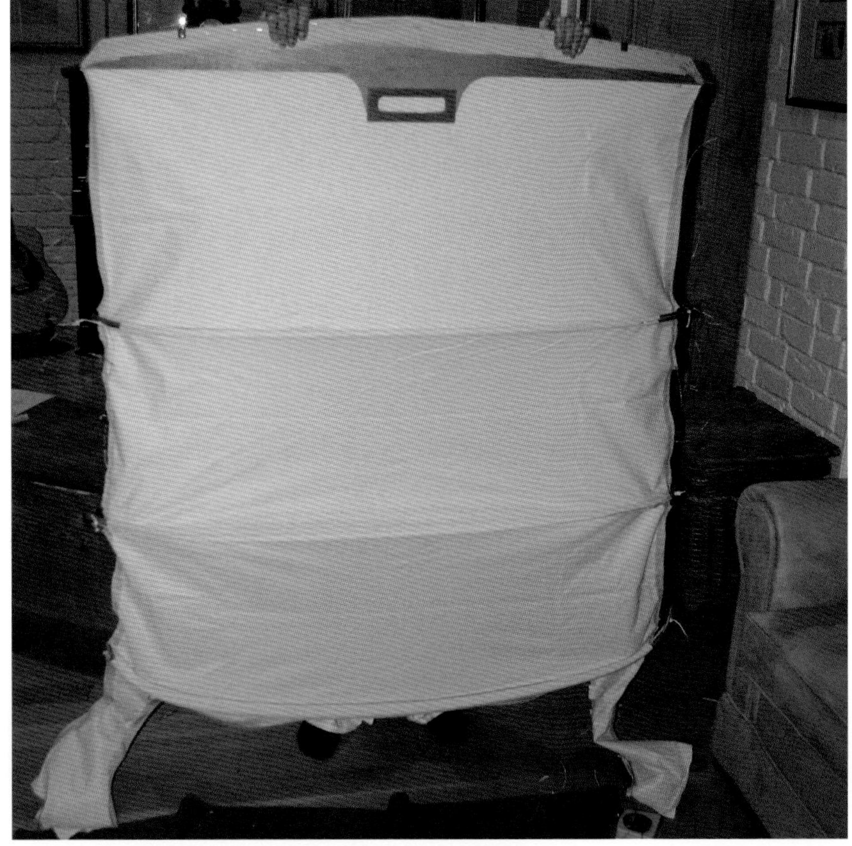

above top: Sound deadening felt was glued in using plenty of 'Kwik Grip' adhesive to reduce the risk of any drumming.

above: My mother-in-law, Faye, happily demonstrating the threaded headlining. Working out the positioning of the wires, cutting pockets and hoop placement took hours.

Headlining Replacement – A Step by Step Guide

1. Examine the original headlining carefully in order to work out how it all goes together.
2. Measure in and cut a 70mm section out of the sleeves that hold the tensioning hoops in place (Do not cut the lining). Repeat this process on all three hoops. Each hoop is curved differently.
3. Make a hole through the sleeve. Tie a string to the end of the tensioning hoops in order to tension and centralise (space – left and right) the lining evenly across the hoops. This will help keep the tension on the lining and stop it gathering in the middle of the roof. This process must be repeated on all three hoops.
4. Using the original headlining as a guide, position and staple the tensioning board in place (check the staple length and staple on the extreme edges where the staples will not be seen).
5. Attach the two retaining clips onto the front edge of the tensioning with bifurcated rivets.
6. Thread the stainless steel wires along the length of the lining. Be sure to insert the wire through the spring eyes on the end of the three hoops. Allow plenty of wire at both ends for tensioning.
7. Thread the wire around the back window section of the lining. Allow plenty of wire for tensioning.
8. Check with the photograph on the left. If it looks like this then you are probably on the right track!
9. Inside the car, loosely position the hood lining in place and fit the hoop edges in the roof reinforcement gant rail.
10. When satisfied with the positioning, insert the tensioning board in place and clip the clips into the front reinforcement gant rail (Make sure this is centred within the windscreen area). Thread the wires down the windscreen pillars and pull through under the dash.
11. Working towards the back, carefully stretch and tension the lining until it is centrally positioned.
12. Thread the tension wires down the 'B' pillars and pull through. Loosely wrap the wire around the Phillips head tensioning screw behind a flat washer.

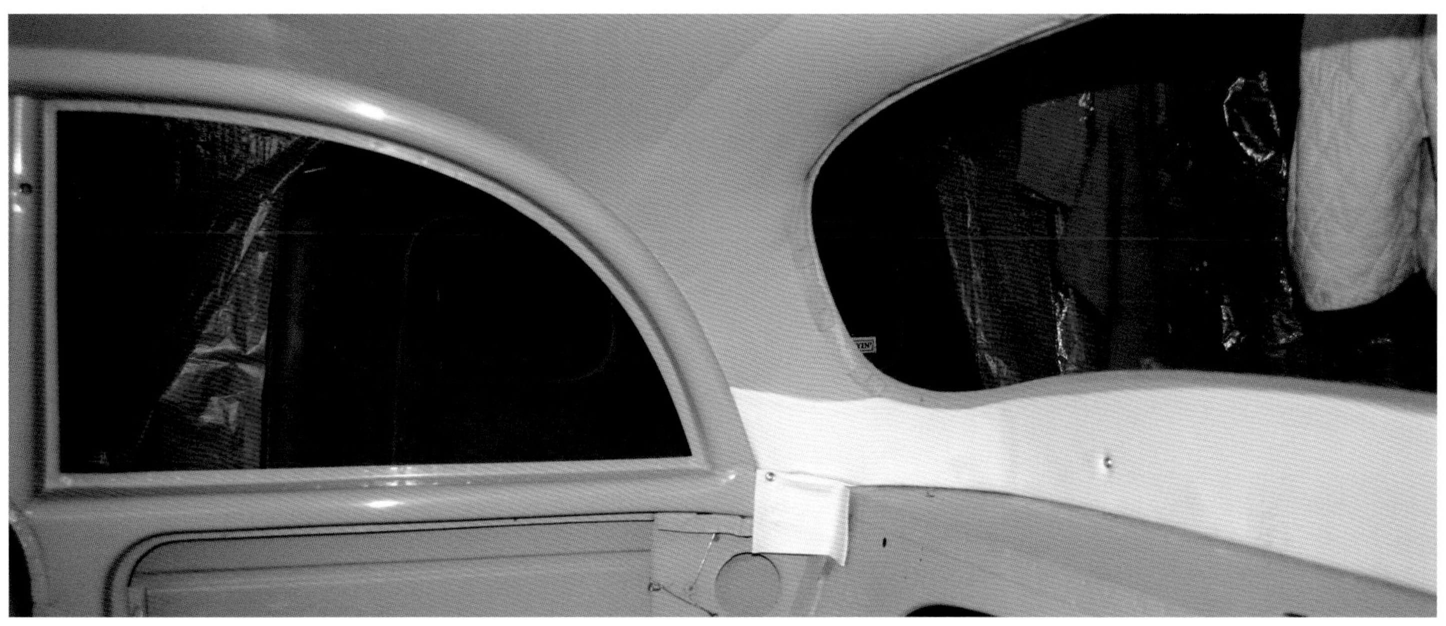

13. Move to the back of the car. Tension and clip the lining over the aggressive 'teeth' at the top of the window. A bit of pressure can be applied here in order to get the lining taut.

14. With everything in place any creases in the lining will slowly start to disappear before your eyes.

15. Carefully position the wires in place, making sure the wire is tucked under the flat washers, then tighten slightly to tension the wires.

This is a delicate operation for the home restorer. The process was not without its problems and at times was quite stressful. For instance when the tension wire on the front was being tightened the retaining washer cut the wire with a resulting high pitched 'twang' Fortunately the wire was rejoined without any problem.

McKellar Tip – If creases remain in the lining after the fitting process all may not be lost. Putting a heater in the car for an hour or so works miracles in helping to remove any small creases.

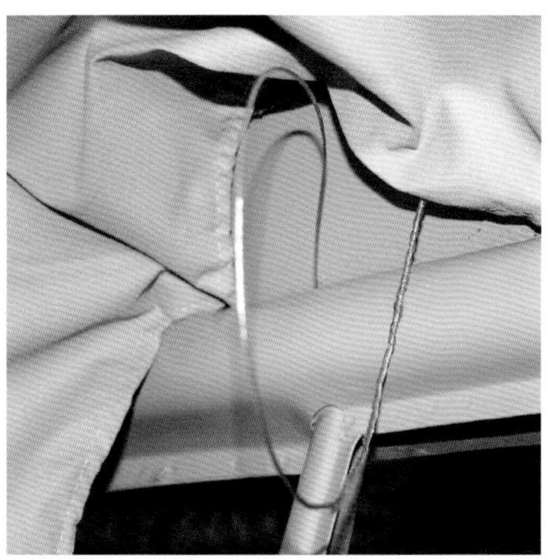

Threading the side tension wire down the 'B' pillar. Stainless steel wires were used.

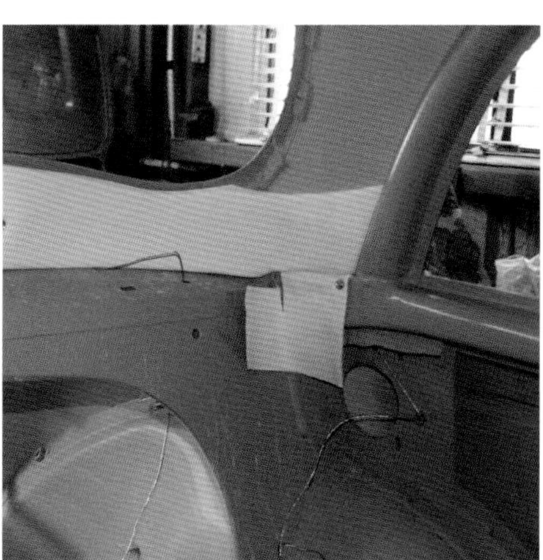

above: A small amount of tension should be applied to the securing screws.

above top: The passenger side with the rear finishing board correctly positioned and held in place by the edges from behind the gant rail. Two cup washers with domed screws hold the middle section in place as per original specification.

The use of a heater helped smooth out any wrinkles.

right: Although the fit is faultless, I am sure an upholsterer would have completed the job in half the time.

Courtesy Light

The Morris Minor Million, as well as most Minors built after September 1958 (with the exception of convertibles), were fitted with courtesy light switches in the 'A' pillars, enabling the interior light to be illuminated when opening the door. It was important to keep this in mind when fitting the headlining and to make sure that the electrical wires were threaded down the 'A' pillars. Before installing the headlining it is essential to attach the wires (even temporarily), to the wooden lamp base which is part of the tensioning board.

After the headlining is in place (and you have had a 'Valium' and a good lie down), the next challenge is to install the courtesy light. Locate the lamp base by feel. Once you have located the base, mark the area lightly with a pencil and go and have a cup of coffee or a walk. After a short time come back and review the marks. Cutting the lining is a point of no return and great care must be exercised. With a small slit cut in the lining in the correct place, wires can then be threaded through the lamp base and the headlining and connected to the globe holder with bullet push fittings. The metal lamp body can then be fixed in place with four Phillips head self tappers. Careful cleaning of the lens and the finisher adds the final touch to a tricky job. All that remains is to check to see if the courtesy light functions as it should. With the above operation it is important to remain focussed, as one slip with the screwdriver could easily put a hole through the headlining and undo, in an instant, hours of patient work.

McKellar Tip of the day – Use gloves when handling the headlining, and change them often. This will save you cleaning dirty marks off the textured surface.

The headlining as viewed from the front of the car. The hoops are sprung and all curved differently to fit tightly against the inside of the roof.

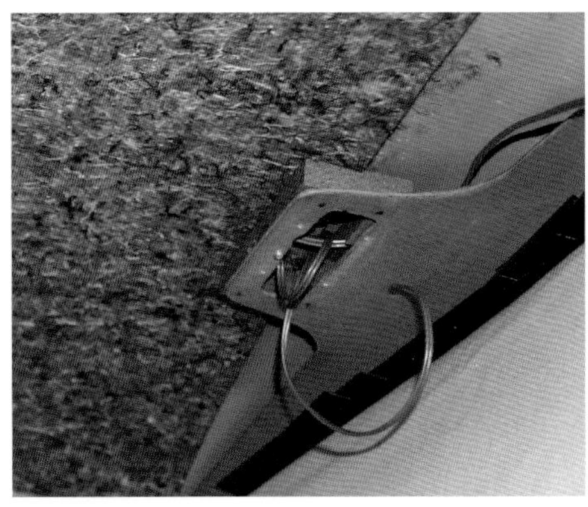

Be sure to run the electrical wires to the courtesy light.

The light screwed in place, wired and tested.

Screwing the visors in with flat head self tapping screws. Extreme care must be taken not to slip and put the screwdriver through the headlining. The brackets were re-chromed at great expense.

The mirror is held in position with three Phillips screws. Be sure to use the originals as they have the correct domed profile.

Black Bits and Other Colours

Home Restoration – A Personal Perspective

As previously mentioned the restoration of the body and panels took place at 'The Shed' in North Harcourt (Victoria).

Undertaking a major restoration at home, particularly if you are confined by space and the lack of a dedicated workspace area, can prove stressful and invasive. I am extremely fortunate in having a very understanding wife and family. Nevertheless, as the following personal account shows, I am certain that on occasions I stretched their patience to the limit. Take for example the photographs here which show our dining room with parts laid out on an 1850 antique English mahogany table. I'm told that there are in excess of 19,000 components in a Morris Minor. I am sure that during the course of the restoration my family have seen most of them. What you don't see here are items such as the rear springs, torsion bars, the prop shaft, or the

gearbox cover, all of which at some stage were placed on makeshift drying racks in the lounge and dining rooms of my home. You also don't see items such as wings, doors, the front grille and the boot lid being colour rubbed on the kitchen table, or my children trying to carry on a normal life, amongst an array of part finished or drying Morris Minor parts.

Everyone embarking on a major restoration project will have their own ideas when it comes to planning and organisation. For me, one of the most significant features was the subdivision of labour and the categorising of different components. Being a designer, with an eye for colour, I decided from the outset to use a colour coding system. It worked well … for me.

The Black Bits

A significant number of the ancillary parts fitted to the Morris Minor were painted black. As the vehicle was dismantled these were set aside for refurbishment or replacement and final painting.

The Green Bits

A similar pattern was followed for the green bits including the starter motor, generator, rocker cover and sump.

The Red and Yellow Bits

The yellow fan blades and top pulley and the red jack and wheel brace were set aside in the same way.

My planning followed my 'small steps schedule' which was essential in my book to keep the restoration on track, while balancing family life, work, band and other leisure interests. Yes, there were some! Completing small tasks at home provided a welcome sense of achievement and reassurance that the whole project was still on track.

Concours Standard Preparation

Stripping back all components to bare metal in readiness for repainting is a priority when it comes to Concours preparation. I was fortunate in acquiring a grinding/polishing machine which was powered by a heavy duty motor which looked as though it had come out of the 'ark'. With a few modifications I was able to have it permanently mounted on a stand in the back garden. Many a happy hour was spent removing paint and rust from just about every component. Each one was viewed as a stand alone part and like a production line the same procedure was followed every time. The paint was removed and the metal was 'buzzed' and buffed until it shone brightly. It was then wiped with Prepsol, hung on a wire and painted using a

above left: My prized eBay purchase. A 'new old stock' (NOS) Smith's speedometer still in the original box with the odometer showing 'one mile'.

This is the correct item for the Minor 1,000,000.

It features a gold face and has only three warning lights. The indicator light had been removed from the speedometer face in March 1959.

above: The freshly detailed Lucas generator model C39 PV-2 with the Lucas LA12 coil.

I kept the aluminium front and back sections unpainted and polished for effect. The M35G starter motor received the same treatment (not pictured).

The polished look was achieved by keeping the polishing strokes in one direction. The decal on the coil provided a neat finishing touch. It was purchased from Bull Motif (UK).

Todd Elliott, a retired Automotive Electrician from Bendigo (Victoria) checked all the electrical components. He replaced brushes and bearings and made any other repairs that were necessary.

The correct engine colour is available premixed in the UK. Due to restrictions this could not be imported into Australia. The closest colour in Australia is Mid Brunswick Green.

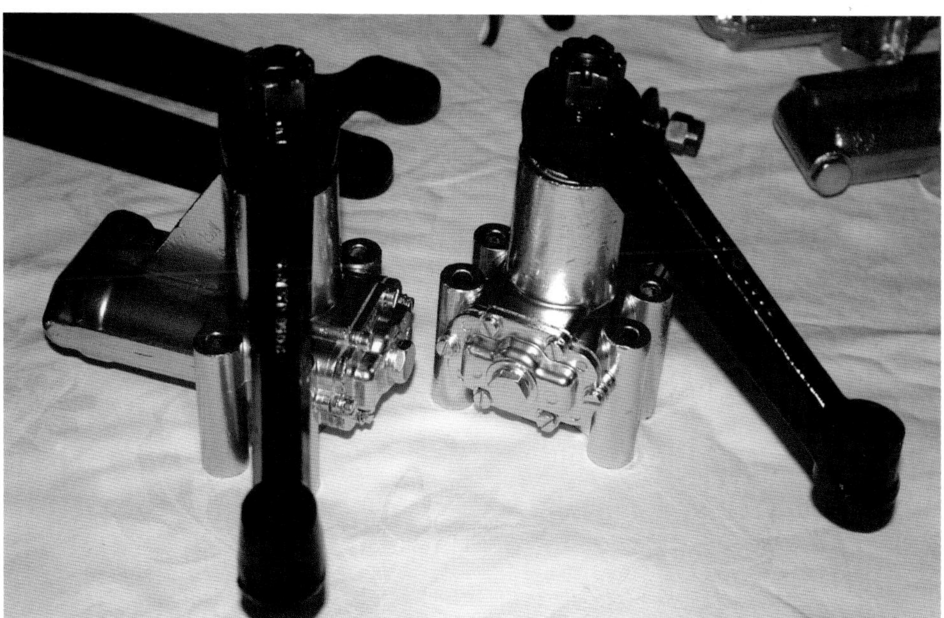

pressure pack (aerosol) of Kill Rust.

In spite of the shortcomings of this product, I found it suitable for my required application. I did investigate an Acrylic paint method. The advantages with Acrylic is that it is quick drying and much easier to use. However, Kill Rust won out in the end due to its rust protection capabilities.

The McKellar Technique

My technique for applying the Kill Rust may be a little different to what the manufacturers recommend. However, it works very well.

Before painting I heated up the component using a hair dryer to make the metal warm. I then applied a light 'dusting' spray of Kill Rust. After about 5 minutes the heating process was repeated, only this time a generous 'wet coat' was evenly applied.

The particular part would then be brought inside and placed in my purpose built drying room. Not to let the truth get in the way of a good story, the drying room was the lounge room with the heater on. My drying rack consisted of two chairs from the kitchen with the kitchen broom balanced across the

above left: The rear Armstrong shock absorbers which have been rebuilt, are an exchange item available from Thorpe, at Morris Minor Australia in Melbourne (Moorabbin) Victoria.

The body of the shock absorber was sprayed in a metal colour Acrylic for effect. This does look very garish in these pictures however, it dulls back very quickly and a natural metal look is achieved – don't panic!

above top: The DAS8/R front Armstrong shock absorbers received the same treatment.

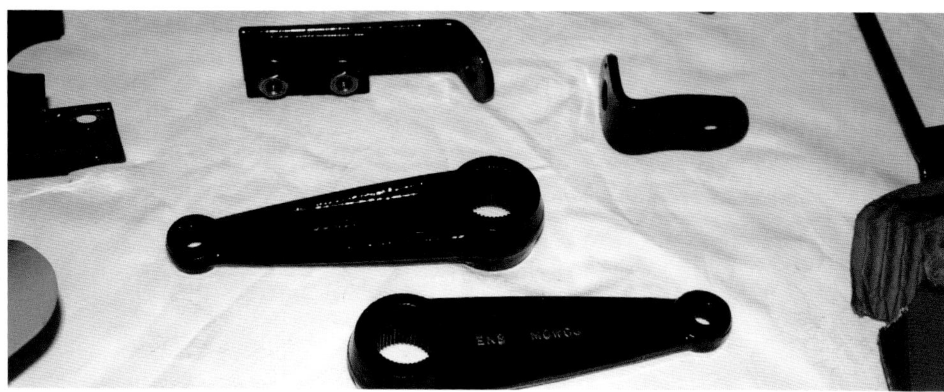

More black bits. Rear end torsion bar levers. The part numbers were painstakingly highlighted with gold paint for effect. This is over restoring to extreme but a nice touch. I get a kick when people discover this attention to detail when underneath the car. These have also dulled back.

The interior rear vision mirror, complete with new glass.

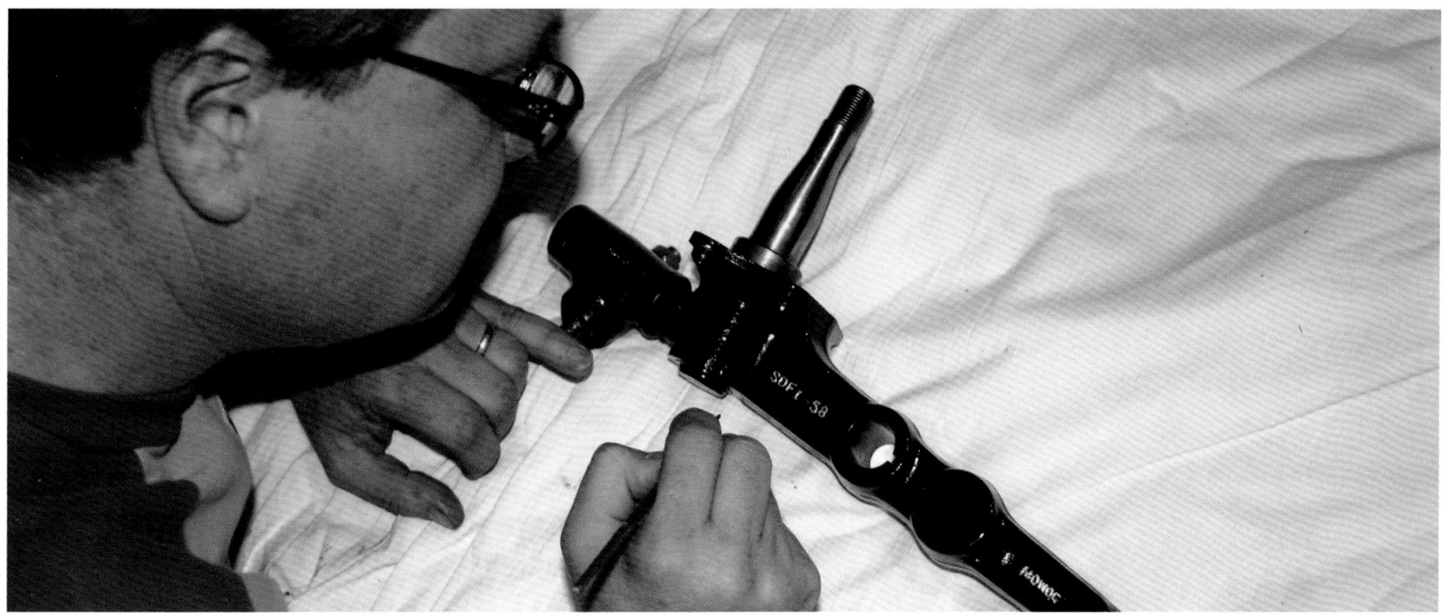

top. On busy days, I had a few drying racks operating at a time. When I ran out of brooms I opted for garden implements, such as rakes and crowbars.

Larger items such as springs, the tail shaft, gearbox cover, flooring from the boot etc., were hung on the clothes line in the back yard, heated by the sun and sprayed the same way.

After about a week, I would then apply another coat if required, sand and touch up, so as to achieve the best possible finish. When completely dry I would then wrap each component in bubble wrap. Eventually they would be taken to 'The Shed' at North Harcourt for storage until the assembly of the Minor commenced. During the winter months, completing these tasks kept me focussed and significantly moved the project forward.

Overspray Warning

The McKellar technique was not without its problems as one 'standout' experience demonstrates. I will share this with you as some times it is good to learn from other people's mistakes.

I was happily spraying the tail (prop) shaft, which at the time was hanging on the clothes line at home in Canterbury. A slight breeze was blowing. I was totally focussed on applying the paint evenly. Having achieved this I stood back and praised myself for a job well done.

My gaze wandered for a moment beyond the pristine tail shaft and to my horror, I discovered I had inadvertently painted my wife's 190E Polar White Mercedes with black Kill Rust... well, the passenger's side and the bonnet and boot. I had also managed to spray the windows as well as some box hedges in the garden.

In utter panic, I telephoned an uncle, who is a signwriter, and he instructed me to remove the overspray immediately with Prepsol. I did this promptly and then spent the next day cutting and polishing the Mercedes to restore the shine.

The box hedges remained black until the next pruning season. They were a constant reminder of my stupidity.

As for my wife, she was as understanding as ever!

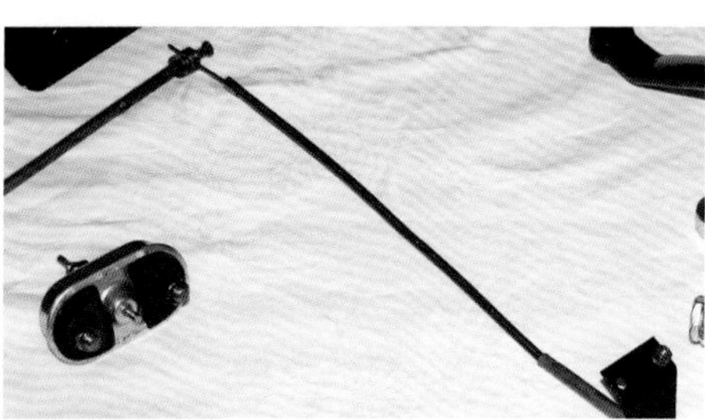

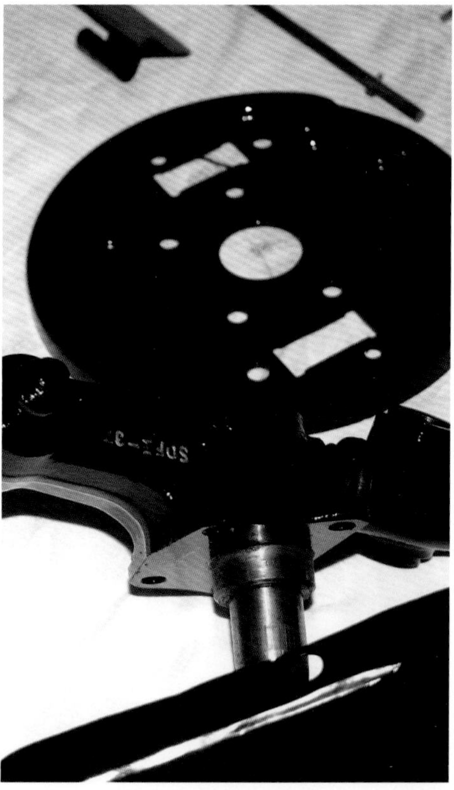

above: Some detailed part numbers on the swivel pin. These are available as exchange items from Thorpe, at Morris Minor Australia in Melbourne (Moorabbin), Victoria.

A front backing plate can be seen in the background.

left: The two piece gearbox cover replaced the earlier one piece unit from the early Morris Minors, enabling better access to the master cylinder. The larger section of the cover was modified in the late fifties allowing a little more room for the right foot next to the clutch. The smaller panel with the circular hole is the master cylinder cover.

Gearbox cross member. Over exuberance and overuse of the gold paint as shown by painting the embossed 'front' word.

Due to the hot Australian conditions, a decision was made to use a slightly smaller four blade fan which was standard on the Sydney assembled Australian cars. Originally the Million would have had a slightly larger two blade fan.

above: Torsion bars stripped and painted silver in the background. They are 'sided' and be sure to mark them left and right. If you look closely the right hand bar can be identified by the cable tie attached.

The lower rear left and right suspension arm. The gold paint found its way to the part numbers. Non standard but a real talking point!

above: An original type radiator was found in the Morris Garden and painted.

I had a conversation with Bill and was assured that the radiator had been tested and repaired.

I made a paper mask for the 'scalding warning message' (cutting each letter out and matching it close as I could to the original). This was sprayed on in white in a similar way to how it was done originally. The radiator was fitted to the car and it all looked the way it should. We later ran into problems when Bill was filling the radiator, as the coolant was running out the bottom as quickly as it was being filled. If memory serves a radiator is designed to hold the coolant. I discovered Bill was referring to another radiator possibly from another decade! Bill engaged Wilson Bunton, a long time friend and radiator technician to rebuild the radiator and fit a new core.

Windows and Glass

Safety First

It is recommended to wear thick industrial gloves and safety glasses when handling and working with glass.

New Glass and Rubbers

A new windscreen was purchased as well as new glass for the side and rear back windows. The quarter vent glasses were reused to keep the original glass standard marks and the rear window glass was retained. This had the remains of the original 'Appleyard of Leeds' dealer transfer still in place and legible.

New rubbers were purchased locally, from Scotts Old Auto Rubber in Melbourne and the side window rubbers were bought from Bull Motif in the UK.

Ray Charleton, an experienced automotive glazier, agreed to lend us a hand to do the fitting. The windscreen was the first to be installed. It was positioned into the rubber. A length of strong nylon cord was inserted into the groove in the windscreen rubber. The ends of the cord were overlapped with plenty of overhang. A liberal amount of kerosene was then applied to the rubber. This acted as an excellent lubricant. With Bill helping, the screen was then lifted into the windscreen aperture and positioned centrally. While Bill and I pushed hard on the inside, Ray carefully pulled the cord outwards, easing the rubber over the aperture edge. Working together we systematically progressed, slowly and carefully. Care must be taken not to tear the rubber, or to leave the rubber on the wrong side of the windscreen. Once the windscreen was in place it was then sealed with mastic between the rubber and the metal, as well as between the rubber and the glass. The excess was cleaned up with kerosene.

The chrome strip was inserted into the rubber followed by the finishing joiners. The rear window was installed in much the same way, although special attention had to be paid to the headlining and finishing strip.

The side windows proved much easier to install.

above: An original BMC transfer is applied to the inside of the windscreen. This was one of those finishing touches I was jumping out of my skin to apply. Care was taken to soak the transfer to remove any excess glue before applying it to a wet section of the windscreen. Air bubbles were removed by using the backing paper. It is best to start from the middle and work towards the edges.

above: Preparing to put the back window in, using the cord method. Much thicker cord was used in the end.

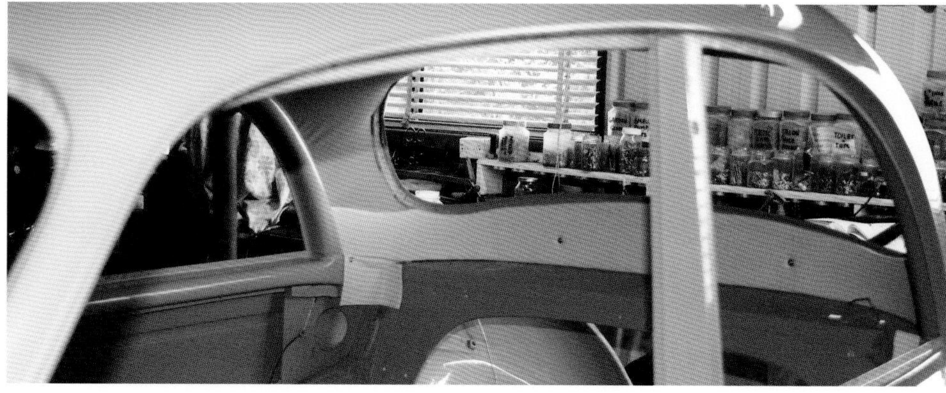

The windows were fitted from the inside outwards. It is normally a two person operation. With one person holding the glass in position the other can use the cord to ease the rubber outwards. Having three people made the installation even easier.

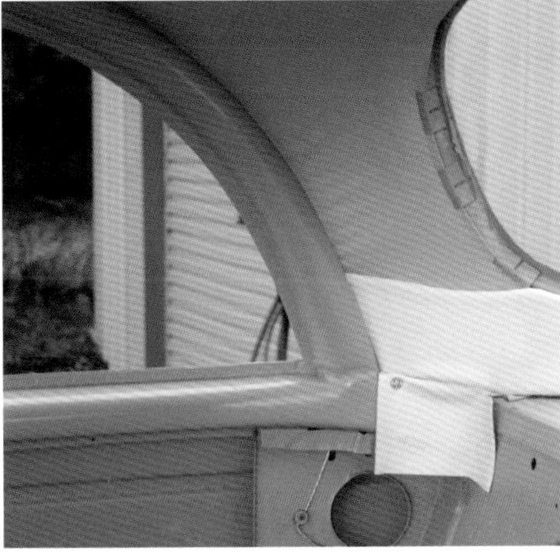

The apertures ready for the installation of the glass.

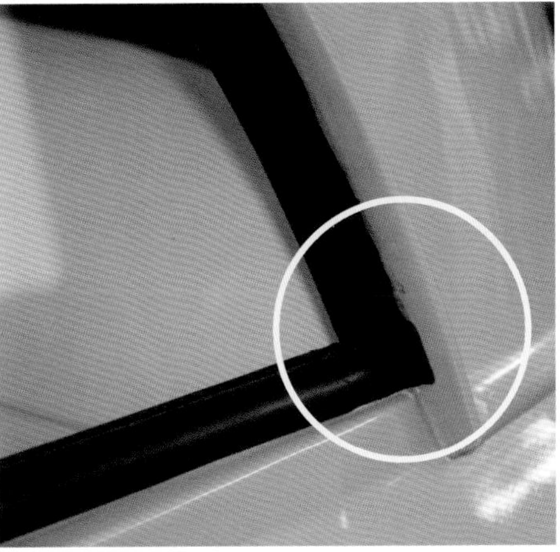

A little detailing makes such a difference. The overhanging rubber on the corner (left) was cut off with a scalpel, making a cleaner line.

above: 'Appleyard of Leeds' dealer transfer.

above: The rear window rubber holds the vinyl covered finishing strip in place. A lot of fiddling was required in order to achieve a good result.

The passenger's side door in the background leaning up against Bill's first ever restoration, a 1928 National Chevrolet. This restoration was completed about 40 years ago, and still presents very well.

All the glass fitted where it should be.

Inspiration

Phil Smith & Ray Newell

Phil Smith from the Minor Million Register (part of the Morris Minor Owners Club in the UK) regularly emailed me photos of activities and events the Million Register were holding.

Phil's images and his informative website provided much needed inspiration and useful information from the other side of the world.

Phil invited my family to stay at his house in the picturesque village of Youlgreave, near Bakewell in Derbyshire in the heart of the UK, for 10 days just before Christmas in 2008. It was an unforgettable family adventure – and there were times when I almost forgot I had a family! We toured all the famous sites including Oxford, home of the Morris Minor and where it all began in 1912, and Goathland – the home of TV's 'Heartbeat', the crime capital of the world, which features Blaketon's Morris Minor Traveller and a Morris Minor Panda Police Car from time to time. We also visited Lord Nuffield's house (not home). Our trip extended to Bath and Bristol, the home of the famous Charles Ware's Morris Minor Centre.

Along the way we caught up with Ray and Sue Newell at Phil's house in Youlgreave where we discussed this book and Ray's involvement as co-author, mentor and editorial assistant.

I am sure most of us would not be required to go on a once in a lifetime family holiday, or to such extremes to gain inspiration to finish off a Morris Minor project, but it all seemed a good idea at the time. It was not all fun. On one particular day, Phil and I had to do some very serious Morris Minor Million research. We visited owners and exchanged yarns and restoration notes. By lunch time we ended up at the Heritage Motor Centre at Gaydon, Warwickshire, where we viewed SMM 501, the first production Morris Minor. I could hardly sleep that night. I think this may have been due to jetlag or Morris Minor information overload, something which I am still getting over nearly two years down the track.

Phil Smith, one of the kindest people you could ever meet, with one of the most photographed number plates in the UK!

My long suffering family: Isabelle, Kim and Madeline at the gates of Buckingham Palace.

Goathland (Aidensfield) home of Heartbeat. The 'woodie' to the left is looking like it needs a little TLC.

One Minor Million owner had three Millions in various states of restoration.

Meeting Ray Newell for the first time – a life long dream.

William Morris' Garage in Longwall Street in Oxford. In this building in 1912 William Morris built his first car, the prototype for the 'Bullnose' Morris Oxford. The huge Motor Works at Cowley changed Oxford into an industrial city.

New Year period, however, the gate was unlocked and I went around the back and had a chat with some of the staff working on their own Minors... Thinking back they may not have been staff at all!

Phil Smith took me on a tour to meet the owners of other Million cars. We ended up at the Heritage Motor Centre at Gaydon.

Firewall

Assembly

This was one of the most exciting stages of the restoration, as it marked the beginning of the assembly process. With the painting completed, the firewall (bulkhead) was given a cut and polish in order to achieve a brilliant shine. The absence of components provided plenty of access to the corners and other difficult to get to areas. It also allowed a welcome opportunity to do any last minute rectification work, particularly touching up any blemishes in the Acrylic paint.

The snap lock freezer bag which contained the nuts and bolts from the firewall was located in 'The Shed'. With Concours in mind, every nut and screw was scrutinised before being buffed prior to fitting. Where possible, original items were refitted. However, occasionally new nuts and bolts were used. All the ancillary components were painted or buffed in order to ensure a factory type finish. The first items to be fitted were the original chassis and patent plates. These were soon followed by electrical components including the starter solenoid, the regulator box and the fuse holder. All the necessary grommets on the firewall were then added.

The SU fuel pump is located on the passenger side along with the windscreen wiper motor. In the interest of long term reliability, a new SU fuel pump was fitted. The original windscreen wiper motor was retained. It had been cleaned, tested, detailed and painted earlier. However, it was mounted using new rubber grommets which were purchased as part of a mounting kit from Bull Motif in the UK. Extra care was taken when fitting the wiper cable and assembly which is positioned behind the dash and held in place with special angled spacers with flat chrome nuts. The wiper cable was lubricated with grease and care was taken not to damage the paint work, especially where the wiper spindles protrude through the bodywork. Before leaving the firewall attention was given to the battery tray. The characteristic large rubber grommet, along with two rubber battery stops were fitted to the back, while a rubber mat was placed on the shelf. To enhance the finished look a rubber bead was put across the sharp top edge of the battery tray.

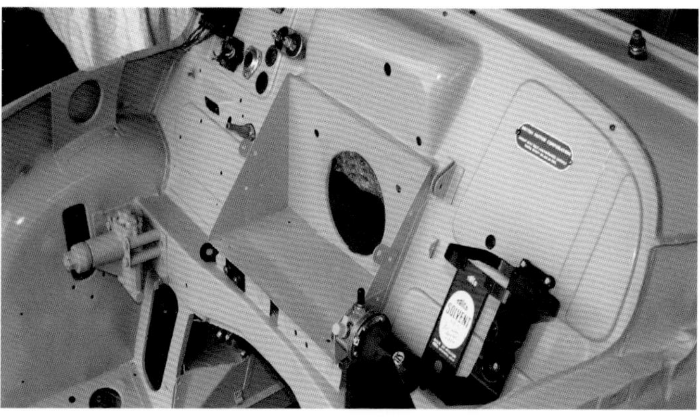

The windscreen wiper assembly fits behind the dash. With the windscreen in place, assembly is a two man job.

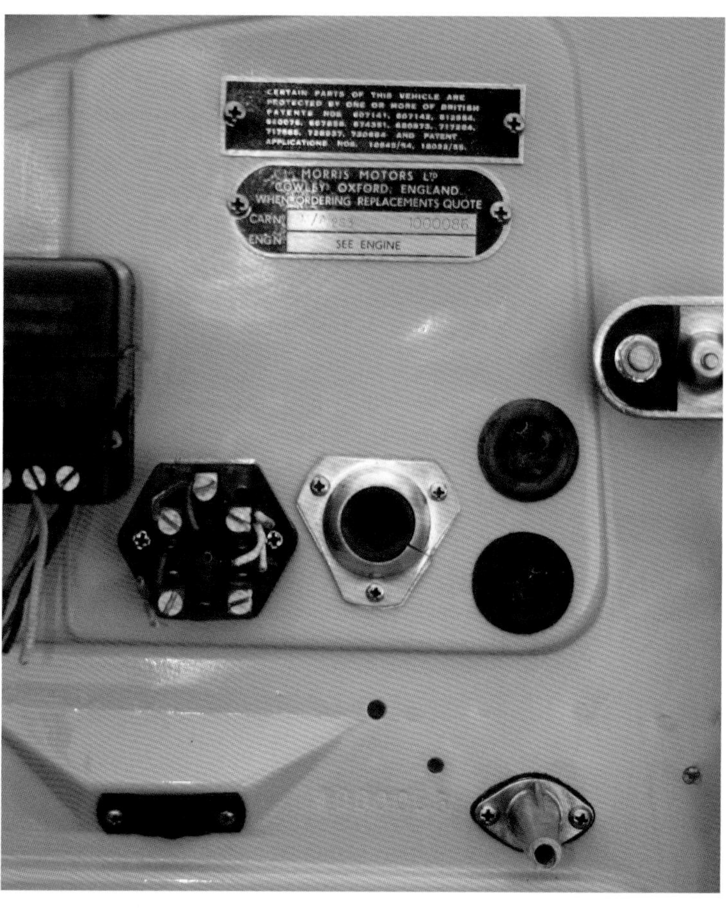

A new style of chassis plate was used from 1958. The patent remained unchanged. The chassis number is also stamped into the bulkhead.

above top: I wish I had reference photos like this to look at when I was restoring this car. A picture paints a thousand words... lucky as this book would be much fatter! A wise old man told me –"the best SU pump is a brand new one".

Motor

Mechanicals

The 948cc engines are bulletproof providing they are regularly serviced and the oil and water levels are checked frequently. We were aware at the time of purchase that the engine had been rebuilt at least once in its lifetime. This was borne out by the fact that even given the recent history with our family as the paddock basher, the engine performed well, never missing a beat. Nevertheless, with this restoration nothing was being left to chance and the decision was made to thoroughly check the engine out. Reassuringly a compression test revealed even compression on all four cylinders. With the engine safely secured on a workbench the strip down began.

Cylinder Head Removal

Though a relatively straightforward task, care must be taken when removing the cylinder head in order to minimise the risk of damage to any of the components. The following sequence was followed. First the manifold was removed by undoing the four brass and two steel manifold bolts. Next the rocker cover was easily removed by

The head complete with new valves and seals and painted with Kill Rust Mid Brunswick Green.

Easing the motor into the engine bay with the hydraulic lifter. Great care was taken not to mark the paint.

above: Having the engine on the workbench allowed for easy access to all components.

Two engine mounts fitted... release the motor!

Rocker cover and gasket.

undoing the two bolts on the top. After consulting the workshop manual the nine nuts which hold the head to the engine block were undone in sequence. A 9/16 AF socket was used to undo these as they were very tight. It is important to release the head nuts in the same order as shown for tightening as there is a chance that the head may get damaged by undoing them incorrectly.

Further dismantling of the head can now begin. Removing the nuts that hold the rockers to the head and lifting out all the push rods is fairly straightforward. However, care must be taken with the push rods to ensure they are put back in the correct order.

McKellar Tip – Make up a wooden rack by drilling holes in a length of wood. Number the holes and then place the corresponding rods in the appropriate hole. Mark 'front' on the face of the wooden rack.

With the split pin removed at one end all the rocker gear can be slid onto a stiff wire. On reassembly the rocker shaft can then be slid into all the rocker gear in their correct order. This wire trick keeps all the springs and other components in sequence.

With a tap of a wooden mallet, the head should be able to be removed. However, care must be exercised so as to avoid causing damage to the head face.

The valves can be removed next. A valve spring compressor is useful to assist with this task. With these tasks completed all that is left is a bare head.

Top End Rebuild

Given the engine's previous performance and the encouraging compression test, we decided to concentrate our efforts on reconditioning the top end of the motor. The valve guides proved to be in good order and even though the valves seemed perfectly OK, new ones were fitted anyway. This was a job we tackled ourselves. We purchased a tin of grinding paste. The grinding paste is coarse at one end of the tin and fine at the other. A valve grinding tool, which is a rubber sucker on a stick was also sourced. Each valve was positioned in the head with a drop of coarse paste on the rim of the valve. The grinding tool was then spun backwards and forwards until there was an even grey ring on the valve. The process was then repeated using the fine paste. Grinding in all the valves took just over two hours to complete.

The next step was to oil the guides with engine oil and reassemble the valves with springs. New type valve seals (which are like a cup) were fitted instead of the original rubber rings, as they are more effective. These fit under the valve collets.

With the head now fitted with new valves and the rocker gear in place, it was time to put it back on the block. Professional advice from retired mechanic Keith White was sought before reassembly commenced. Fortunately the bores were found to be in perfect order. With a new old stock head gasket (copper-asbestos-copper) fitted correctly the head was replaced and great care was taken to follow the three stage fitting process prior to 40 lb. ft. of torque being applied.

Additional components which were checked prior to fitting included a new thermostat complete with a new aluminium cover and the water pump which was fitted with a new seal.

Unleaded Head Conversion

It is worth a mention that most restorers would normally engage a professional to convert the head to run on unleaded petrol.

This was not done in this restoration.

above: The manifold fitted on earlier cars consisted of a two piece inlet and exhaust manifold, with the inlet made of aluminium. Cars after September 1959 had this later type integral cast iron unit fitted.

The engine steady bar fitted. This secures the engine to the firewall (bulkhead). This is a quality reproduction item.

above: The new water pump, bypass hose and thermostat cover fitted. The Mini timing chain cover can be seen with the Mini harmonic balancer front pulley at the bottom of the picture. Note the slightly smaller four blade fan which is standard on Australian Sydney built cars.

The 1¼ inch SU HS2 carburettor. The dash pot top should be black plastic. However, for aesthetic reasons a brass one was fitted.

The later 948cc cars were fitted with this air Cooper-type paper air cleaner in February 1959. This was referred to as the 'saucepan type'. The proportions were more in keeping with the cubic capacity of the engine.

Timing Chain

Timing Chain

To ensure quieter running the decision was taken to replace the single timing chain gears with a duplex one. Eliminating the possibility of timing chain rattle on the Morris Minor is always a desirable outcome. A duplex kit was duly purchased and a timing chain cover from a Mini was sourced.

McKellar Tip – Replace the two main bearing cap bolts with countersunk screws to avoid the heads fouling the bottom gear.

When fitting, it proved necessary to shim the bottom gear until it lined up with the top one. Initially both gears were fitted without the chain and a straight edge was used to line up the faces of the gears. Further work was necessary as the smaller bottom gear was out of line. In order to realign the two gears a shim was removed from the crankshaft. The Woodruff key was then placed into the crankshaft slot and the chain fitted. Care was taken when reassembling to make sure that the timing marks on the gears lined up. The oil thrower disc was then fitted and a new mini rubber oil seal was fitted to the cover. With a new gasket/seal fitted the cover was then bolted back together with particular notice being taken over the different sized bolts used. Finally a harmonic balancer from a Mini was fitted and everything was locked in place with the locking tab which was carefully tapped back.

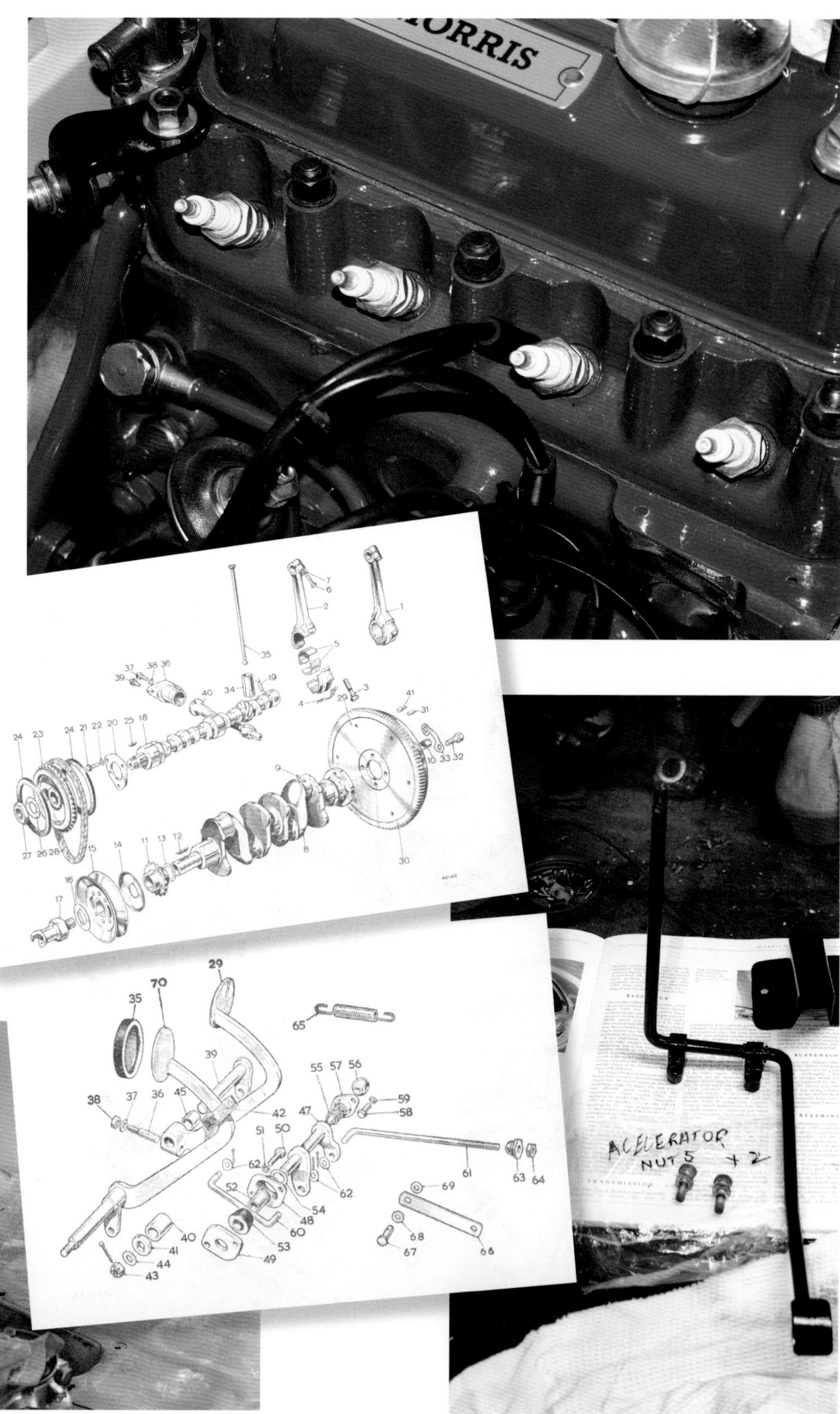

above top: Note the new oil light sender (red). Spark plugs are Champion N5.
above: The brake and clutch pedals fitted. The operating rods were fitted with new bushes and rubbers.

The accelerator pedal and cable cover detailed within an inch of their lives, ready to be installed. Note Ray Newell's 'Original Morris Minor' book in the background for ready reference!

Gearbox Seal

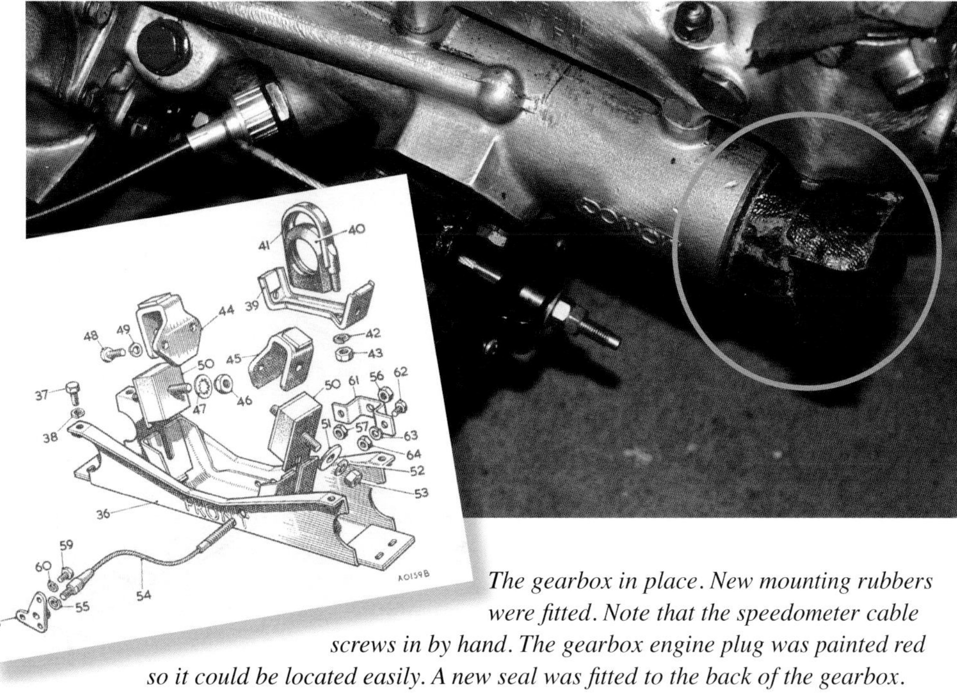

The gearbox in place. New mounting rubbers were fitted. Note that the speedometer cable screws in by hand. The gearbox engine plug was painted red so it could be located easily. A new seal was fitted to the back of the gearbox.

above: The old and new gearbox seal. The old one needed to be eased off the end of the gearbox. The new one was tapped on with a plastic-faced hammer.

The completed engine bay. Distinguishing features of a 1960 engine bay: flat top radiator – HS2 Carburettor – Braided fuel hose – Cooper 'saucepan' dry paper air cleaner – updated carburettor cable system – single piece manifold – bypassed thermostat heater system – vacuum advance pipe running around the front of the motor.

Front Suspension

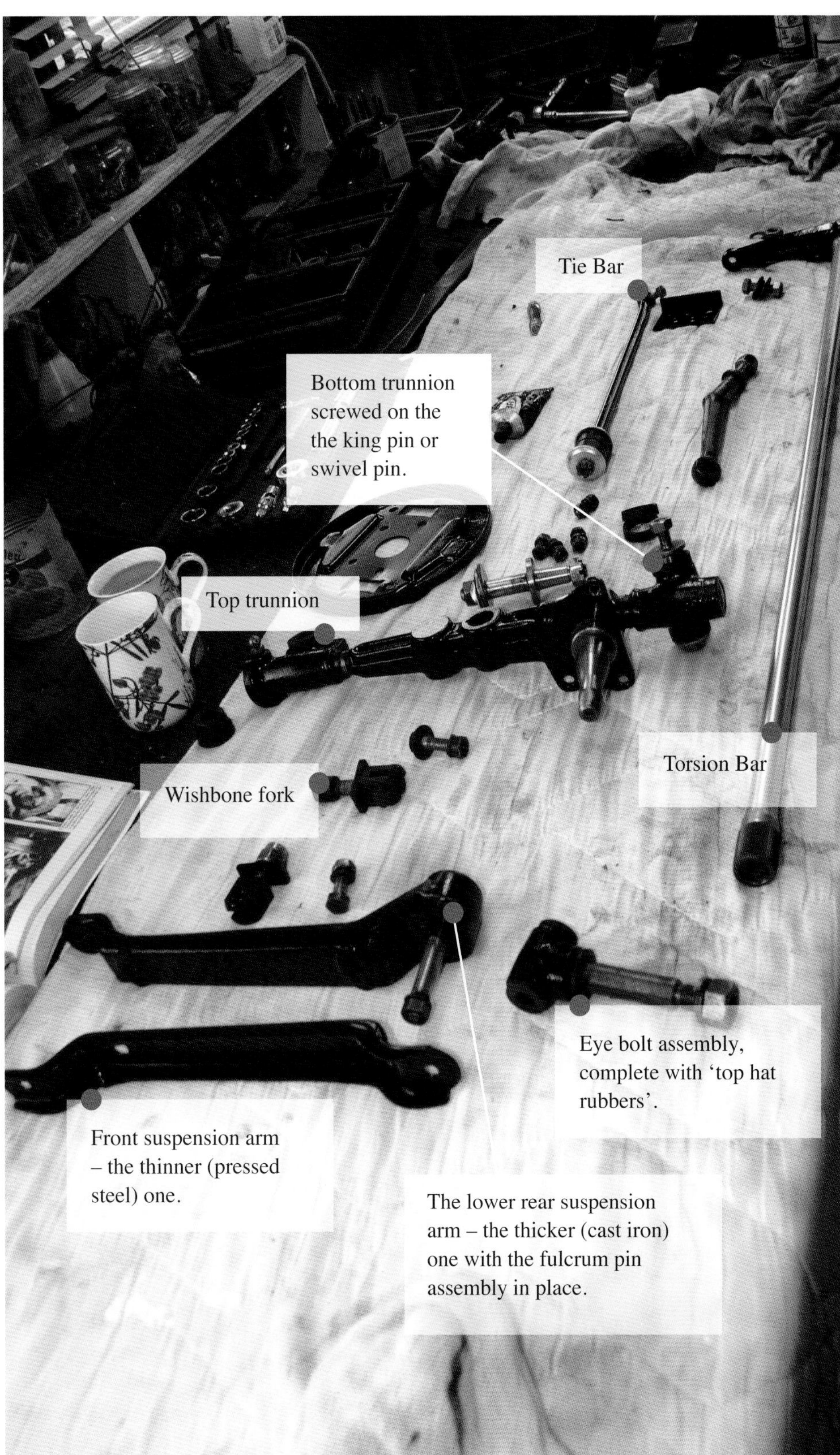

One of Bill's favourite pictures. You will see two cups of coffee. Mine remained untouched as I tried to work out how the suspension went back together.

In 1948 when the first Morris Minor was introduced, its handling and road holding set new standards. The Minors' independent front torsion bar suspension and low centre of gravity was largely responsible for this success and the basic design remained unchanged throughout the cars' twenty three year production history.

Most of the suspension components were painted black with the exception of the torsion bars, which were painted silver. The body of the Armstrong shock absorbers were left unpainted, the arms were painted black.

Refitting the Suspension

This subject required lots of thought and was the topic of conversation on many occasions. With most technical books on Morris Minor suspension refitting, the instructions are *"reassembly is a straightforward process and the reversal of above"*. While this is technically correct it is particularly difficult interpreting instructions in reverse! Looking at photographs or referring to another Morris Minor in full working order helps. However, the assembly of the front suspension caused a great deal of frustration at times. Here are the McKellar instructions/guidelines which, when used with the numbered diagram to the right, may make things a bit easier for anyone attempting the same task.

Before commencing loosely bolt the front shock absorber in place.

1. Refit the torsion bar to the car / put the shaft 72 *(the bolt end with the thread)* through the hole in the cross member and place the 74 *(lever retaining washer– with the slot)* engine side of the cross member and place the 75 *(lever locating – stepped washer with the step facing the front of the car)* back side of the cross member with 77 *(a locking washer)* and then 76 *(a large nut)*. Do it all up finger tight at this stage.
2. Slide 73 *(torsion bar lever)* on the torsion bar. Just leave it dangling there at first (if you leave it off you will have to undo it all and start again).
3. Slide 100 *(The lower rear suspension arm – the thick one)* onto the splines at the front of the torsion bar.
4. Make up the swivel pin (*fulcrum pin*) assembly with 49 *(the pin with the*

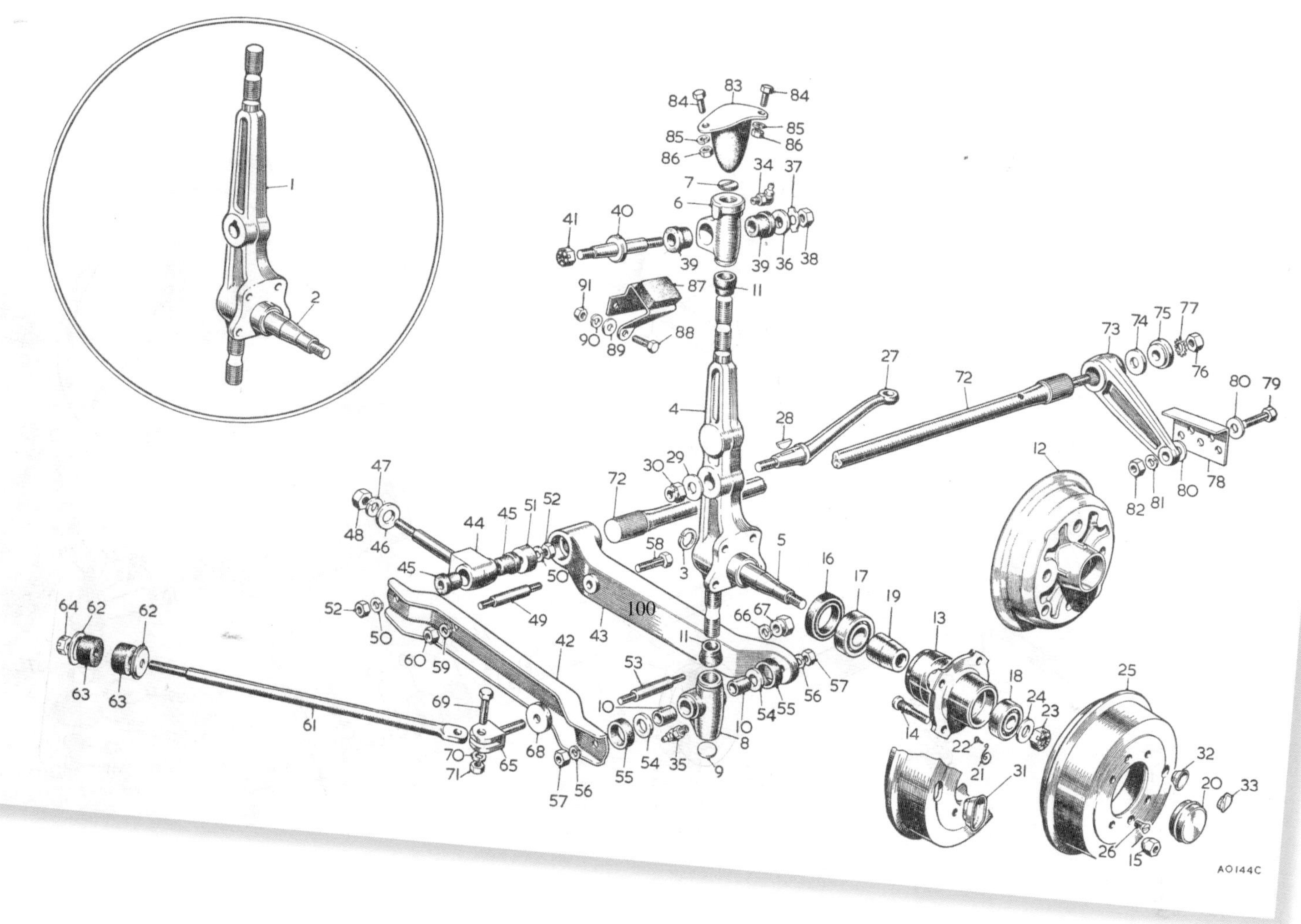

threads on both ends) 51 *(spigot pivot)* 50 *(spring washer)* 52 *(nut)*. Tighten this up.

5. Make up the eyebolt assembly with 44 *(the eyebolt)*, 45 *(top hat rubber bushes)*.
6. Push the eyebolt assembly (rubber top hats) on to the swivel pin assembly. Apply some lubrication such as PBR rubber grease to the swivel pin first.
7. You now should have an assembly consisting of 44, 100, 72. With the threaded bolt shaft on 44, put some lubrication on the shaft and slide into the Chassis Rail.
8. 46 *(washer – eyebolt adjusting washer)* – cut a slot in this (and make up another couple of slotted washers and keep them on hand so they can slide off and on if necessary for front end alignment).

   Followed by 47 *(lock washer)*, and then tighten with nut 48 *(nut)*. Finger tight.
9. Assemble the top trunnion, 39 *(bush for rubber link rubber)* two required, 36 *(washer for rear pivot)* 37 *(tab washer for rear pivot)*, 38 *(nut for rear pivot)*.
10. Screw 6 *(top trunnion)* on as far as it will go to 4 *(the swivel pin)* then turn it back 1¼ turns to give it maximum clearance.
11. Assemble with and place on 40 *(damper arm pivot bolt)*.
12. Lift the assembly of the swivel pin into place and fit the bottom trunnion nut to the 100 *(rear suspension arm)*. Thread the bottom trunnion to the swivel pin, but allow the trunnion the space to turn otherwise you will have no steering.

    The bottom trunnion consists of 53 *(lower link fulcrum pin)*, 10 *(bush... you need two of these)*, 54 *(the thrust washer for the fulcrum pin)*, 55 *(rubber sealing ring for link washer... you need two of these)*, 56 *(lock washer x 2)*, 57 *(the nuts that keep it all together)*.
13. Refit the lower wishbone / front suspension arm 101 *(front arm – the thin arm)*. Insert locking washers 50 and 56, tighten up 57 and 52 finger tight.
14. From the back push through bolt 58 locking washer 59 and nut 60.
15. Fit the 65 *(wishbone front fork)*, attach with 66 *(lock washer)*, and 67 *(nut)*.
16. Fit the 61 *(tie bar arm)*, 62 *(cup washer)*, 63 *(rubber bush to frame)* – one either side of the support and 62 and 64 *(slotted castellated nut)*.

Setting the Ride Height

Measure from the bottom of the large round hole in the inner wing (the one just along from the rectangular hole that the shock absorber arm goes through) to the hole in the rear lower suspension arm. This distance should be 355mm (+ or - 6mm). This is a good starting point for setting the ride height. The final ride height can be adjusted at a later stage – as the suspension may take some time to settle.

The tie bars are the slim rods that go from the end of the lower suspension arms, forward to the body. They are under load when you brake, stopping the suspension assembly from moving around. The rubber bushes at the end wear out and may need to be replaced periodically.

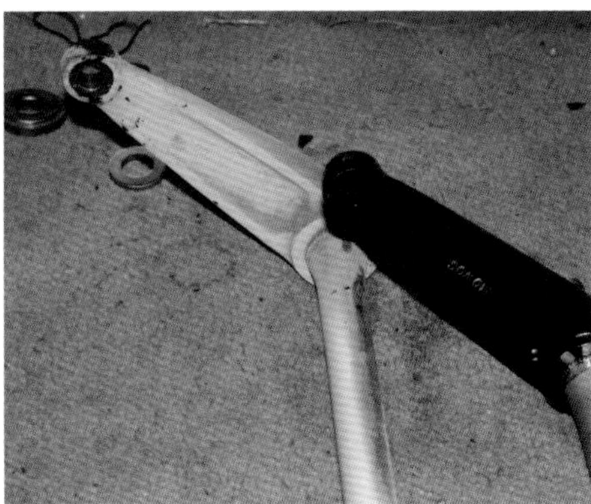

Roughly working out the positioning relationship of the rear end lever and the bar.

The bottom trunnion.

It is essential to give the swivel pin link an end float of .05mm (.002) to ensure the suspension functions correctly. Check the clearance with a feeler gauge. A split pin locks the pivot and shock absorber arm in place.

The tie rod end is bolted to the front suspension steering lever with a nylon locking nut. The tie rod end is an NOS item with a grease nipple on top. Many of the newer tie rod ends are a sealed unit. McKellar Tip – Lubricate the tie rod ends when servicing the car.

Tapping back the locking tab on swivel pin. With the suspension roughly assembled we checked and adjusted the tolerances before locking everything in place.

Alignment

Percy Scicluna, mechanic and long time member of the Morris Minor Car Club of Victoria, agreed to oversee and check the suspension.

Tracking

It is important the tracking is correct. One of the tell-tale signs of incorrect tracking is wear or scrubbing on one edge of the front tyres. The Morris Minor should have 0.4 degrees toe-in. The alignment of the front wheels should be such that they are slightly pigeon-toed in towards each other 2.5mm when in the straight-ahead position. Percy is seen here manually working out the tracking by using a plumb-bob and strings. I was surprised with the accuracy of this method. Adjustment was achieved by winding the track rod in or outwards. Once the correct measurement was achieved a lock nut secured the adjustment in position. It is important that the steering gaiter rubbers are loosened off and rubber grease applied between the rubber and the track rod to enable the track rod to turn freely.

Personal Recollection

Not long after this picture was taken we took the car for a quick test run to check Percy's handiwork. The car certainly tracked in a straight line. I recall speeding along the road and applying the brakes hard... off and on, off and on – off and on, with hands off the wheel to see if the Minor was braking properly and not pulling to the left or right. Glancing over, I caught a glimpse of Percy on the passengers side kneeling (without a seat and without the gearbox floor cover) grasping on to the dash... holding on for dear life *(sorry Percy I was carried away with the moment)*. With the restoration taking place in the middle of nowhere, we took advantage of the opportunity to use the sealed road in front of the property as a testing track.

Brakes – Front

Safety First. McKellar Tips

Always purchase and use the best components available when repairing the brakes on your Minor. Quality brake components are relatively inexpensive and may save your life in an emergency. When working on the brakes remember that brake dust can be highly toxic. Spray the brake drums and linings with soapy water with a hand sprayer. Make sure any asbestos impregnated dust is soaked and thoroughly wiped away. Dispose of contaminated rags and dust in a sealed plastic bag.

Reconditioned stainless steel lined wheel cylinders and new asbestos-free linings were purchased. The brake drums were checked for thickness and our local brake supplier machined the drums and matched the linings to the drums.

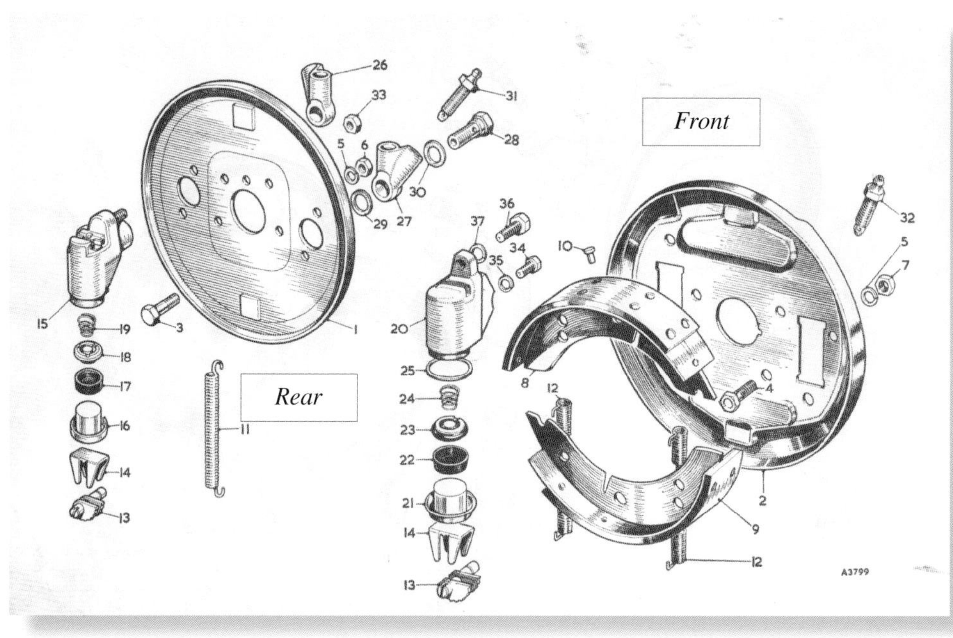

Starting with the Front

The front brakes were assembled on the bench top and fitted to the car with the suspension components. The assembly of the brakes and suspension was then checked by Percy Scicluna to make sure everything was in the correct place. To aid with the assembly reference was made to an 'exploded view' of the brake assembly picture found in a BMC Service Parts publication.

The starting point was bolting the backing plate onto the swivel pin with four bolts. We were unaware at the time that there are left and right hand backing plates. With two right hand sides and no left hand side, a search in the Organic Morris Minor Garden was necessary to complete the set. Incidentally the backing plates are marked left and right and have different part numbers!

McKellar Tip – Before fitting the wheel cylinders, wrap a rubber band around them to prevent the cups from falling out whilst working with them. These can then be cut off later, once the wheel cylinders are fitted. The front wheel cylinders are bolted to the backing plate and the metal equalizer hose is bolted into the back of the brake cylinders. The springs are then fitted to the back of the brake shoes and the bottom shoe is positioned in place. The correct springs are made up of a long coil section and a smaller coil section. The rule here is that the smaller coil section lines up with the adjuster on the wheel cylinder. The springs are fitted into the holes furthermost away from the wheel cylinder.

Once fitted up, the adjuster is then pushed into place, albeit with a little levering with a screwdriver. A new flexible hose is then screwed into the wheel cylinder. Use the copper washer supplied with the hose to seal the connection. A new brake bleeder screw was fitted to the rear of each assembly.

Tricks for restorers young and old. The backing plates are left and right handed. Be sure to use the correct plate.

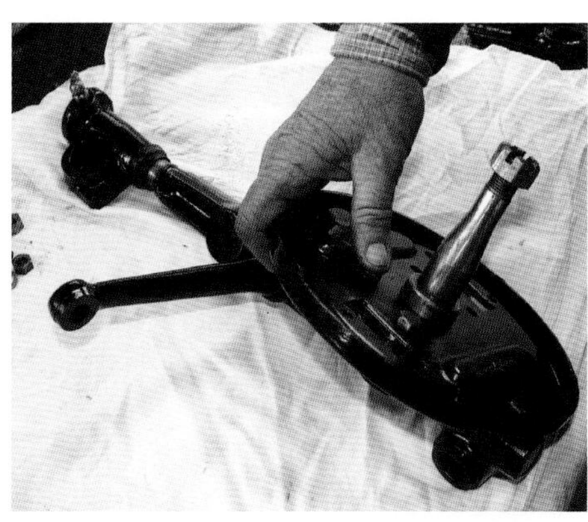

Applying the backing plate to the swivel pin with four bolts.

The backing plate fitted. Spring washers prevent it all coming undone. Check that the trunnion has plenty of movement. Note the holes for the wheel cylinders.

A rear view of the backing plate with the metal equalizer pipe in place. The wheel cylinders are fitted up and the bleed screw is inserted. The nuts and bolts will be touched up with black Kill Rust when assembly is completed.

above top: A new flexible hose was fitted.

above: With safety in mind new asbestos-free linings were purchased.

left: Percy checks that all is in order.

below: The wheel cylinders were reconditioned and fitted with stainless steel inserts. The threads on the wheel cylinders differ from car to car.

McKellar Tip – Make sure that all brake components are compatible before sending them off to be reconditioned.

Brakes – Rear & Bleeding

Wheel bearings and seals were replaced before fitting the hub to the axle. Percy tensioned the nut to the correct specifications. Note the split pin that locks the front wheel nut in place. The ends of the split pins were cut to an acceptable length and bent backwards. The grease cap was then tapped in place with a plastic faced hammer.

Using the pencil trick to hold the brake springs in position while fitting the brake shoes.

The rear hubs only have one brake cylinder per side. These differ in appearance from the front wheel cylinders.

The Back Brakes

There is only one brake cylinder per side. This is a much simpler assembly compared to the front brakes. The rear cylinder has to be allowed to slide freely, so applying a small amount of grease helps aid the movement. When assembling it is important to ensure that the bleed nipple points upwards.
It is imperative to purchase four rubber hats to fit over the bleed nipples to keep dirt and water at bay.

Refitting the Brake Drums

Before attempting to fit the brake drums, make sure the adjusters are adjusted in the fully anti-clockwise (down) direction. The drum should be able to be tapped on with the aid of a plastic faced hammer. Tap the drum sideways and around the edges until it sits flush against the hub. A good trick is to push the brake pedal once or twice to centre the shoes.

Adjusting the Brakes

The brake drum has a large hole in the front to assist in locating the adjuster – a torch may also be required. With a flat screwdriver turn the adjusting screw clockwise until the drum is fully locked. Test this by turning the drum around by hand. Once the drum is locked, turn the adjuster back ONE click anti-clockwise. The front wheels have two brake cylinders, so repeat the process with the other cylinder. The back wheels have only one adjuster per wheel. Before adjusting the rear shoes make sure the handbrake is fully off.

Bleeding the Brakes

It is essential to bleed the brakes to remove any air from the hydraulic system. Any trapped air bubbles in the system will result in a soft or 'spongy' brake pedal.

Always use new brake fluid and never reuse old fluid. Brake fluid is hygroscopic – which means it absorbs water vapour from the atmosphere. Due to the pressures in the brake pipes any water that the fluid absorbs may create a vapour lock, making the brakes ineffective. Water in the fluid will also cause corrosion, the main cause of brake problems. Brake fluid will also melt and remove paint similar to paint stripper, so it is important to remove any spilt fluid.

Partly because of its unique position in the chassis rail, it is most important to keep the area around the master cylinder scrupulously clean and free from any debris that may inadvertently drop into the aperture.

Fill the master cylinder (to the bottom of the filler) with NEW fluid and lightly replace the cap. – The fluid tends to squirt out of the master cylinder when the pedal is depressed. Keep a torch handy to keep an eye on the fluid level in the master cylinder.

The reservoir will empty quickly, so keep in mind to top up every six strokes.

Brake bleeding involves slackening off a bleed screw which is located on each of the wheel cylinders. With the aid of an assistant, the brake pedal is carefully pumped, forcing the fluid out of the system until any air is expelled.

McKellar Tip – Use a 'specialist bleeding kit', as it incorporates a one-way valve, which keeps the air from being drawn back into the system.

Starting with the rear left wheel, loosen off the bleed nipple and fit the tube over the nipple with the other end into a jar with some fluid in it. This also acts as a non return valve for the air. Using a ¼ inch Whitworth spanner make sure you can easily and quickly open and close the bleeder nipple.

With the nipple open, call to your assistant 'down!' At this point the brake pedal is depressed SLOWLY.

When the pedal is fully depressed, tighten the nipple. Repeat this process until no air is left in the line. Move to the right rear wheel and repeat the process. Then move to the front left wheel and then the right front wheel. The whole process may need to be repeated twice to achieve a good firm pedal.

Screw the adjuster fully in the clockwise direction until the hub is locked. Then click the adjuster anti-clockwise back ONE click only. The wheel should be able to be rotated.

Keep an eye on the brake fluid level in the master cylinder. Failure to do so may mean repeating the process a number of times.

A reconditioned stainless steel lined master cylinder was purchased and fitted.

Mum will be pleased. Dressed for the occasion. Bill's in trouble for working in his best shirt. It is a two man job even with a 'specialist bleeding kit'. Note the ¼ inch Whitworth spanner – one of Bill's favourites. The black tape quickly identifies it for easy retrieval from the tool box.

Differential and Rear Springs

Differential

Before undertaking the restoration some serious road-testing was undertaken to assess the condition of the mechanical parts. After all, in the previous five years the car's main duties were confined to teaching the kids to drive and some paddock work.

On our road test the differential passed with flying colours and without a murmur.
As a precaution a new front oil seal was fitted. As for the rest it was just a case of improving appearances.

Replacing the Differential Oil Seal

With the back axle out of the car and the oil drained, things were made much easier.

1. The nut in the centre of the drive flange was removed. These are usually very tight, but fortunately this particular one came off quite easily.
2. The flange was then tapped forward and rotated as the process progressed.
3. The dust cover was then removed and the old seal was levered out.
4. This task was undertaken under the watchful eye of our friend Percy, who modified the new oil seal by carefully taking the spring out – winding the spring into itself to put more tension on it – before placing it back in the assembly.
5. The seal was then carefully tapped back into place and the dust cover replaced.
6. Finally the nut was then replaced and tightened with a torque wrench to 140 lb. ft.

Now for the Aesthetics

With the aid of some automotive paint stripper and an electric drill with a wire brush attached, the paint and rust was removed from the rear axle. The stripping process revealed a number on the right hand side of the back axle which corresponded with the differential number on the production records. Yet another plus point in the authenticity record. After being wiped over with Prepsol to remove any residual grease and oil, the axle casing was warmed with an electric heater for a short time in preparation for the spraying of a good coat of black gloss Kill Rust.

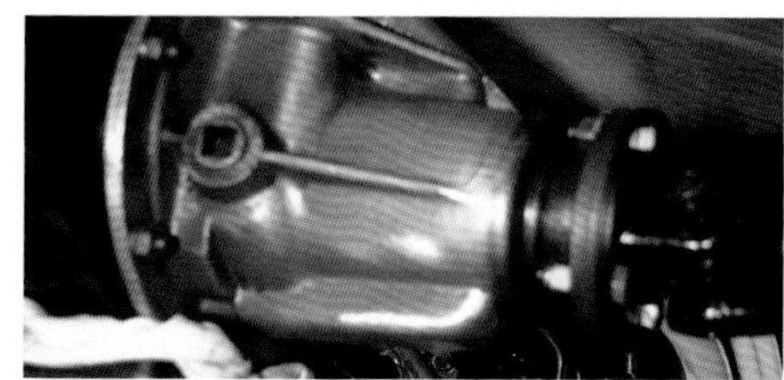

above and left: Removing the paint from the axle housing. The differential was left unpainted and was cleaned and polished up to good effect. The back axle was given a generous coat of Kill Rust.

Rear Springs

This was an area where a compromise was made in terms of originality. In December, 1958 the springs on the Morris Minor were changed from seven $^{7}/_{32}$ inch leaves to five ¼ inch leaves. The seven leaf springs provide better road holding (in my opinion), so the springs from the Green 4 door saloon featured on page ten, were acquired.

In keeping with the high standard of the restoration these were stripped down, cleaned and resprayed to the same standard as the other components.

The assembled springs with the U brackets holding everything in place. Note the original bump rubber. 7 leaf springs were used.

Rear Springs Assembly

The rear shackle plates and all the components that make up the spring assembly were stripped and painted. U bolts, rubber pads, rear shackle pins, nuts, rubber bushes and anything that belonged to the rear suspension was purchased new. The rear bumper stops were in good condition so these were cleaned-up with some thinners. There were no hidden mysteries here and all the components were assembled with the aid of the diagram (right).

McKellar Tip – Ensure the lower shock absorber bolt is inserted through the mounting plates BEFORE the springs are in place.

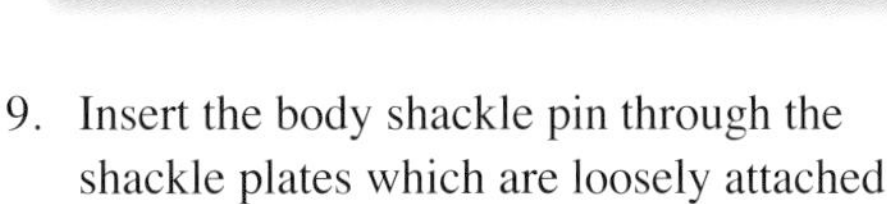

Step by Step Guide to Fitting Rear Springs

Make sure the back of the car is supported by axle stands. With the rear springs loosely assembled to the axle, swing everything round so that it faces the correct way up... (Springs smiling upwards.)

1. Assemble the metal front shackle pin arrangement by bolting the metal plates to the hanger with the four nuts, lock washers and bolts supplied. A new kit which consist of two plates with a special bolt pin arrangement (for each side) can be purchased.
2. Insert the new shackle rubbers into the spring ends. Lubricate with rubber grease.
3. Offer the spring up to the front mounting point.
4. Insert the front shackle pin through the fitting pushing it right the way through to the opposite side.
5. Tighten up the nut which locks the pin in place by pulling it through the mount. Complete this for both sides.

   By this stage the front of the springs will be attached to the body of the car.
6. Place a jack under the back axle and offer the rear of the springs up to the body.
7. Insert the back shackle rubbers into the springs. Apply rubber grease.
8. Insert the body shackle rubbers into the mounts (holes) in the body.
9. Insert the body shackle pin through the shackle plates which are loosely attached with the spring washers and nuts.
10. With the aid of a jack lift the back axle to help align the springs for final fitting.
11. Insert the shackle pins through the mounting points and loosely fit with the spring washers and nuts... don't tighten anything just yet.
12. If it looks like everything is in place, lower the jack a little further so the weight of the car is on the springs. Finally tighten everything up and lower to the ground.

Rear Shock Absorbers

These are easy to replace provided the lower shock absorber bolt is inserted through the mounting plates BEFORE the springs are in place. The shock absorber is bolted in place through the mounting plates. The linking arm is attached with rubbers to a support through the body. Use plenty of rubber grease and bolt in place. The lower link bolts into the shocker arm. Be sure to use locking washers. Keep an eye out for any leaks from the shock absorbers.

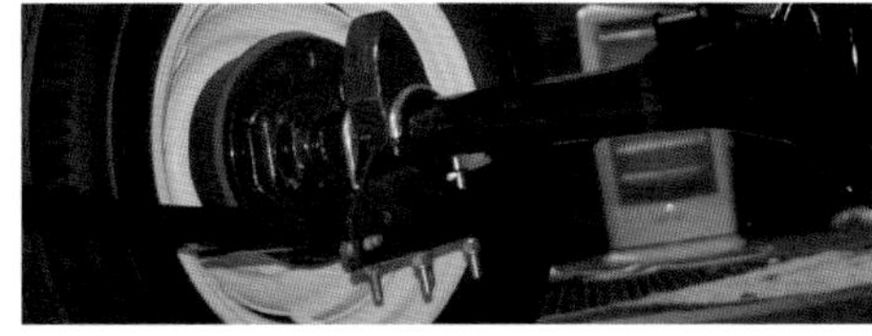

above top: Attaching the U bolts. Be sure to insert the lower shock absorber bolt.
above: The springs are attached to the front shackles via the plates and pin assembly.
above right: The front shackle plates and pin assembly (ready for the pin).

Electrical

Todd Elliott Auto Electrician

Todd Elliott, a retired auto electrician from Bendigo (Victoria) agreed to oversee the installation of the new wiring loom and to check over the electrics. While this may have been a challenge for us on our own, with Todd's vast experience to call upon, any reservations we might have had were soon allayed.

With the loom laid out in position it was relatively straightforward to work out what belonged inside the car and what was positioned behind the dash. A set of wires which service the SU fuel pump and the windscreen wiper motor run along the inside of the dash, and pass through a grommet in the firewall located on the passenger side. The main part of the loom passes through the firewall (bulkhead) on the driver's side and is secured by a metal finisher. The loom branches into two sections once it enters the engine compartment. The first section takes in the regulator box, fuse holder and starter solenoid. It then runs to the front of the car along the top of the inner wheel arch on the driver's side of the engine bay taking in the horn and driver's side lights – then across the front of the car (through a plastic protective sleeve) beneath the radiator to the passenger side front. This is where the headlight, parking light and indicators are connected by bullet connectors. Spot welded retaining clips help hold the loom in place. The second branch of the loom takes in the engine components including the starter motor and the generator. The second branch is joined by bullet connectors and runs briefly through a plastic sleeve, past the gearbox and alongside the prop shaft to the rear of the car. It enters the boot through a rubber grommet in the boot floor. This spur services the indicators, parking lights, stop lights and the number plate light. Once again the loom is held in place by spot welded clips attached to the underbody.

Under Todd's watchful eye, great care was taken to identify the correct wires and bullet connectors and to ensure that wires to the regulator box were positioned correctly before connection. Fortunately this crucial part of the installation was helped by the fact that the original wiring had been cut and left in situ on the factory fitted regulator box. With a wiring diagram at hand, Todd checked the wiring to each component and methodically worked his way around the car. A temporary battery arrangement was rigged up and this allowed for regular checks on the power supply to all components. Even with Todd's expertise there were a number of occasions when the fuses had to be replaced!

Inferior Tail Lights

Up to this point in the restoration there had never been a problem with any of the new old stock (NOS) items which had been purchased from the UK. However, all that changed with the rear lights. Only reproduction units were available. These were not quite up to usual high standard. The quality of the lens and chrome base was exceptional, but it soon became obvious that the globe holder would never function reliably, due to a badly designed, poor quality fitting. To rectify the problem the globe fitting from the original tail light was drilled out and screwed into the reproduction unit. Fortunately, with this modification the units worked perfectly. Just as well, as the tail lights had been purchased six years previously. There was no chance of getting them replaced.

The reconditioned indicator switch fitted.

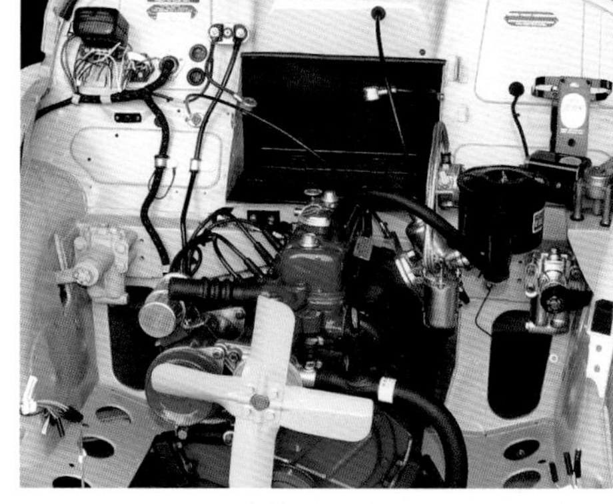

Wires were loosely put in place prior to final fitting to the electrical components.

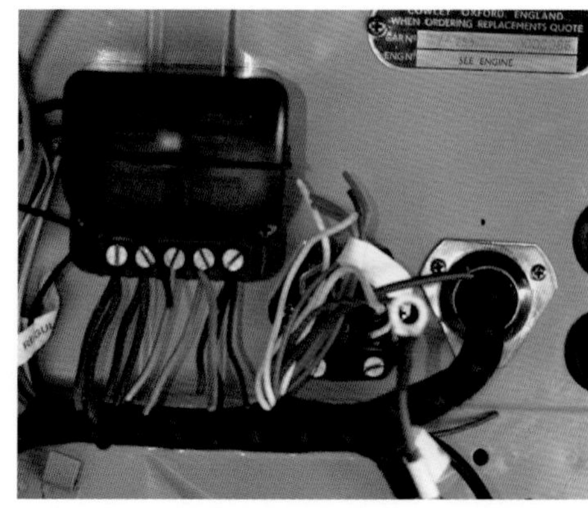

A McKellar Tip that really worked. Leaving the original wires in place on the factory fitted regulator box paid dividends when it came to fitting the new regulator box and wiring loom.

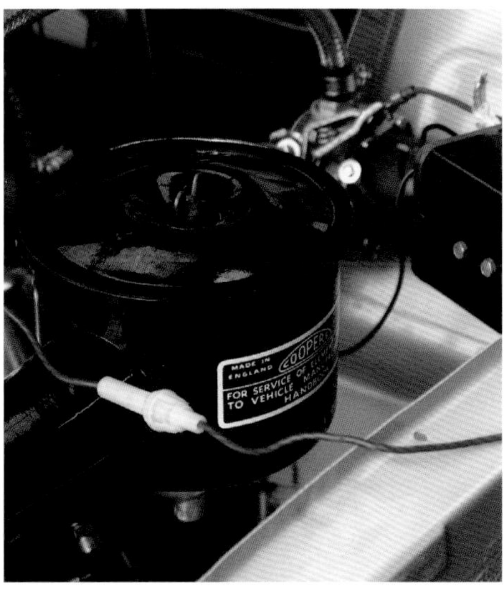

above: Power to the car via a car battery sitting on a milk crate positioned along side the car. This was fused (which blew often).

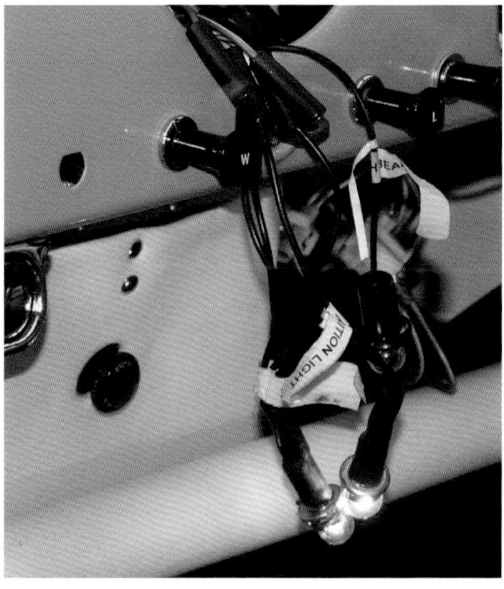

above: This looks promising!

above: The trafficators were taken apart and cleaned. The long pivoting rivets were replaced by screws which were glued in place.

above: Modifications. An original style globe holder was screwed in place using self tappers. This was a more positive arrangement. The offending poor quality holders are in the foreground.

Final adjustments. One of those nice simple tasks that puts a smile on your face and makes restoring worth all the heartache and pain.

The Million almost becomes alive as the power to the lights is switched on for the very first time. Even the brake lights worked... a true Kodak moment.

Parcel Tray and Heater

Parcel Shelf and Heater Shroud

948cc Morris Minors manufactured after February 1959 – built to the Deluxe specification – shared an updated heater shroud and an enlarged parcel shelf with an aperture for the steering column. The Morris Minor Million had this specification.

The original parcel shelf had completely collapsed and the heater shroud had also seen better days. It was an easy decision to import a parcel tray and crash pad kit from Newton Commercial in the UK.

The heater shroud was a light grey colour originally, however, the replacement one was supplied in black. In order to achieve a good match this was covered in white vinyl to match the crash pad. This was completed to good effect. However, the assembly of parcel tray took a long time. The instructions looked like some sort of brain teasing puzzle. Fortunately line drawings were supplied and eventually the cardboard tray was fixed to the white vinyl covering, through the metal support rail with bifurcated rivets, which was then glued to the crash pad. The heater shroud was then attached via a metal bracket to the parcel shelf.

The heater unit was found to be in good working condition. The heater and all associated components were stripped back to bare metal and sprayed black before final assembly. The fitting of the heater unit, the parcel shelf and the heater shroud proved difficult and at first it seemed as though we were adopting the wrong approach. However, with the heater hoses and demister ducts added to the assembly, final fitting proved much easier. With everything screwed in place and the heater working perfectly, suddenly everything seemed right with the world.

above: The newly covered reproduction black cardboard heater shroud covered in white vinyl.

above: This original metal fitting had to be attached. The clip hangs from the bottom of the back of the dash. In the interest of originality some bifurcated rivets were purchased.

above: Before and after.

above: The Smith's recirculatory heater, standard in Minor Millions.

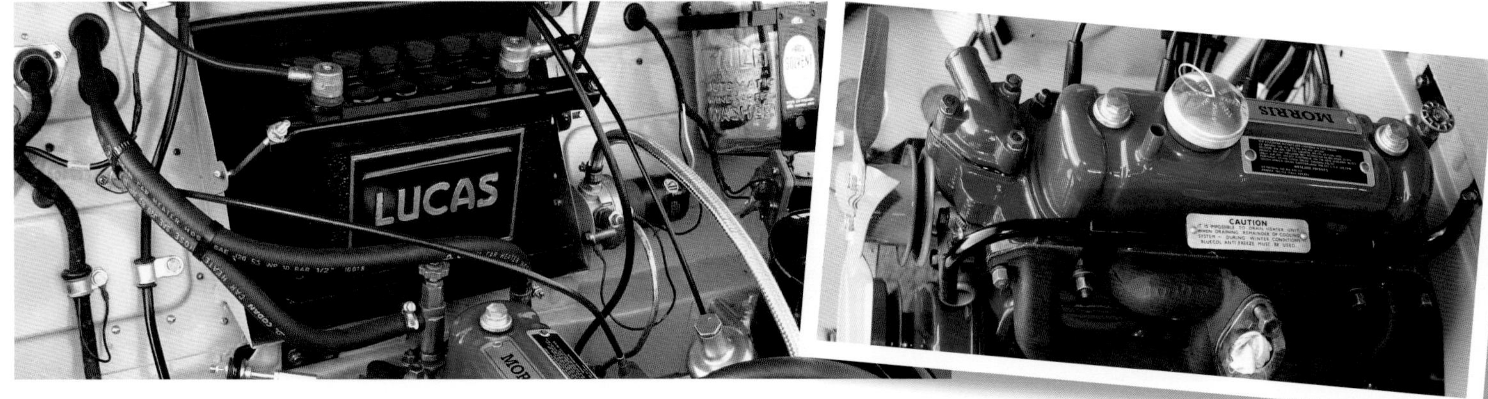

The heater hoses pass neatly through grommets in the firewall (bulkhead). The water flow is controlled by the Smith's brass tap. Unlike Australian cars, water flows from the heater through a black painted brass pipe which runs the length of the manifold, bypassing the thermostat and joining the bottom radiator hose. This method heats the vehicle interior faster as the thermostat is not required to open before the flow of hot water reaches the heater.

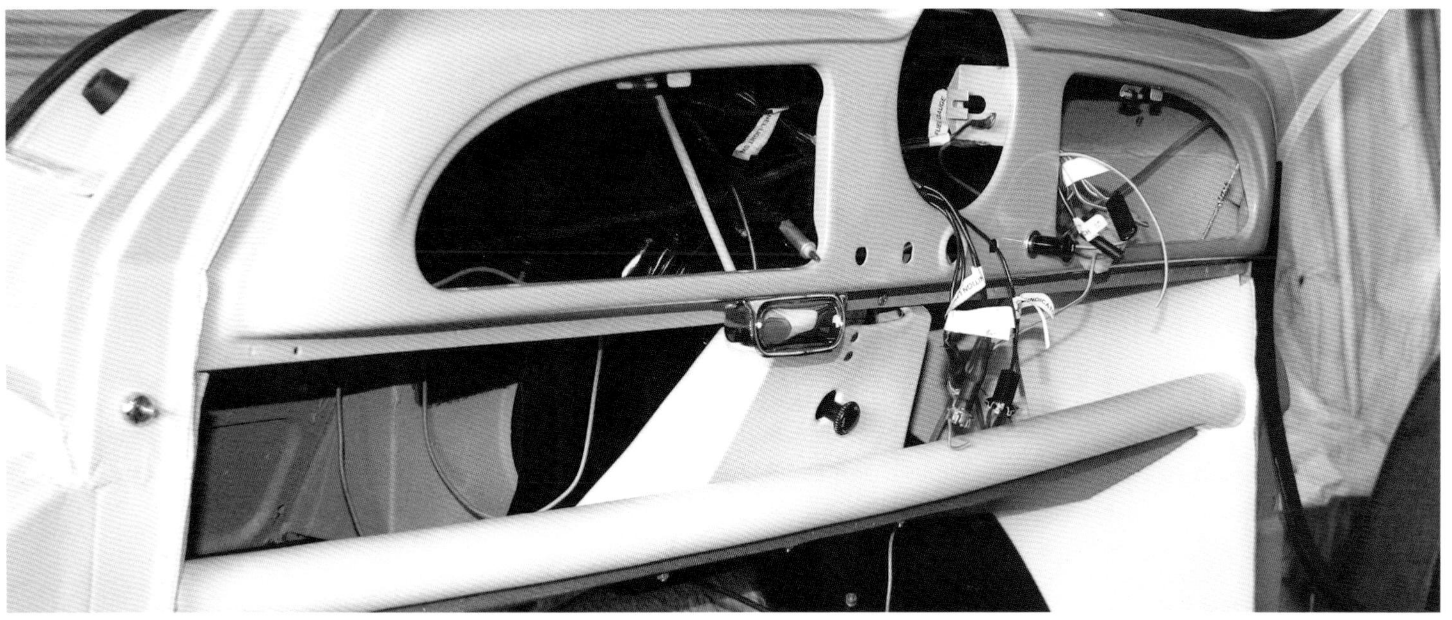

The Smith's recirculatory heater, with the fresh air attachment mounted on the base. This attachment screws to an opening in the floor, through which fresh air flows via a channel running the width of the firewall from outside the car.

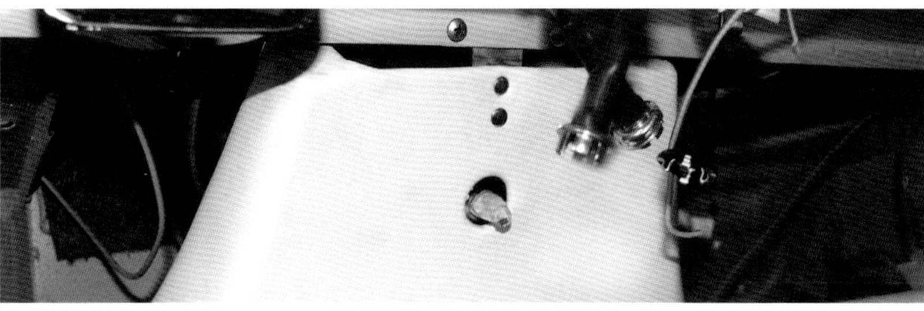

above: The heater is secured to the underside of the dash by two large Phillips head self tapping screws which pass through the parcel tray and are screwed to the fresh air opening. The parcel shelf is fastened to the firewall with nuts and bolts. Large Phillips head self tapping screws attach the parcel shelf to the lower dash side panels.

The fresh air attachment with the cable operated flap valve. The splitter pipe is attached to the upper section of the heater and (feebly) directs the heated air through ducts to the left and right of the dash to demist the windscreen.

Dash – Fitting and Detailing

Spending Some Quiet Time

Visually, the dashboard is one of the most important areas of any restoration, as once seated, this area is constantly in your line of vision. Particular attention was therefore taken with the fit and finish of all the components. Special care was taken with the appearance and assembly of the glove box lids. These were sprayed with a number of coats of Acrylic and allowed to dry for weeks before they were cut back and polished. The glove box lids on the late 948cc models, including the Minor Million, differ in terms of their construction. They are more detailed and better finished. In order to reassemble the refurbished components the small painted handles were first screwed in from the back. Next the fabric covered wooden inserts were then fitted into the back of the glove box lid and secured with long fine screws. These also attach to the chrome finisher around the edges. Finally chrome hinges were screwed with special wood screws to the underside of the glove box doors.

Before any of the components were installed, a black sound proofing mat was fixed to the inside of the firewall and along the back of the parcel shelf. This was purchased in kit form and supplied by Newton Commercial (UK). In the interests of originality, some original brass button headed clips were salvaged from the firewalls of some of the cars in the Morris Garden. These were cleaned and polished before being inserted into the sound proofing and affixed through the holes in the firewall. With the sound proofing in place the process of fixing all the other components could begin in earnest. Replacement reproduction black pull switches had been purchased from the USA. These were a push fit as per the original design. It was important to remember to push in the small locking pin underneath each of the knobs which secure them to the switch shafts. With this in mind, the starter pull was the first to be installed. This coincided with the wiring loom installation. The light switches were then wired up and fitted, along with the ignition and the wiper switch. The choke cable then followed. Due to the fact that there is not a lot of room behind the dash, it is essential to allow plenty of time for this job and to give serious consideration to making yourself as comfortable as possible in a confined space!

The speedometer cable, fuel gauge, dash and warning lights were then connected into the back of the speedometer. With these connected, the unit was then fitted into the dash by sliding it into position and tightening the Phillips head securing screws located on either side of the speedometer. The glove box inserts were fitted next. New cardboard inserts were purchased on eBay and fortunately they proved to be good quality reproduction items. To fit, they fold inwards so they can be inserted through the apertures in the dash. The glove box aperture lip and clips hold the inserts in place and additional support is provided by a bracket which is located on the underside. The glove box lids were attached using special screws which locate through the cardboard inserts into supporting clips.

Final jobs included ensuring that the steering wheel bracket was bolted firmly in place before fitting the driver's side glove box inserts and carefully locating the painted speedometer rim, which needed to be firmly pushed into the dash to secure the unit.

McKellar Tip – Delay the fitting of the glove box inserts until late in the whole restoration. One reason is that the fitting of the bonnet hinges will require access from under the dash without the inserts getting in the way. Final speedometer fitting should be delayed too, as access may be required for the checking and testing of electrical components. Taking the speedometer in and out may cause damage to the surrounding paint work, particularly if the speedometer rim has been put in place.

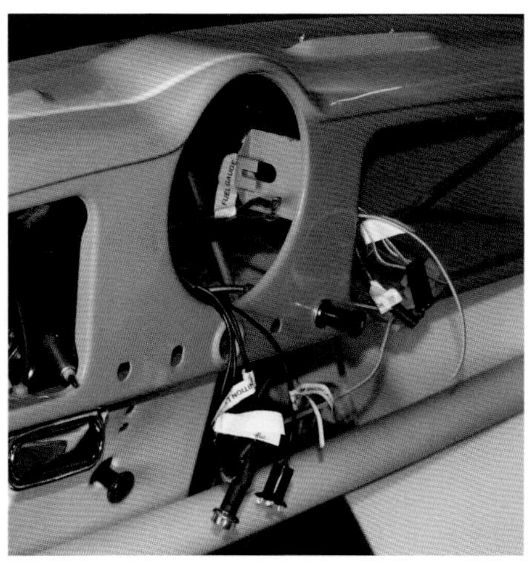

The pull start knob and cable fitted. A large nut secures this from behind. It is important to remember to fit the tiny dash light switch.

A special screw secures the horn push button assembly. The stylish ashtray is secured to the underside of the dash by two screws.

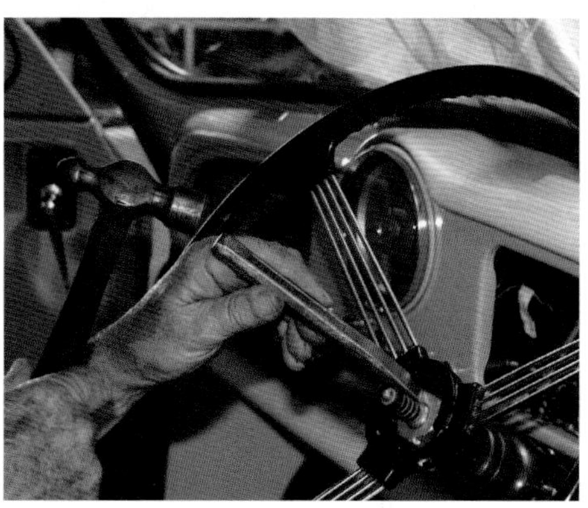

above: A cold chisel was crudely used to tighten the steering wheel nut. The correct socket was later obtained for this task.

below: A view of the right hand bracket that supports the speedometer.

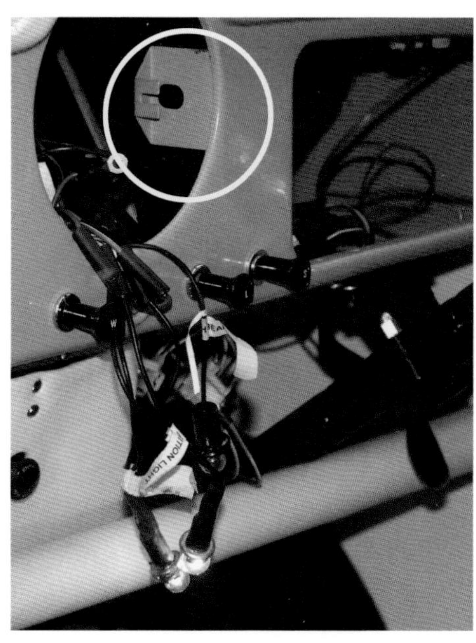

The passenger's side glove box lid has a smooth action. Note the roller locking clip and tab.

Reproduction cardboard glove box inserts with original style rivets.

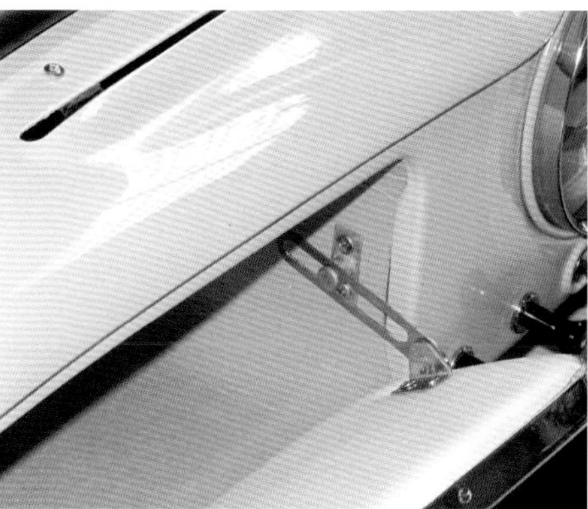

The passenger's side glove box lid support takes the weight of the lid once it is fully opened.

The driver's side glove box lid is impeded by the steering wheel. The lid was removed on the subsequent 1962 Morris Minor update.

A chrome glove box finisher was used from February 1959. The original ignition lock with key number FP713 was retained.

The dash light off-on switch. Black reproduction plastic switch pulls were purchased on eBay from the USA.

The black sound proofing mat was neatly fitted to the inside of the firewall and along the back of the parcel shelf. In the interests of originality, original brass button headed clips were salvaged from the firewalls of some of the cars in the Morris Garden. The parcel shelf is a reproduction item purchased from Newton Commercial (UK).

Door Locks and Windows – Fitting

Assembly

Two door saloons, Travellers and Convertibles all share the same door arrangement.
The four door cars have a slightly different arrangement.

The doors were carefully disassembled before painting. Before removing anything, the screws, nuts, bolts and clips were soaked for over a week in Inox. The screws, special washers, nuts, bolts and hinges etc were carefully placed into snap lock freezer bags and securely stored until required for reassembly.

With the handles and door cards removed, any sealing material covering the access holes in the door was taken off. The door handle assembly and window regulator were then clicked out of the window track and unbolted.

Next, any bolts holding the frame to the door casing on the inside and any of the various bolts holding the window frame in place were removed. Then working up through the two square holes to gain access to the inside of the door, the two nuts on the studs that hold the quarter light window section were released. Extra care was taken here as experience had suggested that these were prone to snapping off. After this the screws that attach the external door handle and the escutcheon plate 'speed nut' were removed.

With any existing felt window seals removed, in order to make a little extra space, a first attempt was made to lift the frame out carefully. However, a fair bit of wiggling and jiggling was required before the frame was finally released. This process was repeated for both doors.

Before starting, clear the workbench and put down some layers of blankets as a pad. The Acrylic paint is often still soft weeks after spraying and can mark easily.

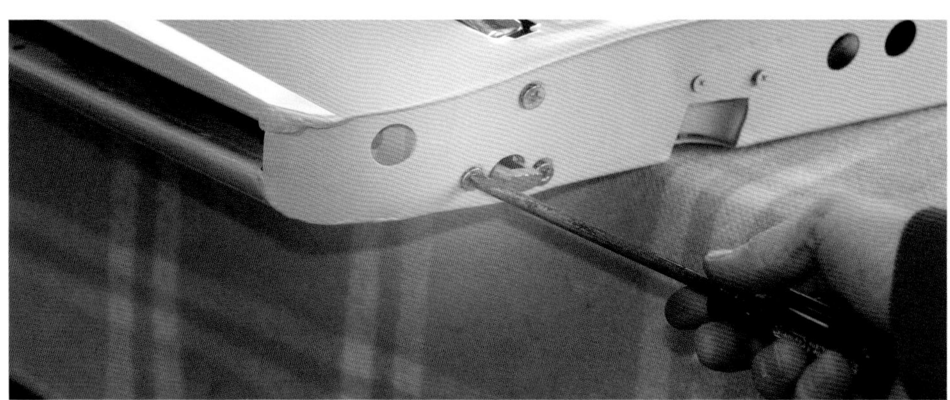

The door handle was slipped in from the back and secured with three countersunk screws and special locking washers. The key number is stamped on the face of the door lock mechanism. It is a good idea to make a note of this. Replacement keys are available on eBay or from the MMOC in the UK.

*The remote control assembly was fitted by threading it across the width of door to where it links to the handle assembly.
It is held in place by four countersunk screws. Be sure to fit it with the folded tabs in the lower position highlighted. They can be fitted upside down in error.
above right: These thick felts tension the long lever and prevent rattles. They were secured using contact adhesive. This was an important consideration in this restoration as rattles and knocks had to be eliminated for peace of mind.*

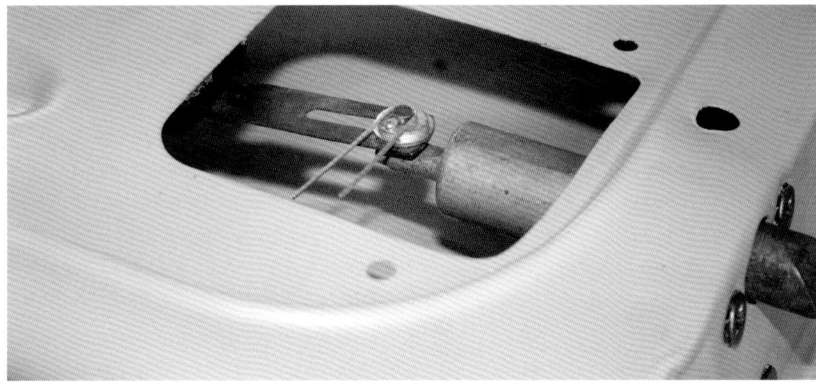

above: The lever was hooked over the pin and secured with a washer and a fine split-pin. The split-pin ends were snipped off with side cutters. The remote door opening operation was then tested.

The escutcheon plate was replaced by sliding it down the fitted door handle and hooking it in to the front end in the door panel cut-out. The peg at the other end was fed through a hole in the handle depression, and fixed in position with a spire lock nut (speed nut).

The window regulator was slid in from the back and secured by four bolts (above). It is advisable to lubricate this with grease prior to fitting as this cannot be done once it is in position.

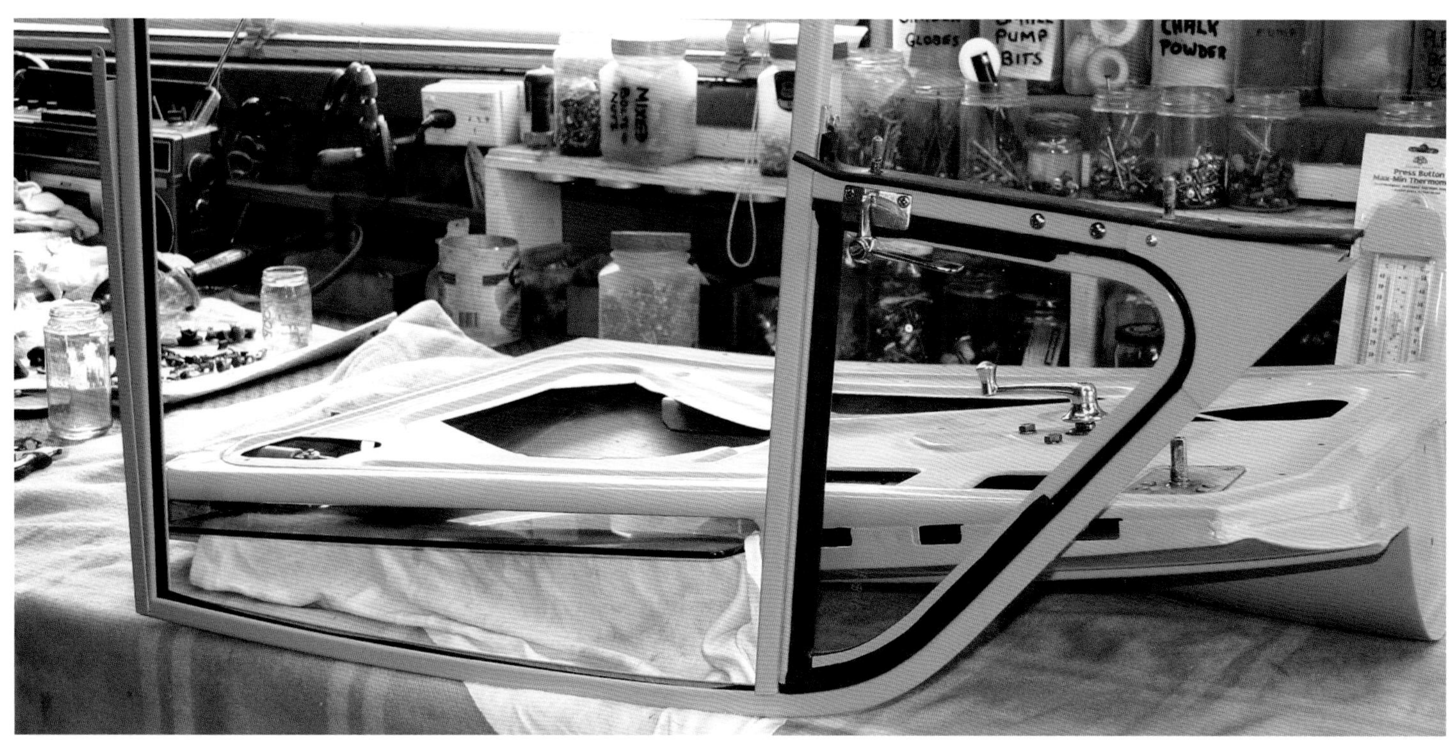

above: The door frame was assembled easily using the correct countersunk screws. The rubbers were pushed into the frame and the thin sealing rubber was slid into the purpose built channel. The quarter light window required some pushing and pulling as the new rubbers were a tight fit.
McKellar Tip – Using rubber grease or washing up liquid makes the rubbers slip into place much more easily.
A fixed pin on the bottom of the quarter light window was then pushed into the tensioning clamp, fitted to the base of the frame.

The quarter light hinge was connected to the window then inserted into the rubber and positioned in the frame – all at the same time (An extra pair of hands were needed here. Fortunately Bill was on hand). The hinge was then tightened up using two countersunk screws. This proved to be a very difficult operation and as a result no photographs were taken to illustrate the process.
McKellar Tip – Make sure you retain the hinges from the original windows as experience has shown that they can vary from car to car particularly with regard to the spacing between the holes!

Positioning the door felts in place. Note that slits have to be cut in the top sections of the upright felts to allow for the glass to pass over a joiner (Joint). Without doing this the window will not be able to be wound to the top.

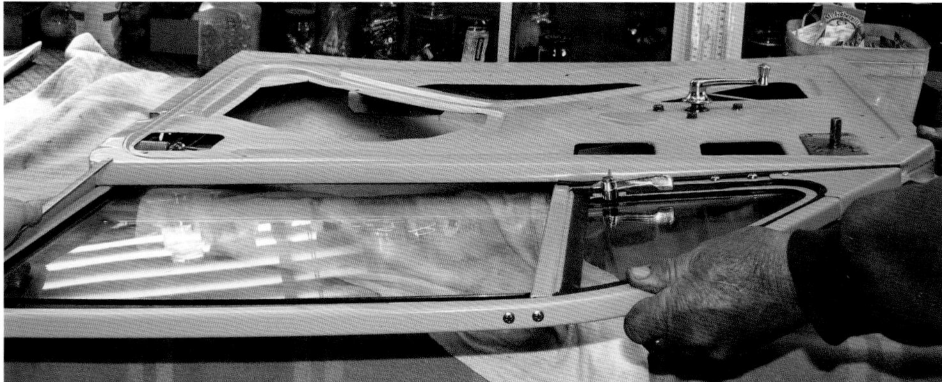

A new rubber was fitted in place between the quarter light window and the door top.
The window glass was slid into the frame and lowered into the door casing... very gently.
As the glass and door frame was lowered, the wheel from the window winder was inserted into the track that runs partly across the bottom of the window. The opportunity was taken to lubricate the wheel and track with grease.
A felt pad was glued to the shelf that acts as a stopper when the window is lowered.

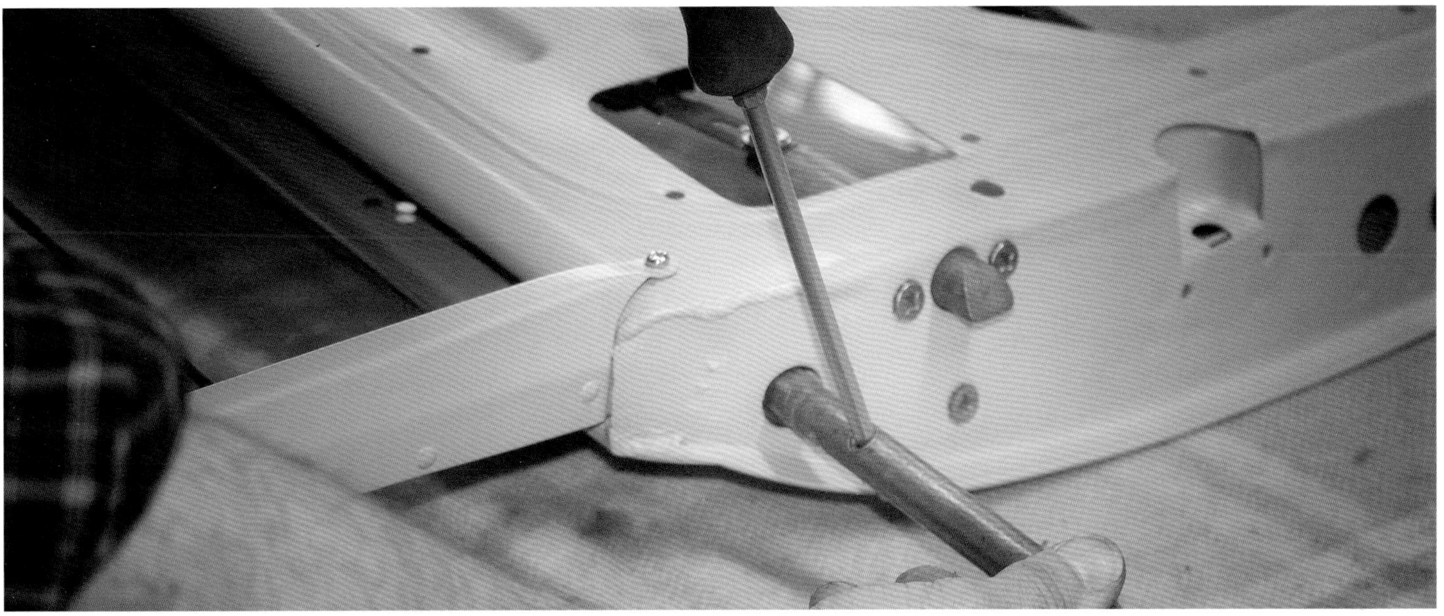

Bill had this wonderful old pipe spanner, believed to have been used by Noah when building the Ark! It proved ideal for tightening the two screws that hold the lower quarter window section of the frame to the door casing.

above top: Tightening one of the three bolts that supports the edge of the door frame. A small chrome domed self tapper adds extra support to the door frame. The two large domed Phillips head screws (above) regulate the tension on the quarter light window.

The weather strips for the top of the door, between the glass and the door are held in place with small spring loaded clips. These were inserted with pointy nosed pliers.

above: The bottom inner edge sealing rubbers are often left off restorations, leaving tell-tale holes in the lower section of the door. Not so here! With the help of some rubber grease the lower sealing strip was easily slid into place and nipped up with some flat nosed pliers.

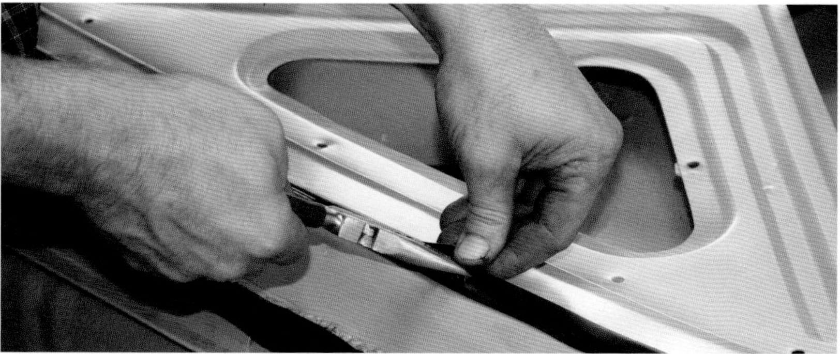

The rubber seal strip held on by a slotted metal fixing strap which is tightly held in place with small spring loaded clips. The clips were carefully inserted using some pointy nosed pliers.

Fitting the Doors to the Body

Door Fit

With the doors fully assembled, it was time to fit them to the car. The hinges were in quite good condition considering the weight of the doors. Precautionary checks were made for any excessive up and down movement. Fortunately there was no excessive play in either set of hinges despite the age of the vehicle and the use it had had. The hinges had been painted during the summer months and put aside. Before fitting the doors, the threads on the special door screws were cleaned with a wire brush and the captive threads were tapped out on the door and the 'A' pillar. Before putting the door on, the chrome plated striker plate was positioned in the maximum outer position. This was a useful ploy which worked well and helped reduce the risk of paint damage.

The passenger side door was the first to be lifted on and bolted into position. This was a two person operation. Fortunately the door fitted flush into the door frame without too much adjustment. Flushed by the success of the door fit, attention turned to fitting the draught excluder around the door opening. Two types were available. Even though the plastic type is much easier to apply and the rubber edge is much softer, in the interests of originality, the correct specification, black cotton covered metal type had been acquired.

Fitting the Draught Excluder

In order to reduce the possibility of making errors on this critical job, a dry run was undertaken to check the length of the door draught excluder required for each side.

McKellar Tip – Be generous in the amount of draught excluder you purchase and always allow plenty of overhang when fitting, as somehow the draught excluder seems to mysteriously shorten when it comes to fixing it in place with the clips. Use the McKellar 'Baby Steps' method. This requires a fair degree of patience, however, it can pay dividends in terms of door shut and panel alignment. Loosely position the draught excluder in the aperture and then try shutting the door. If it is too difficult to shut, then use the 'Baby Steps' method. This involves fitting a short section of excluder and then attempting to close the door. If this proves difficult, then using a pair of wide blade multi-grips, bend the edge slightly inwards. By trial and error adjustments can be made until the door shuts perfectly. A lot of bending may be required, but, if taken in small steps a good result can be achieved. With the fit and alignment provisionally agreed, the metal retaining clips can then be put in place using a plastic hammer. As the clips tend to push the excluder out slightly some final adjustments may be necessary. Generous use of the metal clips can ensure a good fit and provide added grip.

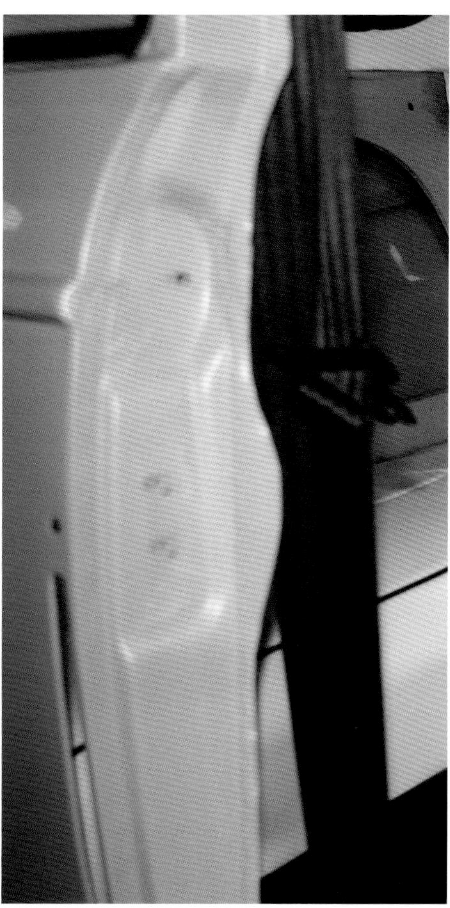

The captive adjustment in the 'B' pillar for the striker plate and door locator. The threads were carefully tapped out.

Striker Plate and Locating Pin

McKellar Tip – These are fastened with tapered Phillips head screws. For a Concours finish it may be prudent to purchase a few sets as the heads tend to become damaged with constant adjustment. The striker plates as fitted to the two door saloons are often hard to get when you want them, so it may be good to purchase some when they are available. Ensuring a good door fit can be achieved by adding a spacer behind the locating plate and/or by filing out the door locator with a round file.

right: Bill used a sensational pair of multi-grips with a wide blade to make adjustments to the door aperture. This was the secret to an excellent door fit. Bending the seam edge back (as needed) to accommodate the door seal was a useful ploy. This enabled the door to fit flush into the door frame. Masking tape was applied to the blade to minimise the risk of paint loss.

The striker plate is fixed with two tapered Phillips head screws (new ones were purchased).

above: The chrome door locating peg with correct rubber grommet is fitted with two tapered Phillips head screws.

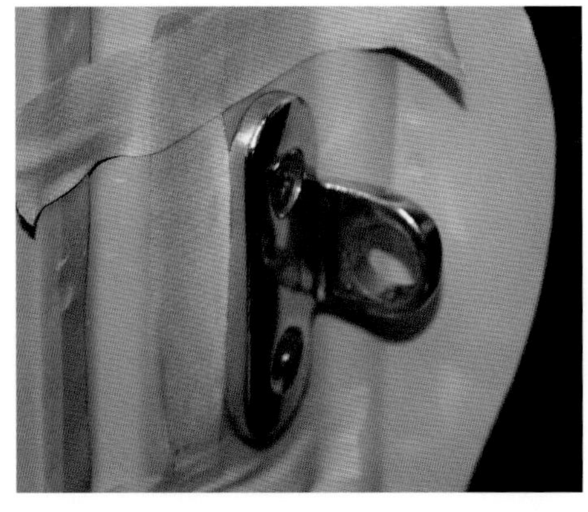

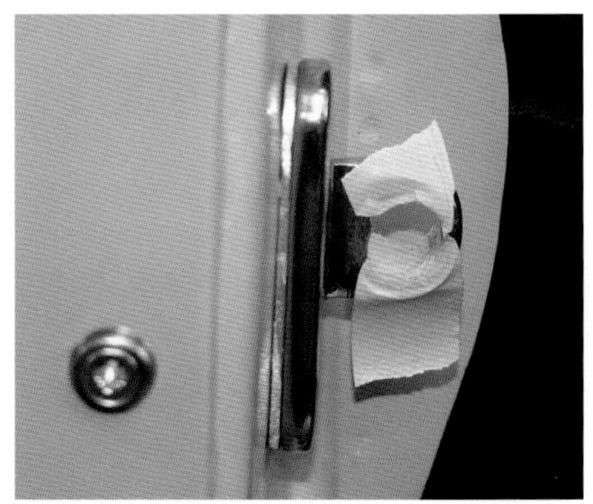

The chrome door locator required adjustment. On first adjustment the locator was moved slightly forward. A long spacer was made up out of mild steel, which mirrored the shape and was inserted as a spacer. McKellar Tip – The use of the masking tape, pictured here, is the best way to position the locating peg from the door. It is worth spending some time to locate this in the correct position. Further changes may need to be made if the door requires readjustment.

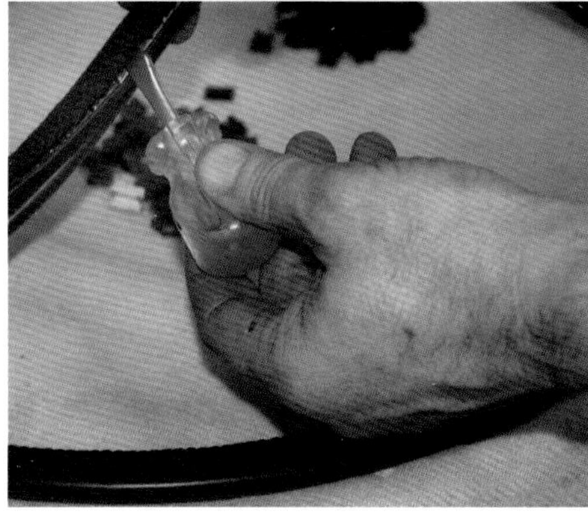

above: Using a wide screwdriver, the metal clip grippers were carefully opened along the length of the door draught excluder. This made the fitting process just that little easier.

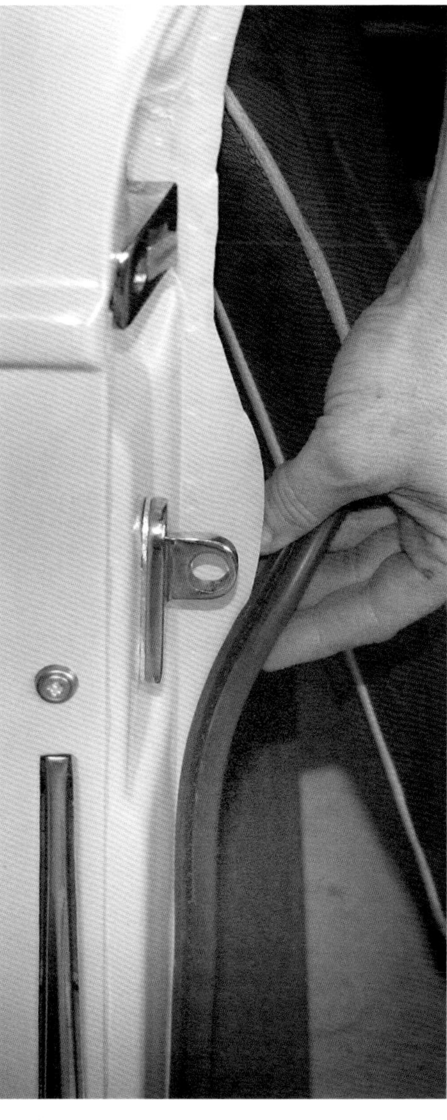

left: A dry run was necessary to check the length of the door draught excluder. This provided an indication of which areas might be problematic. The 'Baby Step' method was used. Small sections were fitted and then the door was closed – then a little more was added – and this continued until the door draught excluder was fitted. With any tight areas the seam edge was gently bent inwards until the door draught excluder was in the correct position – so the door did not need to be slammed. The retaining clips were then fitted (which pushed the door seal out slightly). More door draught excluder than required was used. This was cut to length after it was fitted using some sharp side cutters.

above: The door draught excluder in place. The door was still tight to close, however, the seal eventually compressed making the operation easier.

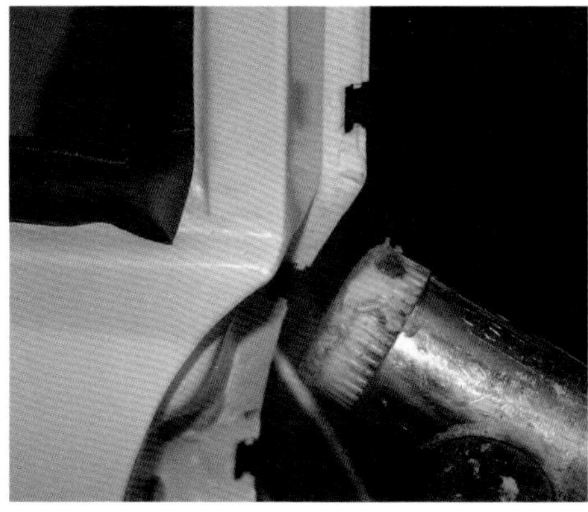

The waist line area required bending to make the perfect door fit. Double the amount of draught excluder clips were purchased to ensure that the door draught excluder did not come off in a hurry. A plastic-faced hammer was used to tap the clips into place and position the draught excluder.

Driver's Side Door Fit

The fitting of the passenger side door *(right)* went like a dream. However, the driver's side was a different story. Reinforcements were necessary and so the services of panel beater Robert Tingay were enlisted to show the door "who was boss." Robert is a genius and miracle worker when it comes to panel fit. The frame had to be hit violently with a rubber mallet and the door was bent and bowed (alarmingly) by jamming a rubber mallet in the hinges and pushing on it – in order to achieve an acceptable fit. No photos were taken due to the stress of watching the above performance! The results were spectacular but it was not a task Bill or I would have undertaken ourselves!

Sill Cover and Side Panel Finisher

Before fitting the sill cover panel the carpet that covers the inner sill was glued in place. The cover was then carefully positioned over the lip on the top edge of the sill. The inner edge rests on the carpet and helps keep it in place. The holes were then lined up with a scriber before the domed Phillips head screws were loosely screwed in place.

Nuts and bolts were also 'hung' in place on the bottom edge of the sill finishing panel. The side panel was slid into position from above. Adjustments were then made to make sure that the alignment of the side finishing panel was flush with the door. This was achieved by using flat washers to force the finisher outwards. Once everything was aligned, all the screws, nuts and bolts were carefully tightened, starting with those on the outer edges. Time and patience here paid dividends with an excellent finish and no damage to the paint on either the sill cover panel or the sill finisher.

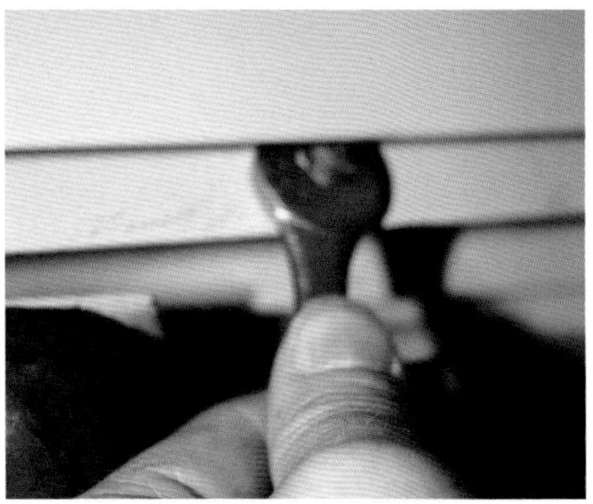

The bottom edge of the sill was adjusted outwards with spacers before being bolted into place.

The sill cover was affixed with domed Phillips head screws.

above and top: An excellent panel fit was achieved on the passenger's side. The driver's side took more beating into place.

The sill cover holds the carpet in place. The side cover can be adjusted outwards for a better fit by using flat washers as spacers. A flush fit is achievable with time and patience. above top: The black cotton covered metal draught excluder in place.

Back Guards/Wings – Fitting

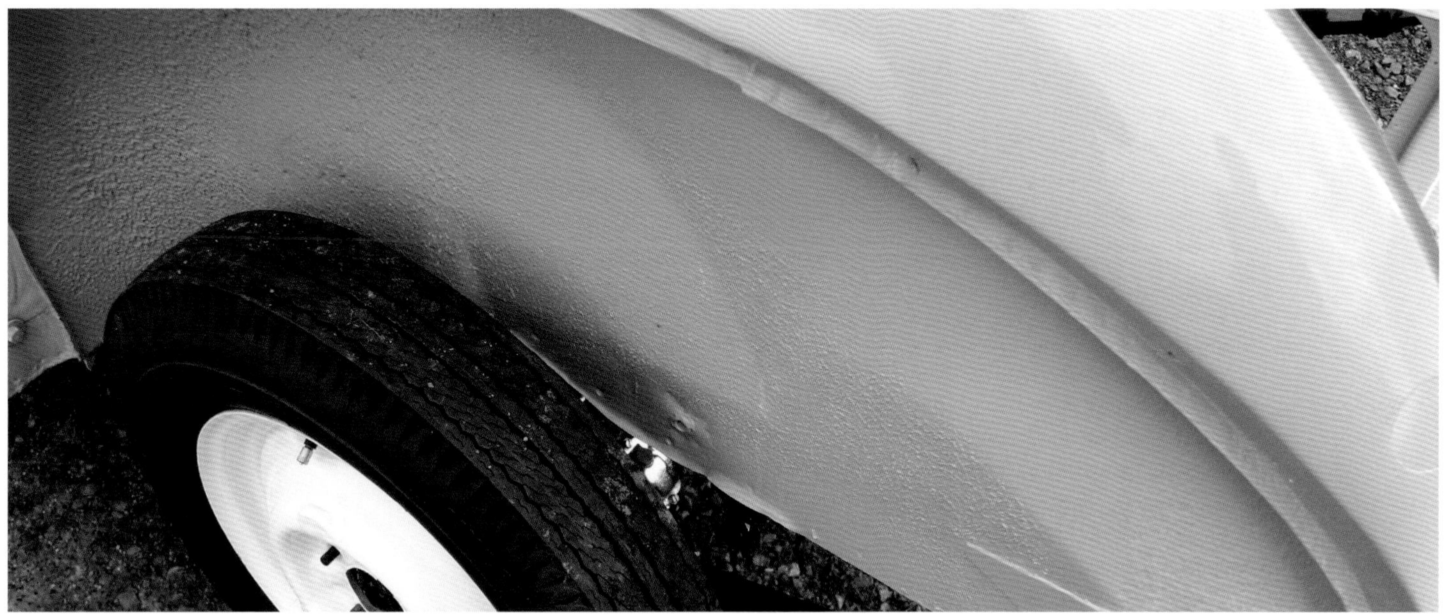

Assembly

With the back guards/wings painted and polished, preparations were made to fit them. Bill, as if by magic sourced the zip bag with the original nuts and washers. He had also tapped out the captive nuts around the wheel arches in readiness for this much anticipated event. Holes had been punched into the white wing beading using the original as a guide. Each guard/wing was offered up and bolted in place. Surprisingly, little adjustment was necessary. They looked just as they did on December 13 1960, perfect!

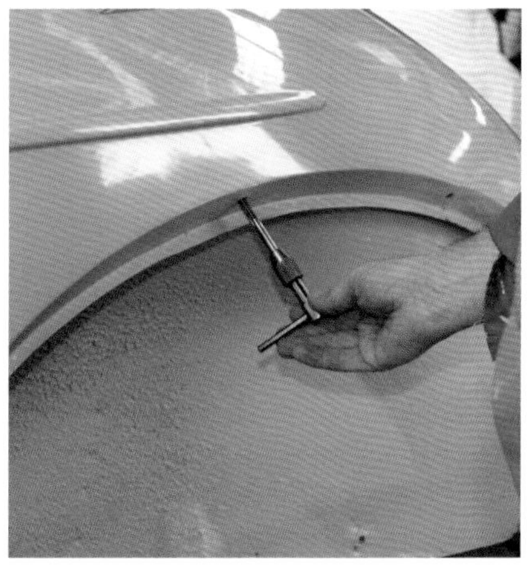

Tapping out the captive nuts.

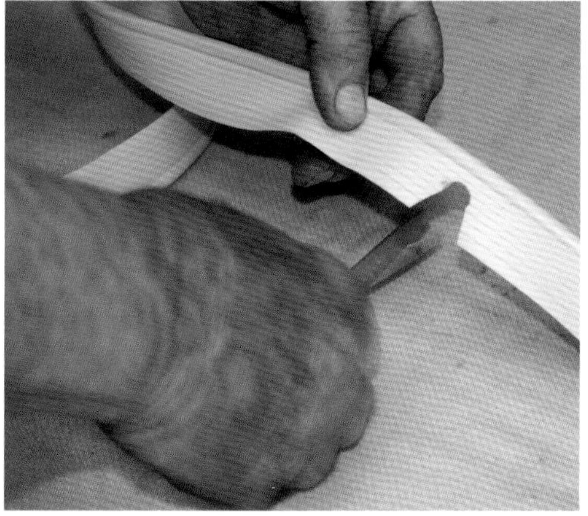

New wing beading is a must for a restoration.

The original nuts and washers ready to be put back into service.

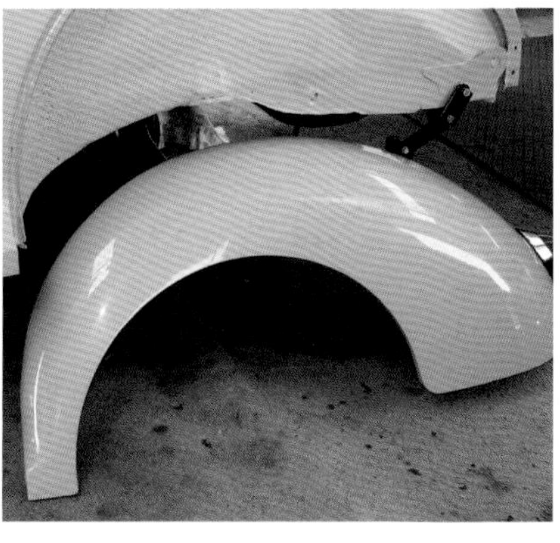

above top: An unusual shot of the wheel arch – looking very tidy.

The finished item. The later Minor guards/wings from 1956 were updated and concealed more of the inner wheel arch giving them a fuller look.

Fuel Tank – Fitting and Detailing the Boot Area

The fuel tank was stripped of paint and surface rust using a self made wire brush system. This messy job was completed behind the garden shed at home in Canterbury, Victoria, before the tank was painted twice with black gloss Kill Rust. In true McKellar fashion it was then hung on the clothes line in the sun to dry before being moved inside to join a collection of other parts hanging on makeshift drying racks in front of the heater. Unfortunately during this process half of the fine brass bolt that is attached to the sender snapped off. I was hopeful that it would still work and fortunately, my optimism based on the fact that everything was working prior to dismantling proved to be well founded.

When it was eventually taken up to the Harcourt property for fitting it was checked by Bill using a multimeter. After several anxious moments it was found to be working perfectly. Phew! What a relief.

Fitting the Tank

A bead of Mastic was laid down around the fuel tank aperture area. The tank was then carefully manoeuvred around the boot floor stay, and then positioned in place with the mastic edging outwards, sealing up any gaps. Some 24 or more self tappers were then screwed into place. The fuel sender wire was then connected to the now very short sender bolt and tightened. The next task was to fit the delightful looking red rubber 'Morris' branded hose to the top of the tank and to the filler pipe with the original large jubilee clips.

The tank was then filled with a few gallons of fuel, and checked for leaks. Much to our relief everything checked out just fine, with the SU fuel pump ticking away nicely to start, and the fuel gauge registering for the very first time!

The wooden boot floors were painted with semi gloss Acrylic and fitted. Four self tappers were required for the back and eight small nuts and bolts with spring washers were required for the sides and front.

McKellar Tip – When fitting the wooden boot floor, slide in one side only, pushing towards the front of the car, then move it back towards the back of the car, so the front of the board positions underneath the metal lip. Once one side is in place, proceed with fitting the other.

It is advisable to protect the boards as they can be easily marked and damaged. Black carpet was used. Of course, this would need to be removed if the vehicle was presented for judging in the restored category at a Concours event.

above: A bead of Mastic was laid down around the fuel tank aperture area. The paint finish is smooth to touch and has a natural sheen. The aim was to achieve a factory finished look so much restraint was needed so as not to over polish. Polishing was limited to removing any overspray!

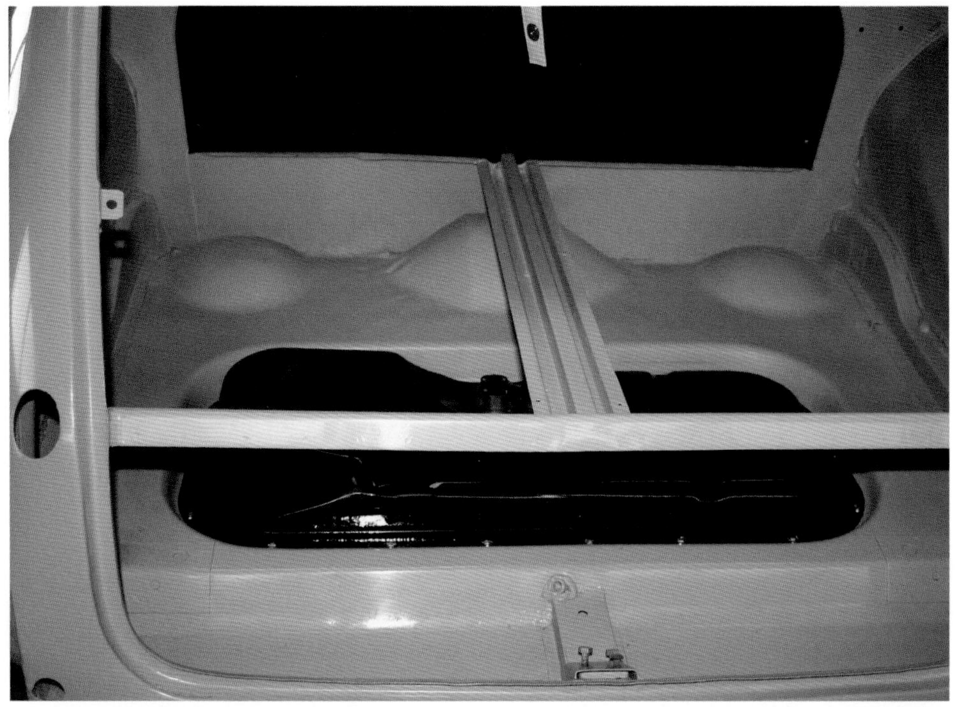

The colour contrast between the black tank and the lilac body is quite magical.
The white strap hanging down from the top of the frame has a lift-a-dot connection which fastens the rear seat back onto a pillar bolted to the back shelf. This new position was part of the Minor 1000 updates introduced in December 1956.

above: An interesting view from underneath the back of the car showing the aperture in the body for the fuel tank.

left: The fuel sender unit wire connected to the now very short sender bolt. Everything worked fine.

left: The fuel tank screwed into position with the brass drain plug positioned in the centre of the tank.

Shortly after the car was restored there was no fuel gauge reading on the gauge in the dash. Lining up for a vasectomy was preferable to taking out the fuel sender unit and replacing it. A day was allocated for the expected removal of the boot floor and the replacement or rectification. While unscrewing the sender unit I had an inspirational moment. What if it is just a bad earth? I turned the ignition on and the gauge was working. It was a bad earth! Time for reassembly, a coffee and time to reflect on a lesson learnt.

Front Guards/Wings and Grille – Fitting and Detailing

Fitting the Front Panels

Plenty of time was allocated for the fitting of the front guards/wings and the grille panel. The main concern, apart from panel fit, was damage to the paint. With this in mind, this particular job had been left as long as possible. Even then the Acrylic lacquer was still quite soft. In order to protect the paintwork the edges were covered with some low tack masking tape and some cardboard strips were prepared to use as spacers. Bill cleaned the threads out on all the associated captive nuts before assembly commenced. This made a big difference as the threads could be located quickly and without fuss. The driver's side guard was offered up first and quickly bolted into place. Once secured, the passenger's side was offered up to the body and bolted in place.

The front panel grille was then temporarily bolted into position with nuts and bolts. Great care was taken here as the bolts that are attached to the chrome hockey sticks are easily damaged. Experience has shown that it is best to position all the panels before fitting. Bill made up some spacers (washers with sections cut out) which could be moved and removed enabling us to achieve the best possible panel fit. Once the correct balance and fit was achieved, the spacers were then systematically removed. Such a simple description does not do justice to the time, care and precision needed for this crucial part of the restoration. It is definitely a two person operation which requires considerable patience.

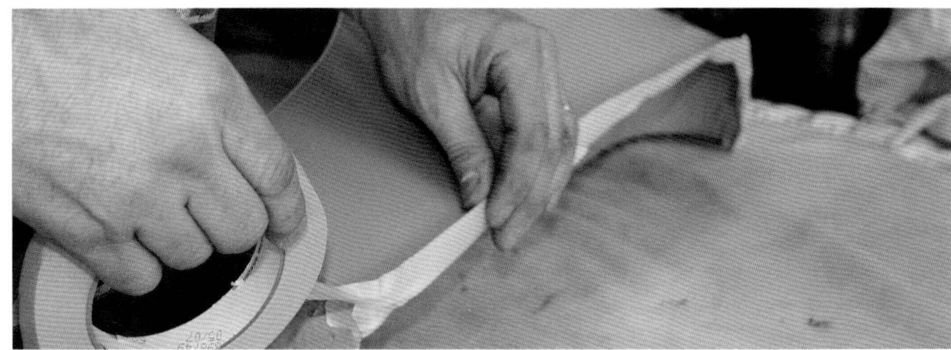

Paint protection was the number one priority. Taping the edges sure helped, although some edges were damaged. Acrylic lacquer is soft and can be marked easily. However, as explained previously, it is quite forgiving and can be easily touched up.

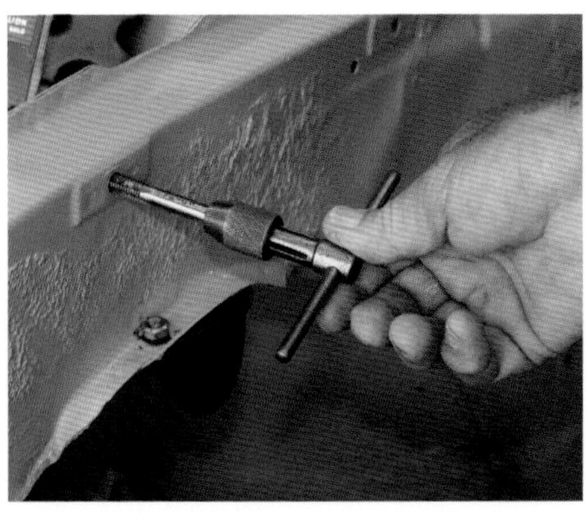

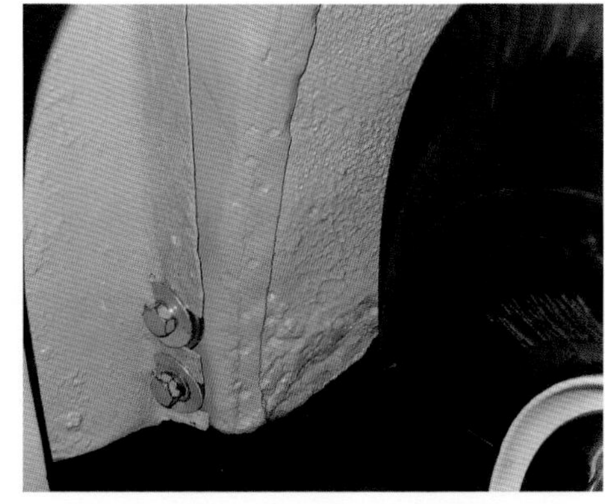

above top: Carefully manoeuvring the driver side front guard into place. The key here is not to chip too much paint off... expect it to happen.
above: Bill cleaned out the threads in the captive nuts.

The lower guard/wing bolts and large washers. These were touched up with Acrylic paint.

The Top Bar and Hockey Sticks

Whilst judging cars at Concours, Bill and I often comment on the poor fit of the top chrome bar and the hockey sticks. A good trick is to carefully place some washers behind the top bar lifting it forward enabling it to line up correctly. In order to achieve equal space between the top bar and the hockey sticks (the same space each side is desirable), it is possible to carefully cut a small amount from the end of the tightest side of the top bar. While this is a minor task to perform, it can change significantly the overall appearance of the front of the car and gain a few more points in the panel fit department, come Concours judging time.

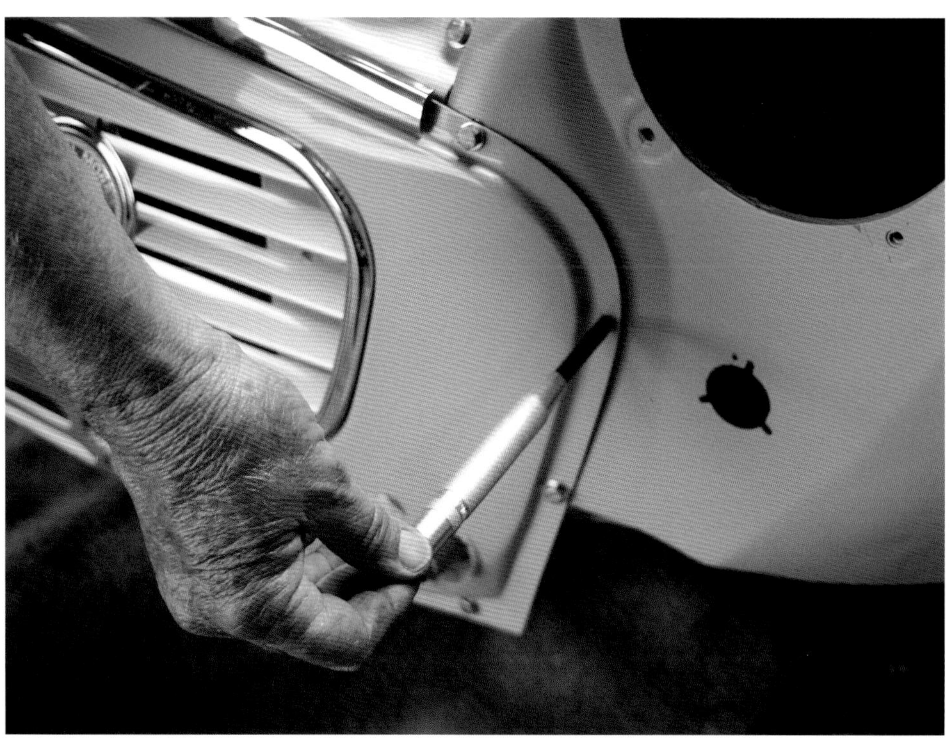

above: Bill using a punch to line up the holes so the grille can be temporarily held in place. The threads on the hockey sticks are easily damaged.

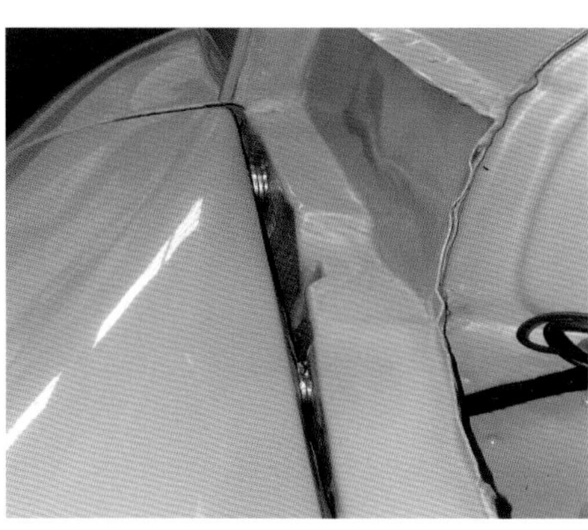

Not an attractive gap at all! The spacers were a big help and were later removed. The gaps were seam sealed when finished.

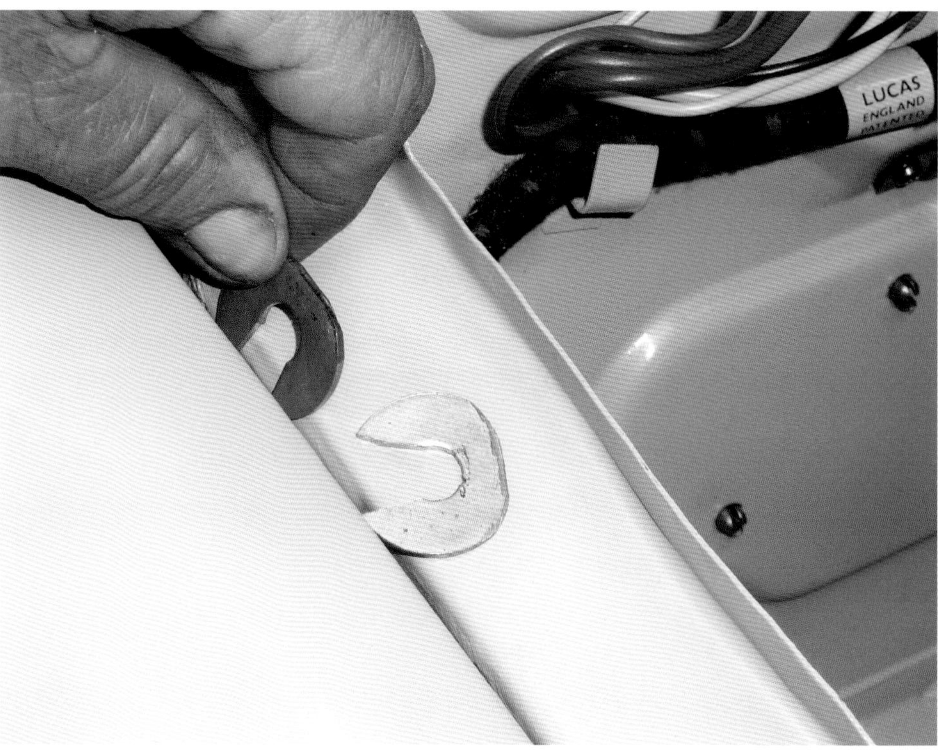

Spacers were used to work out the line of the guard/wing in order to achieve the best fit. Many of the spacers were removed once the grille was in place.

Attention to Detail

The grille tends to be the focal point on the front of the Morris Minor. Surprisingly, the lower part of the grille (the section that lives under the bumper) is often overlooked by restorers. It is also the portion of the grille which is most likely to suffer from damage, road traffic grime, and ultimately rust.

For this reason particular attention was paid to this area and some small stainless steel nuts, bolts and washers were purchased and fitted. These added to the overall appearance and gave a professional look to the finished job.

Once the fitting up was completed, the next step was to seal the gaps with automotive seam sealer. After the sealer hardened (after a day or so) it was painted with Acrylic or Enamel. Seam sealer applied between the gaps makes for a very professional looking restoration. We matched the lilac with automotive Enamel paint for under the guards and on the inside floor of the car. Enamel paint will go over Acrylic and provides better protection for harder wearing areas.

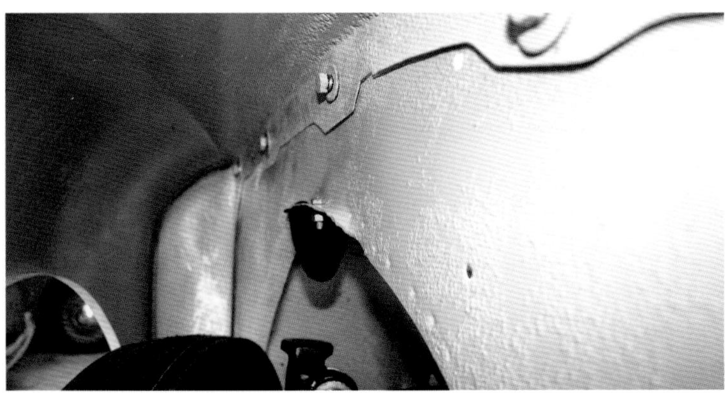

above: The large washers and locking nuts are bolted into the captive nuts. This is the view from under the front driver's side guard.

The lower section of the grille panel. Bill purchased some stainless steel nuts, bolts and washers in order to improve the overall appearance.

Pulling on the front of the front guard/wing will change the panel gap on the lower edge of the guard/wing (between the guard/wing and the door).

Two rubber spacers separate the bumper valance from the guard. Fitting these is often overlooked by restorers.

The top chrome bar can be carefully cut with a fine bladed hacksaw to achieve equal spacing between the hockey sticks.

This magic piece of cardboard saved many chips and allowed us to achieve the desired gap.

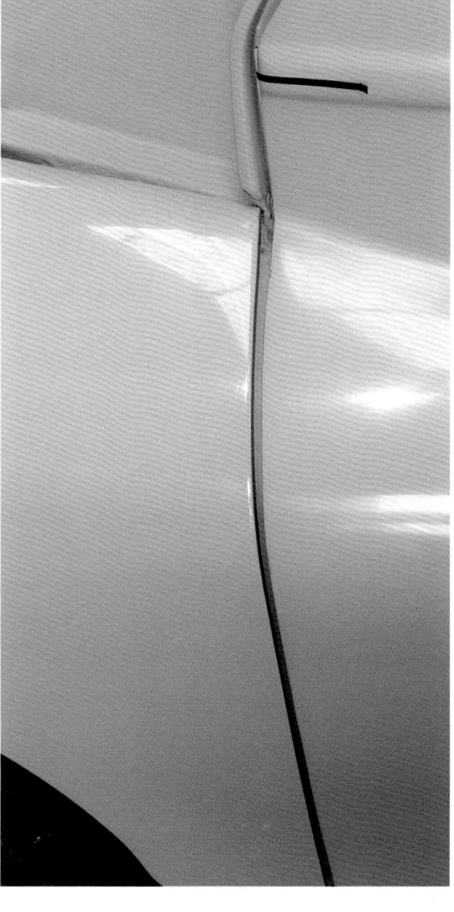

The gap on the passenger's side.

The driver's side gap.

Lighting – Fitting the Headlights

Fitting the lights is one of the most rewarding stages of any restoration. In the case of 6396 WX, with the front of the car nearing completion, it meant that at last there was a glimmer of light at the end of the tunnel of the restoration odyssey.

The lights are very much the eyes on the face of the Minor. The correct Lucas pre-focus head lamps, still in original boxes, had been purchased at the start of the project, so I could hardy wait to fit them. This was a very low stress, straightforward process with no surprises. For the headlights to operate correctly they must be aligned, or they may dazzle on coming drivers (highly unlikely with original globes fitted) or restrict driver vision. The alignment was set up initially using a trial-and-correction method. Final adjustments were made by a local garage using specialist optical test equipment.

The apertures for the lights in the guard/wing. The threads were tapped and cleaned for easy application.

Two of the four special brass screws for holding the headlight bowls to the guard/wing.

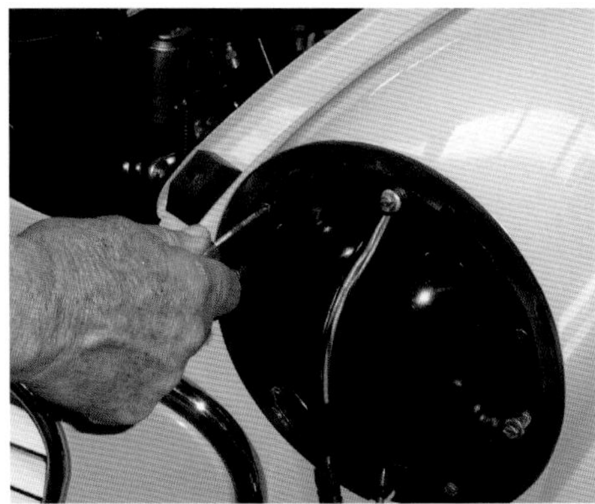

The rubber grommet lined up and fitted in place. The bowl can then be screwed in place.

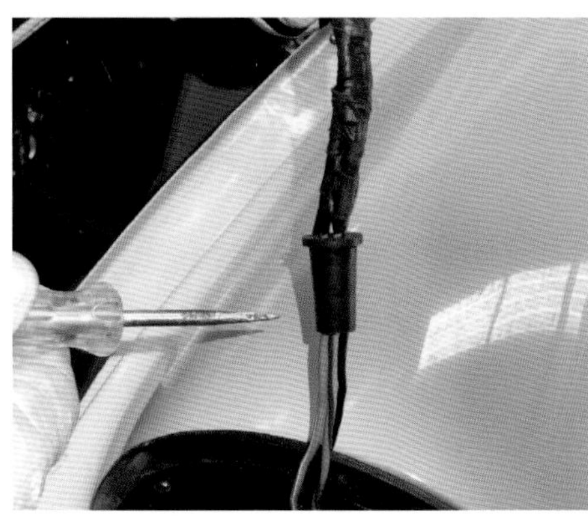

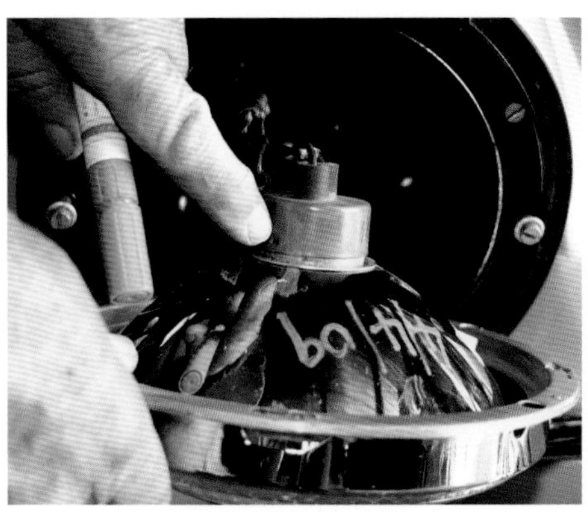

This grommet keeps any water and dust from the assembly. It is a tight push fit into the top of the bowl. Applying a drop of washing up liquid makes the fit easier.

The globe inserted into the holder – it has a locating slot so it can only go in one way. The terminal is then fitted. For posterity's sake the date of fitting was penned on the inside of the lens.

The unit is fitted on to spring loaded screws and then rotated anti-clockwise. The beam is adjusted by screwing the screws forward or back. Adjustment should be fined tuned by a garage that has the relevant optical equipment.

Parking Lights and Indicators

The parking light lenses were also new old stock items, still in the original boxes. I had purchased (NOS) these many years ago as a boy! Surprisingly the Million has the older Series II parking light configuration due to the trafficators. For safety reasons the parking lights were modified to take in a double filament flashing globe for the indicator and parking light. This was achieved by cutting the back off a later Morris 1000 bulb holder assembly and riveting it to the earlier body/assembly. This was a fun job to do and it was made even more pleasurable by the fact that it worked well when finally fitted. Incidentally the Million was one of the last Minors to be fitted with trafficators as they were discontinued in favour of flashing indicators in 1961.

The rubber body with the globe holder was inserted into the guard/wing. This holder was made up using an early front section and a later 1000 back section in order to accommodate the flashing indicator.

The holes were lined up with a scriber.

Self tapping screws originally held the assembly in place. Out of personal preference some small nuts and bolts were used for a neater more professional job. (I don't think anyone will ever notice behind the back of the guard/wing, but I know it looks better!)

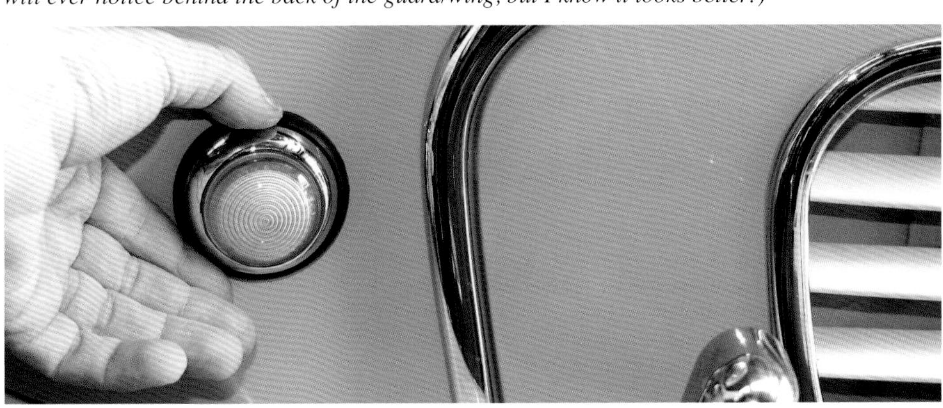

With the parking light base in place, the lens and chrome bezel were added. This is a push on fitting which tucks neatly into the rubber.
above top: A sealing dust excluder is fitted and the chrome rim completes the fitting. A few drops of dish washing liquid applied to the rubber helps with fitting as the rim has to be pushed and turned anti-clockwise to seat. A chrome domed Phillips head screw secures the unit from underneath. As part of the detailing process, the rather oversize rubber grommet was cut back with a scalpel in order to obtain a neater, more original look.

Boot – Fitting and Detailing the Boot Lid

The Important Boot Area

The boot area is often overlooked by restorers. Both the inner boot area as well as the fit and alignment of the boot lid seem to warrant less attention and, as a consequence, when some cars are on display with the boot open the overall appearance is compromised. With this in mind, both Bill and I were determined to make sure that the same high standard adopted with the rest of the restoration would be maintained when adding the components to the boot lid, and when aligning it prior to final adjustment.

In preparation for the fitting of the boot lid the new old stock hinges along with new under hinge rubbers were fitted to the main body of the car using the original large washers and some new nuts. Attention then switched to the lid itself. To begin with the new old stock boot lock and handle was screwed into place using the original screws which were rescued from a carefully labelled snap freezer bag. Next the soft boot sealing rubber was then adhered to the inner channel using Kwik Grip. Care was taken to remove any excess adhesive at the time using thinners. The wiring for the number plate light was then neatly clicked into place using the original clips.

The lid, which had received its first cut back and polish, was then carefully turned over and with a certain amount of pride the number plate light rubber grommet, lamp base, glass and black cover were fitted. The unique Minor 1,000,000 boot badge was then carefully clipped into place using speed clips.

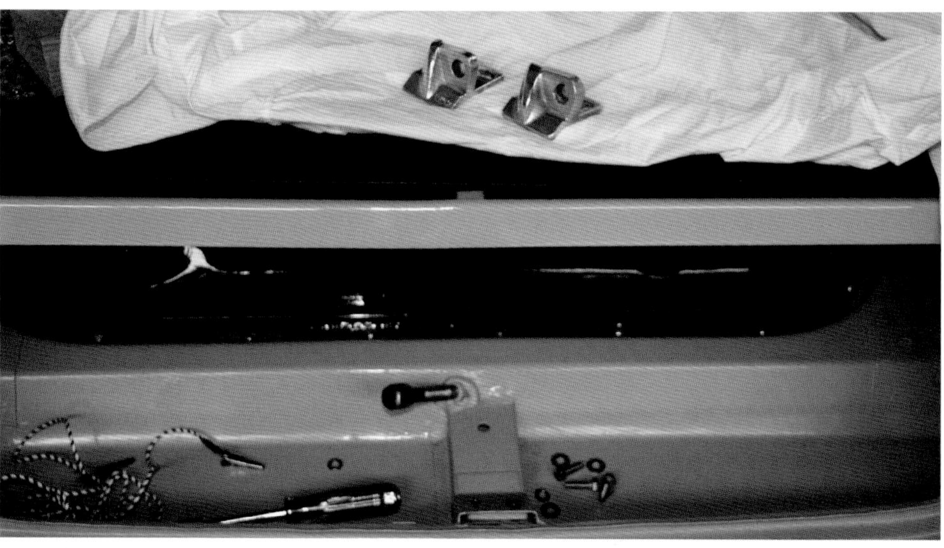

above: The wooden boot floor panels were painted with semi gloss Acrylic and fitted. An edged black carpet was placed over the boot floor area for protection.

A new old stock glass number plate lens, purchased at the Bendigo Swap Meet, was fitted.

The 1,000,000 badge is made up of two sections because of its length. It is joined behind the last (0) in 1000. The back (000) section has a tab that fits under the pin in the 1000. It shares the same pin. It is then attached to the boot lid using speed clips. It is quite fascinating (to a purist) how it joins!

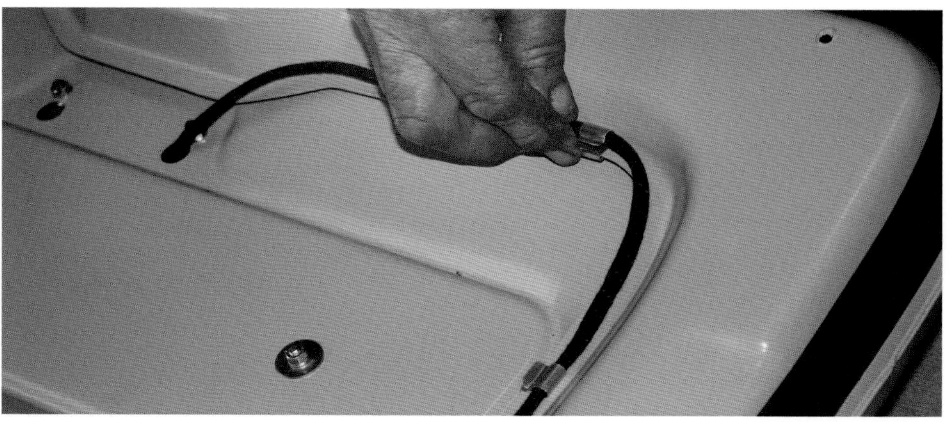

The wiring loom connected to the number plate light and held in place with the original clips. The clips were taken back to bare metal and sprayed with a metal finish paint for protection, thus achieving an original looking factory finish.

This was a special moment which signalled the closing stages of the restoration. The 1961 silver on black alloy original type number plate was then carefully fitted and tightened using new nuts, bolts and washers.

With all the fittings on the outer side completed, the boot lid was turned over again in order to fit the rubber boot stay clip and boot stay, complete with the correct spring tension connector, washer and split pin. It was then time for the all important final fit and adjustment. With Bill on hand to help, the lid was lowered down until it was resting on the rubber hinge grommet. With the lid held steady, flat and spring washers, were secured onto the hinge bolt with a nut. With the boot held in the open position, the process was repeated on the other side. Final adjustment was then made by carefully lowering the lid up-and-down and moving it slightly from side to side until the best panel fit was achieved. The nuts were then tightened.

The final job was fitting the original boot striker plate and adjusting it so as to ensure a flush fit.

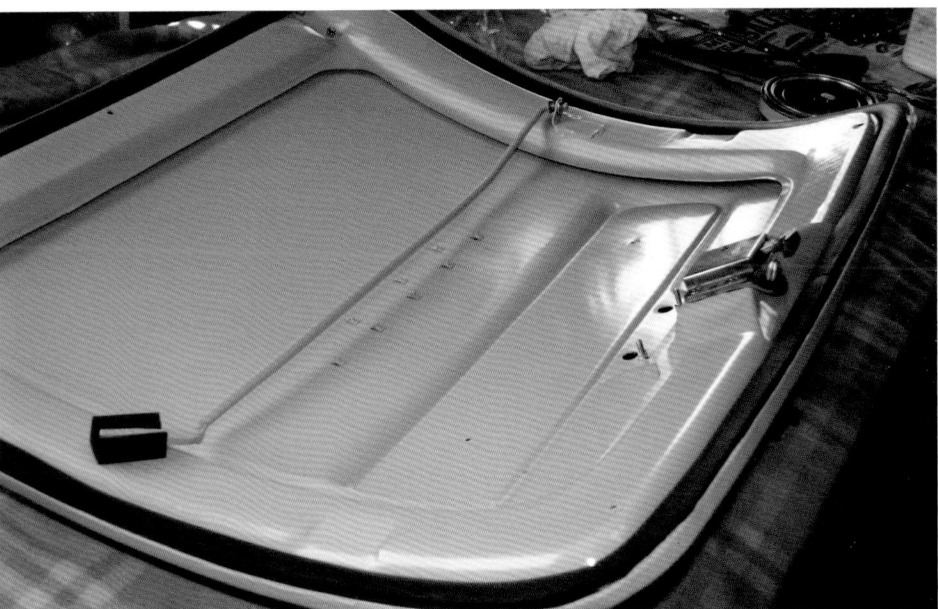

right: Attaching the fittings to the underside. Note: the boot stay attachment (rubber block) was a modification on saloons and convertibles from February 1959. The holding capabilities are not as 'positive' as the original metal clip. The McKellar theory is that this was changed due to 'vibrations at speed.' This is based on having owned earlier cars with the original metal clip, where a vibration sound is quite audible from the boot at road speed (at times).

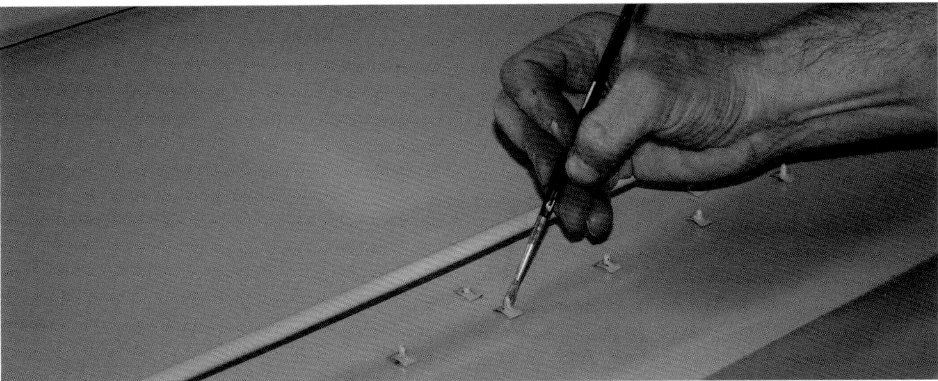

above: Clips (originally metal colour) painted lilac for protection.

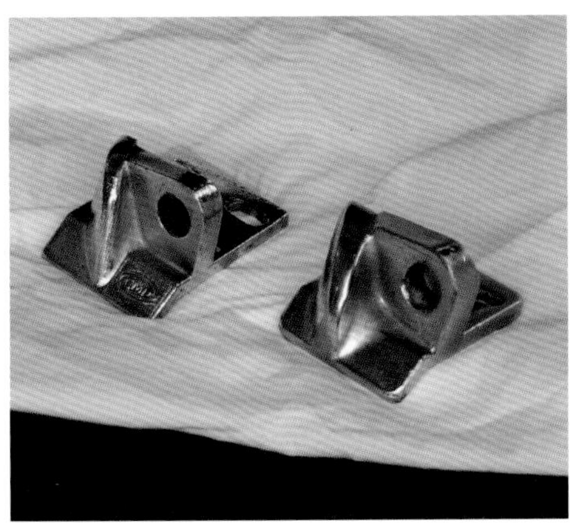

The reproduction boot striker plate on the right was rejected. We opted for the original, which was polished with Autosol.

The original black number plate light cover was retained in the interests of originality. Chrome covers were an optional extra. A stronger boot handle and lock was updated across the Minor range in December 1956. Original type number plates are available from the UK. This is the original Registration number for this Million, first registered in Leeds in January 1961.

Front and Rear Bumpers – Fitting and Detailing

Valance Troubles

The restoration of the front and rear bumper assemblies lagged behind in comparison with the rapid progress made on the rest of the car. The valances, which had been badly damaged following years of touch-parking, gate opening and closing by younger drivers proved to be the most time consuming items to repair. Panel guru Robert Tingay spent nine hours straightening, fitting and aligning the valances with the chrome bumper bar blades. Following the repairs, extra care was required to make sure the valances fitted without buckling, particularly when the bumper irons were fitted and tightened.

In preparation for fitting the chrome bumper blades, any sharp edges and burrs were removed by filing the chrome edges.
For rust protection, silver enamel paint was applied to the back of the chrome blades.

Helpful Tips for Fitting

Though it seems a straightforward enough job, fitting and aligning all the various components that make up the bumper assemblies is more difficult than it first seems. Particular care must be taken not to damage the paintwork or catch the guards/ wings when lining up the bumpers for final adjustment. All did not go according to plan first time round when attempts were

The front bumper valance in undercoat. Note the elongated holes for adjustment.

The freezer bag with the fasteners. The metal ferrule hides any adjusting shim washers.

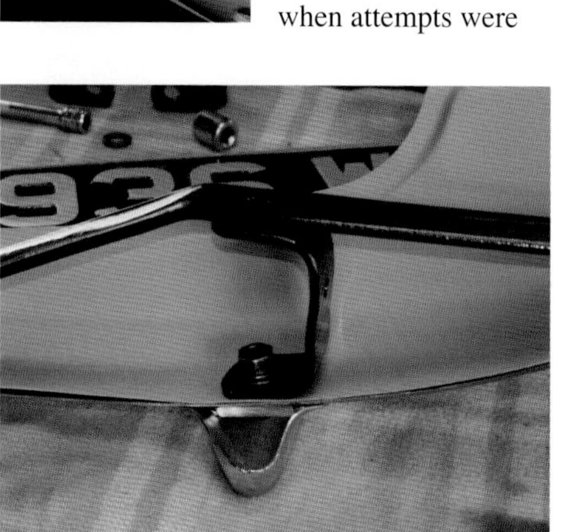

The overrider bolt holds the assembly together.

Working out how it all goes back together. The overriders have to go on first. This was a lesson learned the hard way! The chrome was re-plated locally at great cost. New overriders and bumper blades could have been imported from the UK at half the price. Hindsight is a wonderful thing!

made to put all the components together. Looking back, completing the assembly on the bench before attempting to fit the front and rear bumpers on the car was a good idea. Having to fit overriders was an added complication as the bolts which secure these have to pass through the chrome bumper blade, the valance and the bumper bar support. Getting the positioning right for this was a bit of a fiddle. With everything loosely assembled, the front assembly was then carefully located on the two threaded bumper irons before two metal ferrules were added. These serve to conceal some flat washers which can be added to help pack out the bumper so that the alignment in relation to the guards/wings is equal on both sides.

The rear bumper was secured to the car in a similar way to the front. A rubber grommet was fitted over the bumper support and pushed back so that it sat flush with the body. With this in place, the rear bumper assembly was bolted in position and adjusted where necessary with flat washers. Unfortunately they could not be concealed as there are no metal ferrules fitted to the rear.

McKellar Tip – Elongating some of the holes on the bumper assembly can be helpful in ensuring proper alignment. This can be done using a round metal file.

Bolting on the front bumper.

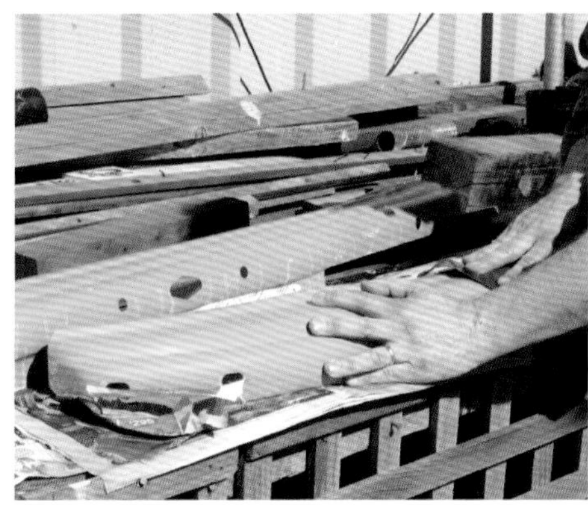

Rubbing the undercoat with some fine wet and dry in the sunshine.

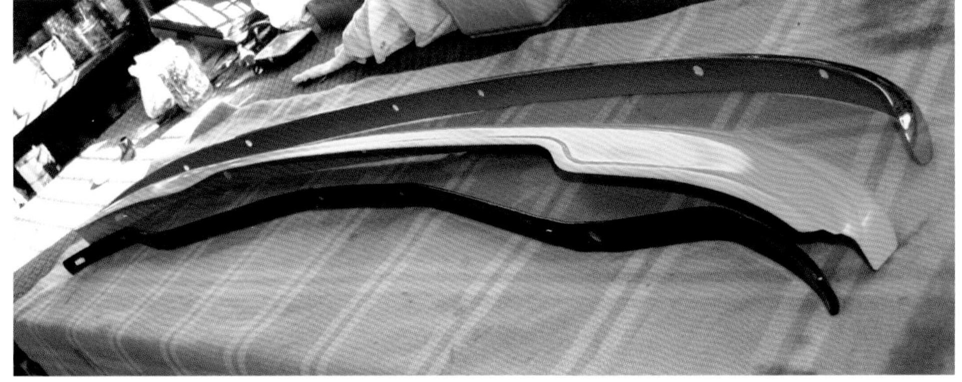

above top: The moment when everything comes together. The spaces around the two bumper irons can be sealed with an inner grommet or mastic. The threads on the studs were cleaned and lubricated with drops of oil.
above: Two small irons for the overriders were temporarily mislaid. These were later found.

Checking the fit of the chrome bumper blade. Any sharp burrs on the edges were removed.

Bonnet – Fitting and Detailing

The bonnet was one of the last items to be sprayed. An excellent result was achieved, as by this time with lots of practice my technique had improved. Nevertheless, due to events described here some rectification work was needed... all was not as it seemed! With the paint still quite soft, a blanketed pad was made on the workbench and any sharp objects were cleared well out of the way. Extra caution was taken with the bonnet due to a previous bad experience with the bonnet from a 1955 convertible. The panel had been painted and polished and had a glass like finish. While other work was in progress it was placed upside down on the lawn. When retrieved the bonnet has a deep imprint of the lawn etched across the top.

In order to be able to handle the bonnet more easily the bonnet motif (flash handle) was fitted first. Great care was exercised here as there was a lot of free play in the area where it slides into a locating slit in the bonnet. In spite of our best efforts the paintwork was damaged. The flash needs to be positioned and be tightened up firmly. If it is able to move around, it will badly mark the paint. It is also advisable to remove any sharp burrs from the flash for the same reason. Having an extra pair of hands around at this stage would be a big advantage.

Before any attempt was made to fit the bonnet, the central anti drum strip and the left and right stiffening supports were fitted.

This was done with the bonnet laid on its back on the bench.

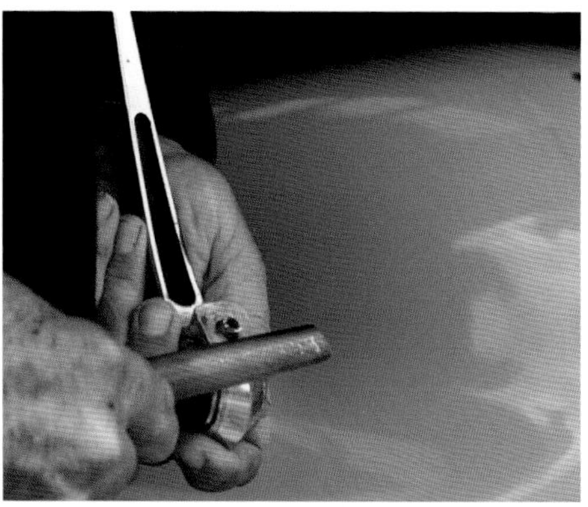

Removing any sharp burrs from the bonnet flash helped reduce the risk of paint damage.

Decisive action is needed when positioning and fastening the bonnet flash to avoid marking the paint.

Thick felt was applied to the central anti drum strip with Kwik Grip adhesive.

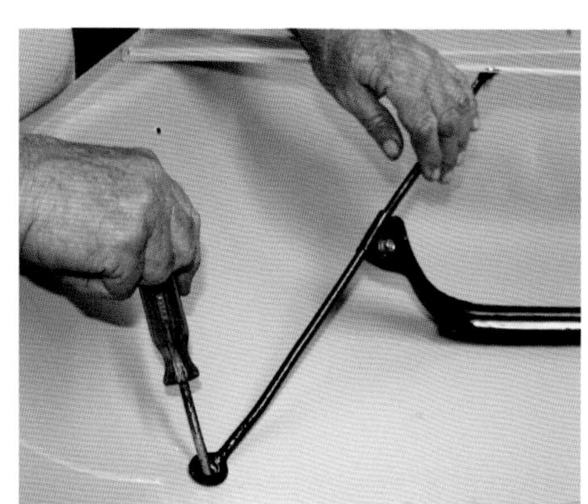

The left and right stiffening supports were bolted to the central anti drum strip. The front bolt on the hinge holds the unit in place.

The strip beading (minus coach line) being secured using push on retaining clips which are fitted from behind.

With the bonnet turned again, the strip beading on the bonnet sides was securely attached using push on retaining clips.

With the glove box inserts not yet fitted, the hinges were bolted to the windscreen opening panel. As access to the hinge studs can only be gained from behind the dash, this is quite an awkward operation. With the hinges in place, and rubber hinge grommets fitted, the bonnet was bolted into place and loosely positioned to achieve the best fit. Once again great care was taken to avoid damage to the paintwork on the bonnet and to the car body. A blanket was used to help keep any marks down to a minimum.

Once an acceptable fit was achieved, the blanket was removed and attention switched to fitting the bonnet striker pin assembly. The assembly has ample adjustment.

The hinges bolt through the windscreen opening panel – access to the studs is from behind the dash. Fitting nuts and washers is quite awkward.

Extreme care was taken when fitting the bonnet badges. These are the originals and replacements were not available at the time of the restoration.

The prop assembly was fitted and attached using two clevis pins/washers and split pins. The spring assures a positive action.

The bonnet striker pin assembly has plenty of adjustment. Consequently a good fit can be achieved across the front panel.

The 4 inch wide swage line/strip up the centre of all Morris Minor bonnets is a reminder of the eleventh hour decision to widen the prototype design prior to production.

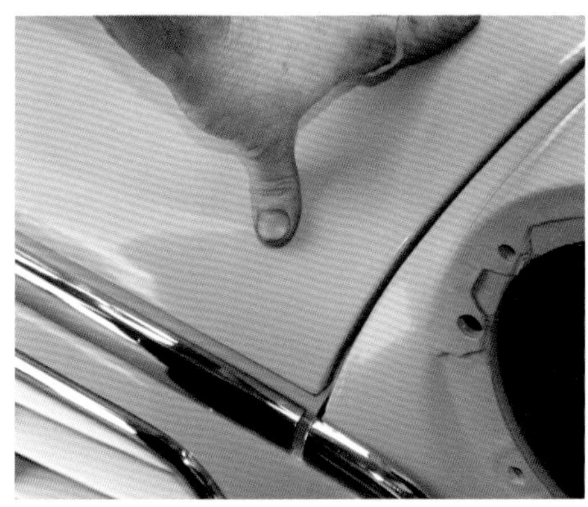

Checking and adjusting the panel fit line. The buffer rubbers help position the bonnet. For adjustment these can be carefully trimmed until the desired line is achieved.

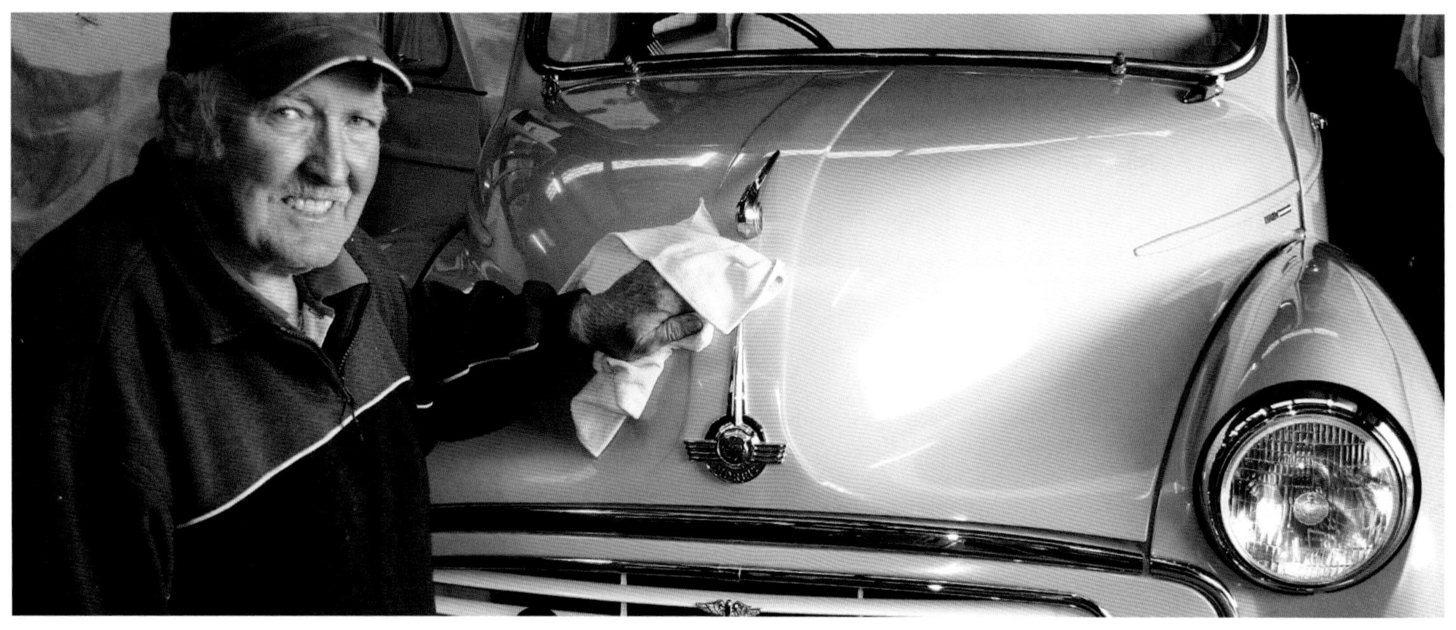

Retaining bolts allow the bracket to be moved from side to side and the length of the pin for the lock striker can be screwed in and out. The front buffer rubbers also helped with positioning the front of the bonnet.

McKellar Tip – For final adjustment the rubber buffers can be carefully trimmed with a Stanley knife until the desired line is achieved. Placing a washer underneath the rubbers may also help with alignment.

With the bonnet finally in place, and opening and closing correctly... the long awaited moment finally arrived... fitting the 1,000,000 badges. These have a three pin fitting and three small spire nuts to hold each badge in place. Care was taken not to break the pins off, as the badges were the originals. The front bonnet badge was then added using the original special screws and washers.

With the bonnet completed and a 95% panel fit accomplished, it was time to step back and admire what had been achieved. However, that was not quite the whole story!

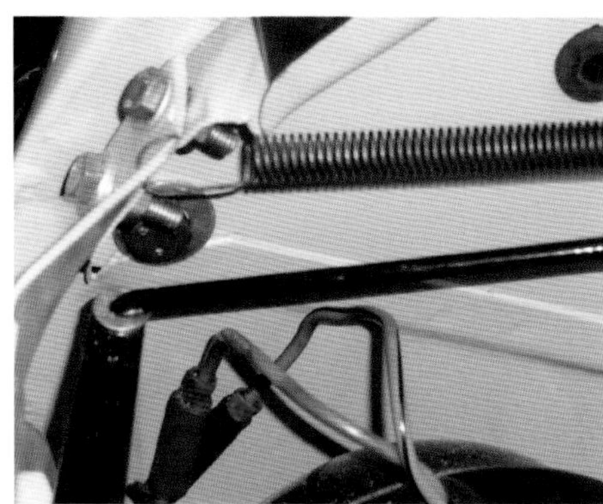

The rod lock control is connected to the lever and held in place by a small washer and split pin. A long anti-rattle spring provides the tension to aid in the bonnet opening operation.

above top: Bill sighs in relief that the bonnet is finally fitted and no paint was removed during the fitting process. A heart starting machine (defibrilator) was not required and the ambulance was cancelled... but we required some coffee to calm down and reflect.

The female slider support assembly lock was fitted when assembling the grille. The spring loaded safety catch is polished up to good effect. The underside spring and pin are fiddly to fit.

Bonnet – Big Problems

"Letting the truth get in the way of a good story!" Confession time!

The description of the bonnet fit tells how it should have been first time round, and as with the rest of the book, is offered as a guide to any potential restorer. However, the truth of the matter is that in the case of the Million, the panel fit of the bonnet and lots of other panels was terrible. Looking back, this was partly due to my over enthusiastic and excitable nature and my desire to get on with the job. With a previous restoration of a Morris Minor 1000 Traveller, the 'Woodie', Bill and I engaged the services of Robert Tingay. Robert's skill in fitting panels has already been praised and with the Woodie, he spent many hours working the panels and fitting them to the body. The guards/wings, bonnet and grille were taken on and off many times. The body and the panels were beaten, pushed and pulled until the panel fit was faultless. The panels were then primed and painted and, come assembly time, they fitted like a glove.

If only we had followed the same procedure this time around. Yes, we engaged Robert's services again, but this time we asked him to work on individual panels. They were not fitted to the body. In my haste and excitement I just primed and painted them thinking nothing would have distorted while undertaking the rust repairs. I was sadly mistaken as the pictures on these pages reveal.

The good news was that all was not lost. Robert took on the challenge of rectifying the painted panels while keeping paint loss and damage to a minimum. Inevitably there was some, but this was a small price to pay for the pleasure of seeing all the panels properly aligned… even if Bill and I nearly had heart failure on occasions when watching the master at work.

The lesson to be learnt is 'After repairing the body or the panels, fit and align the panels on the vehicle before final painting'.

Robert Tingay worked his magic to improve the alignment of the bonnet so that it matched up with the profile of the left hand guard/wing. The stress of watching him bash the metal not only impaired my photographic ability but also affected most of my bodily functions!

Driver's side door and guard/wing… not a good fit at all.

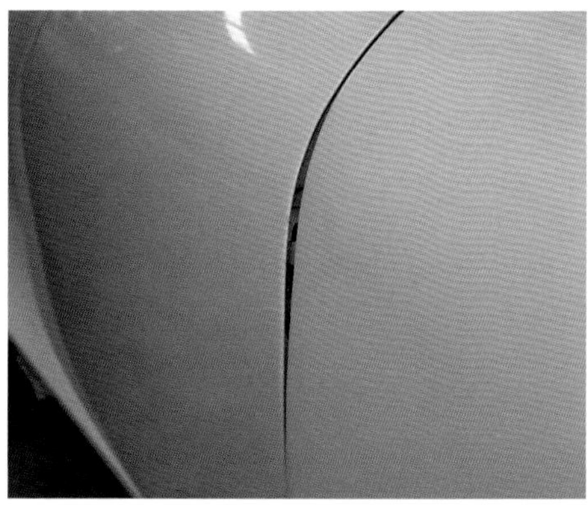

Further work was needed here too.

It was hard to believe the guards/wings were from a Morris Minor as the fit was so bad.

Carpet – Fitting and Detailing

The Cabin Floor

A carpet kit was imported from Newton Commercial in the UK and was easily installed. New underfelt had been purchased from The Bendigo (Victoria) Swap Meeting. Prior to fitting the carpets the inner floor had been painted with lilac enamel paint which matched the Acrylic used on the rest of the car. This was done in order to provide a more hard wearing surface. It had the added bonus of dramatically improving the appearance of the inside of the car.

To begin with, carpet was glued in position on top of the inner sills, along the foot and heel sections in the front of the cabin and below the back seat. A strip of carpet was also glued under the parcel shelf – on the back of the firewall. Using Kwik Grip adhesive, the carpets could be slid into place allowing for any gaps to be butted up making for an accurate fit. This was allowed to dry completely before any further work was undertaken. The inertia reel seat belt units were then mounted on top of the carpet on the inner sills.

The gearbox cover was next to be fitted. This is held in with special brass screws and large washers. Brass screws were used to enable the cover to be easily removed in the future. A bead of mastic was applied to the edge of the gearbox cover before it was fixed in place. This created a seal with the floor (important to prevent the ingress of water).

The underfelt was then fitted around the handbrake and across the tail/prop shaft tunnel. The flat sections of the carpet were used as templates so that the underfelt could

above top: The side panel carpet was glued in place first.

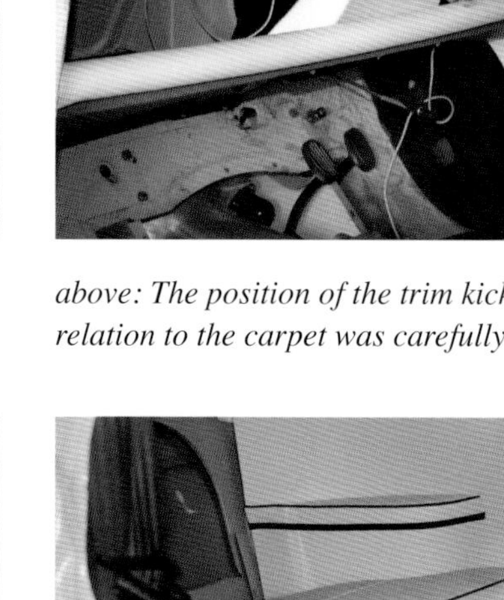

above: The position of the trim kick panel in relation to the carpet was carefully checked.

The carpet was used for a template for sizing the underfelt.

Carpet for the sill panels and heel area below the seat were glued with Kwik Grip adhesive. The small detailed pieces of carpet made a big difference to the end finish.

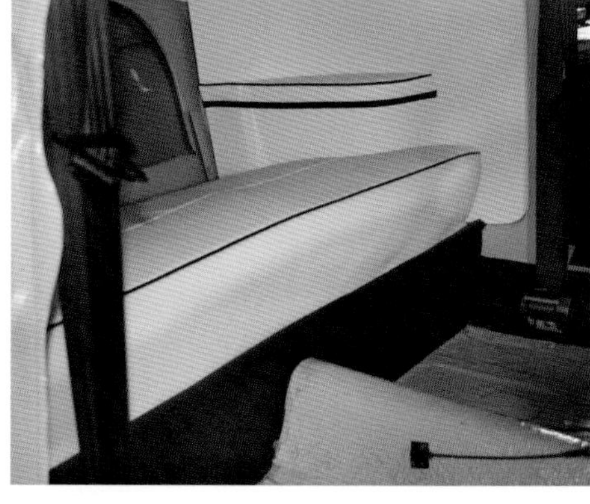

The back seat fitted neatly in position. A metal lip behind the carpet holds the seat firmly in place.

be cut to size and fitted. With the underfelt in place, the carpet was then fitted over the gearbox, handbrake and tunnel to the rear.

The gear lever grommet and surround that hold the middle carpet section in place were attached using the six original domed Phillips head screws. A scriber and wire was used to locate the original holes. The rear middle section of carpet was carefully positioned before the ashtray, which helps secure the carpet in place, was mounted on the transmission tunnel using four domed screws.

Seat belt mountings had to be taken into consideration. Slits were cut into the underfelt to accommodate the extensions for the belt clips. Eight small slits were cut in the carpet to allow for the mounting of the seats. For a tailored fit the seat mountings were fitted on top of the carpet. Due to the thickness of the carpet and underfelt, some longer bolts were purchased. Press-studs and clips were supplied in the kit to attach the outer edges of the carpets to the floor.

Fitting the carpets was an enjoyable job and one where taking time and giving attention to detail really paid off.

McKellar Tip – Placing some spacing washers under the longer seat mounting bolts helped stop the mounts from squashing the carpet and allowed for a much flatter and eye-pleasing look to the carpet fit.

.

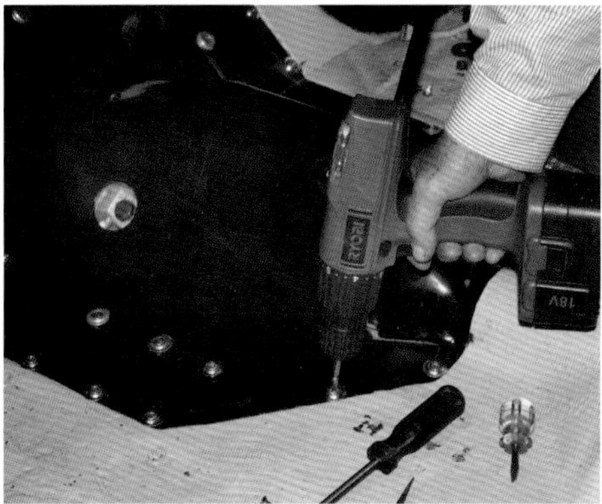

A power screwdriver speeded up the job of affixing the numerous brass screws that hold the gearbox cover to the floor. Unlike earlier Morris Minors, the updated 948cc models had a small additional cover which allowed for easier access to the master cylinder.

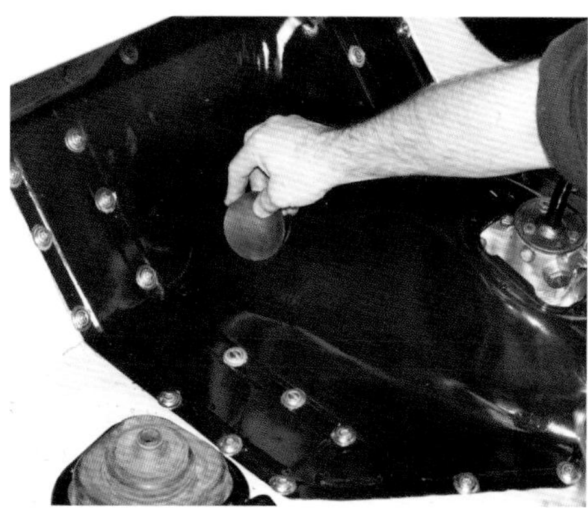

Inserting the gearbox filler grommet into the inspection hole in the gearbox cover.

Seat belts being bolted to the floor. A slit in the underfelt provides a gap which keeps the fittings flush with the floor.

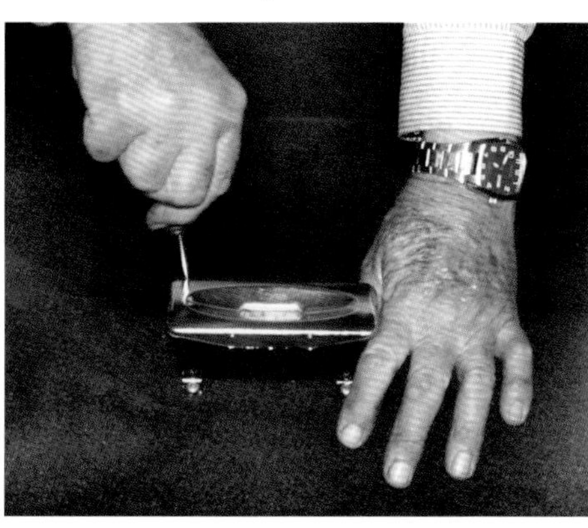

The rear ashtray secures the carpet in place. This box-frame is screwed to the top of the transmission tunnel.

The gear stick grommet surround secures the carpet over the gearbox cover. A wire (right) was used to locate the holes for the screws.

1955 Morris Minor Series II Convertible

My Mother – Claire McKellar 1964.

Richard aged 4 (1969), with the remains of a 1913 Hillman.

Mum and I were run off the road by 'Mad Max' type delinquents in 1985.

Restoring the Minor to original specification in 1986.

My Dad's First Car

My first memory of a motor vehicle was of a 1955 Morris Minor Series II which my Dad bought in 1956, from a used car yard in Wangaratta (North East Victoria) – Allan Capp Used Cars. The dealer allowed Dad to pay off the car in instalments. The Minor was nurtured and loved and was always kept scrupulously clean. Mechanically the car lacked for nothing and I remember that the engine was detailed even to the point of having a chrome rocker cover. Back in the late 1950's there were not many cars on the road and the Minor was considered quite sporty with its convertible hood which was often down during the summer months. The car was promised to me when I grew up. I was four at the time!

The Minor had to be sold in 1969 to make way for a larger 1964 EH Holden (which we still own today) due to a new addition to the family. When I turned eighteen, I was successful in locating the Minor again. The owner was still the lady to whom Dad had sold the car in 1969. It was in a sad state of repair, having been stored in a rusty shed with a dirt floor, but still registered. Margaret Wood, a nurse at the local hospital, agreed to sell 'Amanda Jane' for AU$1,000 (which was all I had). I gladly handed over the cash. I returned the car to the road but unfortunately Mum and I were involved in an accident in 1986. The car was badly damaged so Dad and I decided to restore it back to original specification. Other cars were purchased for parts. The car won a trophy in the 1987 National Rally in Adelaide (South Australia) and still wins them from time to time. Amanda Jane has been restored for over 23 years, driven huge distances but still looks as good as the day she was restored. The car has been promised to my No. 1 daughter when she grows up. (Daughter No. 2 has claimed Edward the 'Woodie'). The McKellar Morris Minor legacy lives on!

Trim – Fitting the Door Cards

Fitting the Door Cards

This is one of the more straightforward and pleasurable jobs to do on a restoration.

It was made much easier due to the fact that a door trim kit had been purchased from Heritage approved trim specialist, Newton Commercial in the UK. The kit is very comprehensive and includes pre-drilled door cards with precisely positioned locators for the spring loaded retaining clips. The holes are also pre-drilled for the door pull and handles. Care must be exercised when setting out the work area so as not to inadvertently damage the vinyl. Extra caution must be exercised if it proves necessary to drill the door in order to locate the door pulls.

McKellar Tip – Make sure a short drill bit is used so as to avoid marking the window glass.

above top: A vinyl fabric was used to seal the door holes in order to keep any moisture away from the door cards. After the glue dried the material was neatly cut to shape.

Plain door trims were part of the Minor Million specification, unlike other 1961 Morris Minors which had a more attractive three panel pleated design.

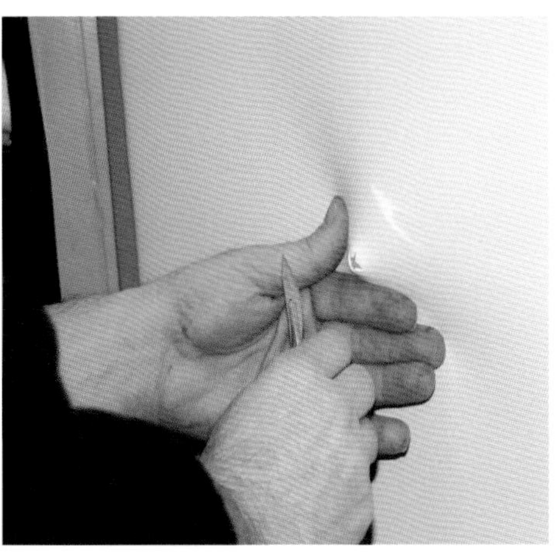

1. *Planning the placement of the holes. Measure twice cut once!*

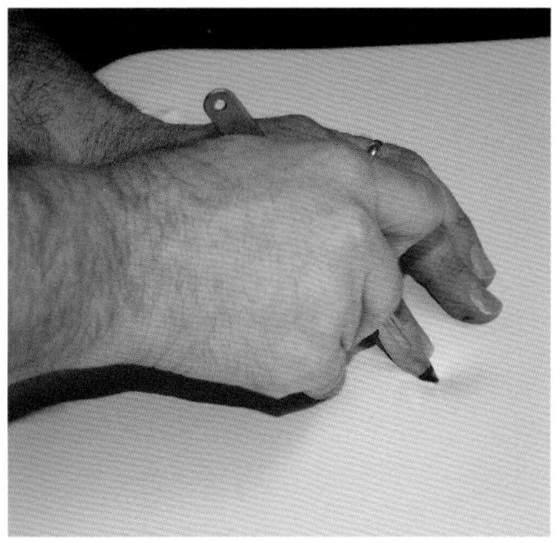

2. *Cutting two small slits with a scalpel helps to make sure alignment is correct.*

3. *Using a large round sharp hole punch to make a neat job of the holes.*

4. *Retaining clips came as part of the kit from Newton Commercial (UK). It really is a quality kit – money well spent.*

5. Other components were prepared in advance.

6. Using a scriber carefully locate the door pull holes.

7. Gently clip the door card clips into the holes in the door. Gloves are essential when doing this job particularly with the white upholstery.

8. Have a coffee or a beer and admire your handiwork. It's not a job to be rushed.

9. A Dremel is the perfect tool for this type of drilling. Make sure you use a short drill bit.

10. Screw the door pull and finisher into place. Use short screws to avoid marking the glass when operating the window.

11. Place the fibre washers on the shafts.

12. Screw on the handles. Check position of the winder orientation to ensure there is no interference with the driver's knee.

far left: As magnificent as the white leather upholstery looks, it is almost impossible to keep clean. Every time the car is driven marks have to be wiped off.

The black piping contrasts beautifully with the white seats.

Photo Gallery

The Journey

It has been a very rewarding experience restoring this car back to its former glory. Like any restoration it was full of heartache and pain, excitement and joy. Certainly the highs and lows let us know we were alive.

There was the panel-fit horror and the joys of fitting the dash and upholstery. The upholstery arriving from Newton Commercial (UK) was a highlight. We were very impressed with the quality of their workmanship and customer service. Then there was the relief of finally getting the panels to fit. There was the large unexpected chrome bill, and on the other side of the spectrum, the incredible help and generosity from people like Norm Deumer and Keith White, Wilson Bunton, Todd Elliott, Phil Smith (Minor Million Register) Ray Newell, Ian Tindley, Phil Plumbe, Percy Scicluna, Mark Coutts, Thorpe,

above top: With the 1,000,000 complete, the final stage was paint protection. 'Toughseal 'a Teflon polish was applied giving the Acrylic paint protection against the elements, particularly bird droppings, as well as a brilliant wet-look shine!

The finishing touches. The coach line was the light at the end of the tunnel, and the final "Kodak moment'. The black coach line tape was easily applied by stretching along the length of the panels until it was in the correct central position on the swage line. The tape provides a crisp clean line. Originally the coach line was applied using a 'dagger brush'. Bill had one on hand, which I have used to good effect painting the lines on the wheels of earlier model Morris Minors. Due to the length of the lines required the tape was a better bet!

Kate Hutson, Graham Bulluss, Barry Hodder, Gillian Bardsley (BMIHT Archivist, Heritage Motor Centre) Keith Philpot, Jack Field as well as a sea of others who gave help and advice. The support and help of Car Clubs, local and overseas, all played a part in the success of the project.

There was the support of family members and in particular my immediate family, wife Kim and daughters Madeline and Isabelle. Not forgetting my Mum, Claire, who helped throughout with tasty meals, the use of her studio, assistance with the proofreading but most importantly by showing incredible patience and unwavering support, sometimes in very trying circumstances.

And, of course, Dad (Bill). Without his sense of humour and his willingness to help without question the completion of the project would not have been possible. Both of us often think what a gift it is to share a common interest and be passionate about the projects we undertake together.

I am the pushy, highly strung creative force, Dad is laid-back and a little more calculating (put that down to life experience!). Together we make a formidable team… and once again we got the job done.

Keith White, mechanic and good friend, gives the engine a quick tune before road testing.

Our original aim was to have the car ready for the 2009 Brisbane National Rally, but we missed out by only a few weeks... due to my extravagant overseas 'Inspiration' trip with the family. In any case we were really not sure how we were going to get a newly restored car, not been tried or tested, to the Brisbane Rally which was 1,800 kms (1,120 miles) away.

The restoration is quite accurate to how I imagine the car would have looked as it left Cowley on 13 December 1960. The only exceptions are the four blade fan, the rear springs and the inertia-reel seat belts. The temptation was always present to over-restore – the painted part numbers on the suspension components is possibly a good example of one that I let "slip through to the keeper". I would have liked to have used the Dunlop tyres, but due to importing costs this was quite out of the question.

I must add that I relived the enjoyment of the project by writing this book. It was rather like doing it all over again... certainly the thought process was identical to what I experienced while restoring.

Ray Newell's input as mentor and friend has been greatly appreciated. His support in reviewing the manuscript and revising and amending the text has been invaluable. I am constantly impressed by the depth and extent of his knowledge regarding the Minor, and it has been a pleasure to work with him on this project.

Where possible I have mentioned the suppliers I have used for parts and advice.

It has been and enjoyable experience and I would recommend the adventure... if you have the patience, time and space. However, if you do, consider the benefits of joining a Car Club as the support available from their members is invaluable for anyone embarking on a project of this kind.

What's in a name? Prompted by our 'inspiration trip', my wife Kim named the Million, Elizabeth. (Oh, how very English!)

History of the Minor Million

The colour photographs on the following pages are four of a series of seven BMC publicity photos of a Million, all taken at Blenheim Palace (Winston Churchill's ancestral home).

The completion of the restoration of Minor Million 1,000,068, apart from being a euphoric moment for Richard and Bill McKellar and all associated with the project, was significant for a host of other reasons. In being fully documented by means of a comprehensive photographic record, it created the opportunity for further investigation into the possibility of sharing the adventure with other like minded enthusiasts and led to the publication of this book. It also demonstrated the feasibility of restoring a limited edition vehicle almost half a century after it left the production lines at Cowley, Oxfordshire, in a location on the other side of the world. It proved – beyond doubt – that with persistence and determination, it is still possible to source new old stock (NOS) and reproduction parts for the Morris Minor. This was done using the internet, local contacts, club members, traders and fellow enthusiasts around the world.

For Minor Million devotees and Million

Register members, it has added a new dimension to the fascinating Minor Million story which continues to interest, excite and amaze given that only 350 of these vehicles were ever produced.

The significance of the Morris Minor Million cannot be overstated. Its production was a means by which the British Motor Corporation Ltd could bring to the attention of the world the magnificent achievement of being the first British car manufacturer to produce one million units of the highly acclaimed Morris Minor, which had been designed by Alec Issigonis. The fact that a large percentage of the million vehicles produced had either been built in assembly plants in other countries including Australia, New Zealand, South Africa, India, Holland and Ireland, or been exported to virtually every country in the world, was not lost on the staff in the Publicity Department who were anxious to mark the occasion and secure future sales.

Once the decision had been made to build a limited edition model to mark the production of a million units the question remained how many commemorative vehicles should be produced. The somewhat arbitrary figure of 350 was agreed. This number included the actual millionth car and 349 replicas.
In reality it has been suggested the extent of the BMC dealer network in 1960 may have influenced the final number produced. Of the cars built 30 were built to left hand drive specification and these were dispatched mainly to North American and European destinations. With the exception of the Millionth car which remained with the Publicity Department, the remaining models were released to the UK dealer network.

The vehicles were allocated a batch of consecutive chassis numbers starting with 1,000,000 and ending with 1,000,349.These numbers were allocated out of sequence though. Research undertaken in 1980 by Anders Clausager, former Archivist at BL Heritage Ltd, revealed that any thoughts of these vehicles rolling off the production line one after the other was wide of the mark.
The first of the cars was built on 22 November 1960. With the exception of the Millionth car the rest were assembled during the period 13-20 December.
The 1,000,000th car was actually assembled on 22 December 1960 and is believed to be genuinely the millionth car built.

Specifications

The Minor Million cars were all 1960 2 door saloons and the mechanical specifications were identical to that of standard production models. The differences related to the paint colour, the interior trim and the external embellishments. The lilac paint colour, although distinctive did not find universal favour. The interior trim on the other hand was tasteful and complemented the exterior finish very well. The sun visors and headlining were light grey in colour while the seats and other trim panels were white. Carpets were black as were the draught excluder and upholstery piping. The seats had 'white gold' leather facings in the same pattern as those fitted to other production models of that era.

Externally the badging on the bonnet sides and on the boot lid was cleverly amended to read 1,000,000 and a nice touch was the addition of wheel embellishers which complemented the overall appearance.

ONE MILLIONT

B M C Photo

Further Information:
Ian Paterson,
Austin Motor Co. (Canada) Ltd.,
Morris Motors (Canada) Ltd.,
737 Church Street,
TORONTO - WA. 4-3341

above: Amidst a blaze of publicity this Minor Million was handed over to its new owner in Toronto, Canada. The exported 1,000,000's differed slightly in specification to their UK counterparts. The exported cars were upgraded by stainless-steel door tops and flashing front and rear indicators.

Mr L. Bowles chats with Morris Minor designer Mr Alec Issigonis some eight days after this Millionth car was built.

The car was used extensively by the BMC Publicity Department until 20 April 1961, when it passed into the hands of the National Union of Journalists. The choice was made for its publicity value, as it was sure to get the car mentioned in every newspaper!

From the Journalists Union the car apparently passed on to the British Red Cross, who raffled it off. It was registered in Bristol on 1 June 1961, perhaps the last of the Millions to be registered, and given the number 1 MHU (one million in engineering terms).

The winner of the raffle was a young girl in Wales who was too young to drive! The car went to her, then to the firm her family owned, and in later years to another owner in Wales.

Promotional Material

Promotional Material

Such a landmark occasion provided a real opportunity to celebrate the success of the Morris Minor as well as to promote the limited edition Minor Million. All the major motoring publications of the time reported on the historic nature of the production run. Ably assisted by the Press and the Public Relations Office in Cowley, many of the parts manufacturers and component suppliers were successfully persuaded to advertise their long association with the British Motor Corporation. To ensure accuracy and to reinforce the perception that the Morris Minor still represented a value for money vehicle, a specially produced booklet entitled 'Morris Minor 1,000,000. The Story of Great Engineering and Commercial Achievement' was issued. The opening paragraph summed up the magnitude of the achievement and the tenor of the publication.

'The production of 1,000,000 vehicles of a common design is a feat never before achieved by the British motor industry, the magnitude of which can be exemplified by saying that if all the units which have left the production lines at Cowley were spaced at intervals of 407yds 11 ½ inches the first would rest in Oxfordshire and the millionth would have its wheels on the Moon.'

In spite of such hyperbole, many trade suppliers were keen to acknowledge the achievement. As the illustrations here show, many were proud to reaffirm their association with the production of the Morris Minor.

Advertising from associated companies promoting their involvement in the Minor Million milestone.
The advertisements which appear on the following pages are printed courtesy of 'The Autocar', and come from 6 January 1961 edition.

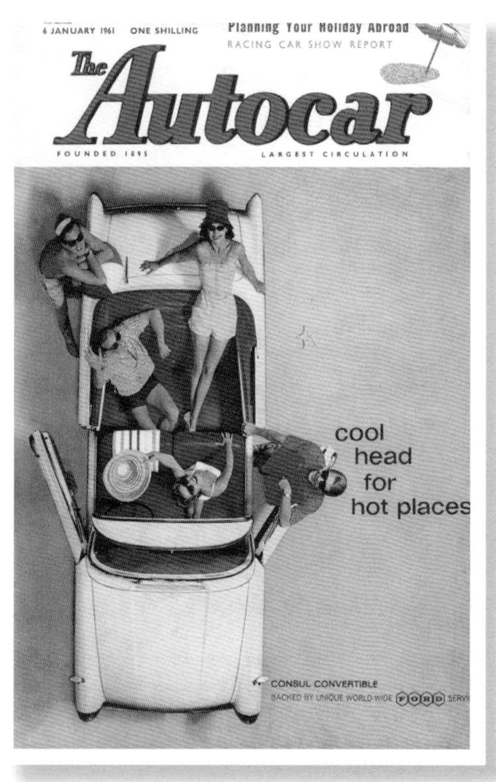

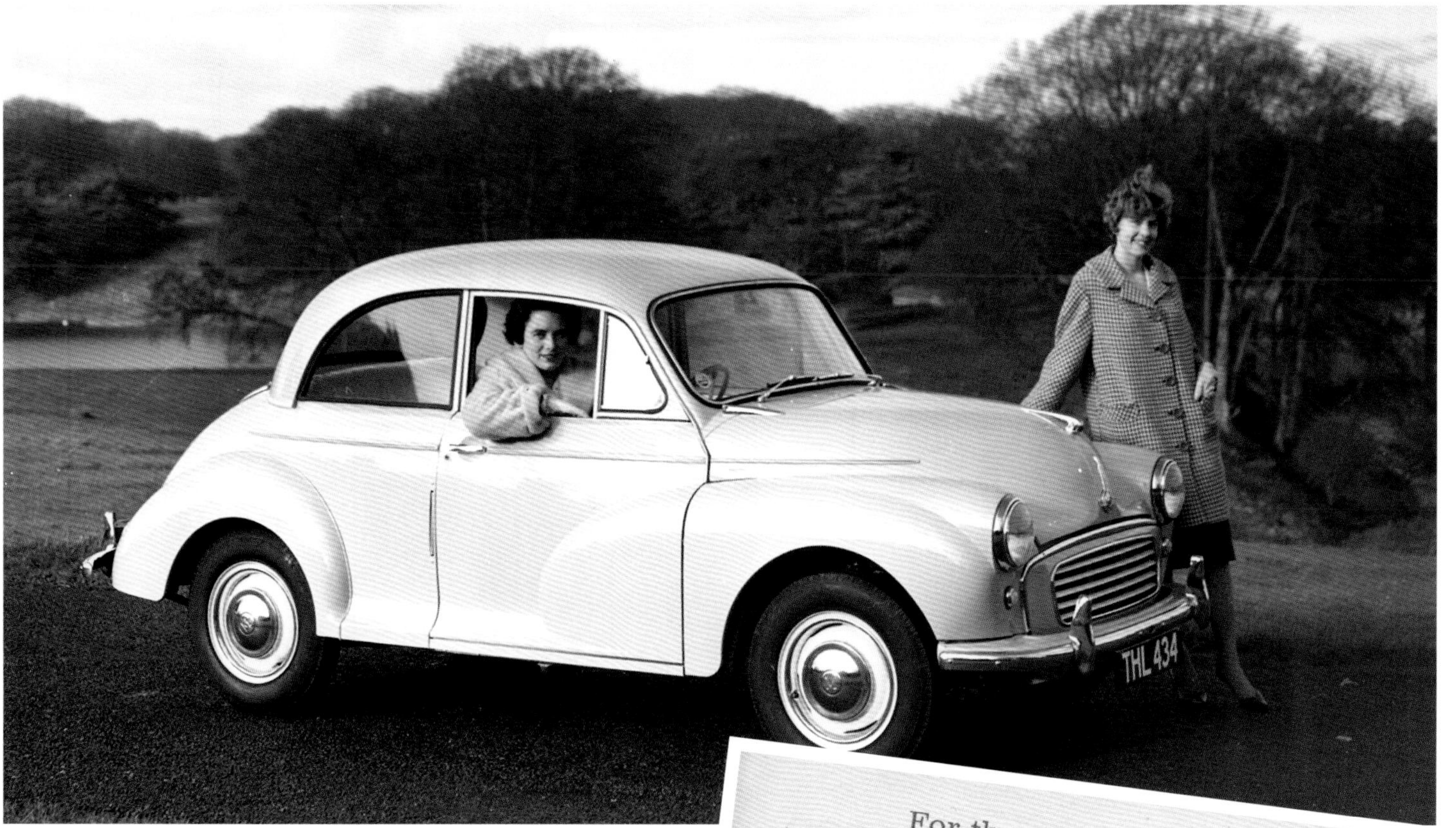

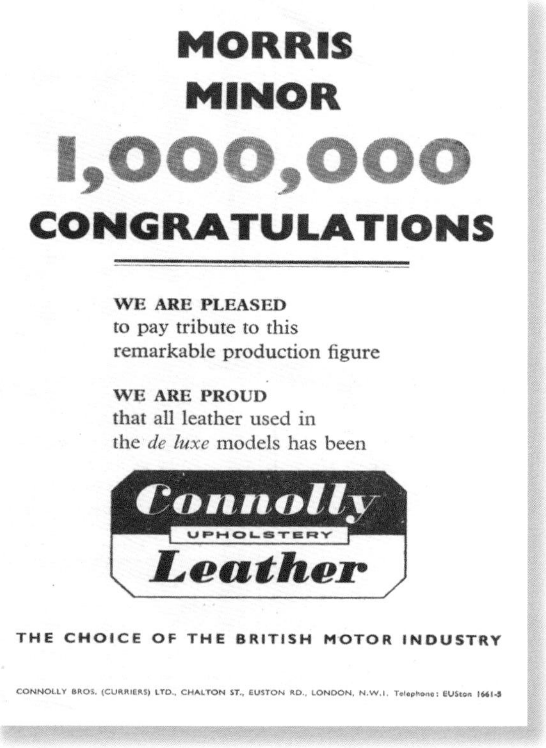

MORRIS
MINOR
1,000,000
CONGRATULATIONS

WE ARE PLEASED
to pay tribute to this
remarkable production figure

WE ARE PROUD
that all leather used in
the *de luxe* models has been

THE CHOICE OF THE BRITISH MOTOR INDUSTRY

CONNOLLY BROS. (CURRIERS) LTD., CHALTON ST., EUSTON RD., LONDON, N.W.1. Telephone: EUSton 1661-5

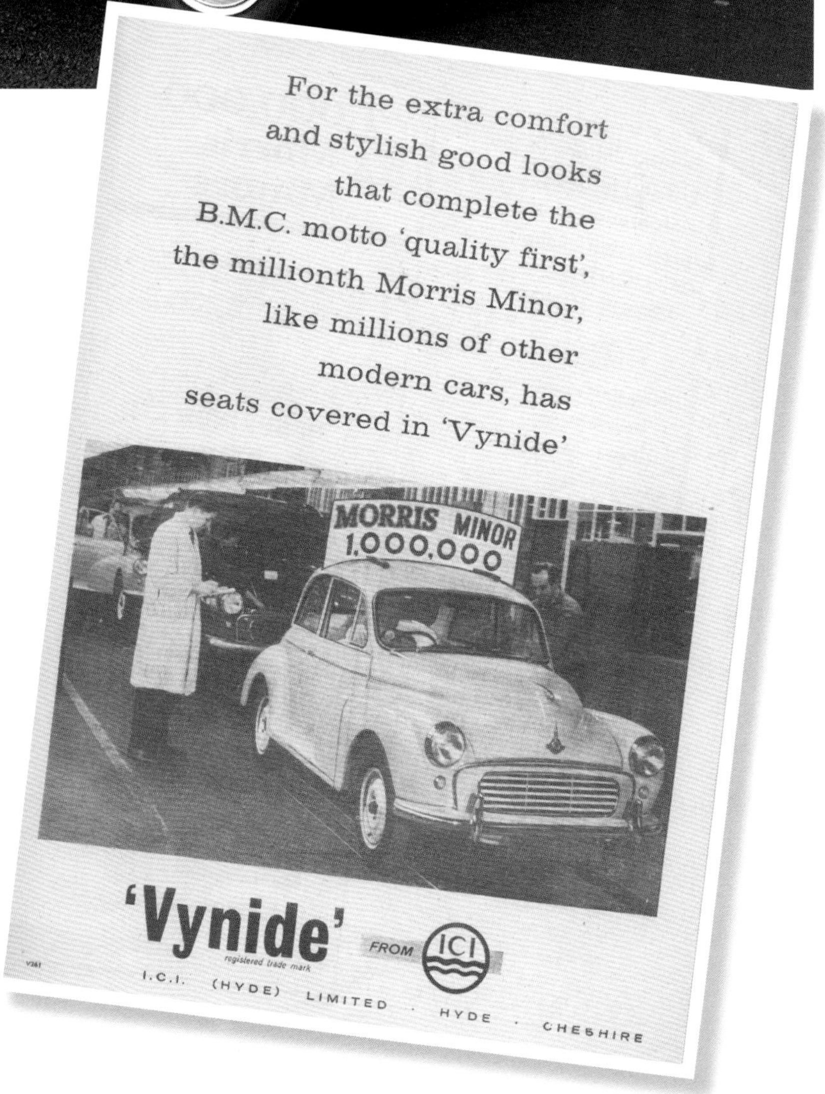

For the extra comfort
and stylish good looks
that complete the
B.M.C. motto 'quality first',
the millionth Morris Minor,
like millions of other
modern cars, has
seats covered in 'Vynide'

'Vynide' FROM ICI
registered trade mark

V261

I.C.I. (HYDE) LIMITED · HYDE · CHESHIRE

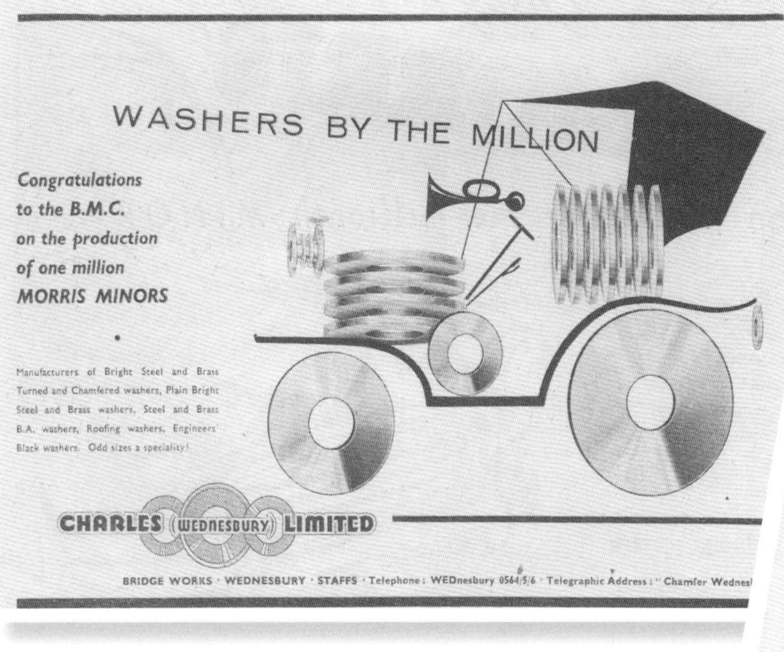

A MILLION MORRIS MINORS

have been fitted with

products

The Millionth Morris Minor has rolled off the production line — fitted, as are all Minors, with products. A powerful hydraulic braking system, a thoroughly dependable clutch and 'Micronic' oil filters — these are the products that have contributed towards the tremendous success of this supreme family saloon.

Lockheed HYDRAULIC BRAKES

BORG & BECK FRICTION CLUTCHES

PUROLATOR OIL, FUEL & AIR FILTERS

1,000,000 Morris Minors!

The first of the post-war series was introduced in 1948, since when, apart from numerous refinements and improvements, the brilliant basic design has remained unchanged up to the present day. So many of these popular little cars have now been sold that there are now more of them on British roads than any other single model of any make.

and that means 1,000,000

HARDY SPICER

PROPELLER SHAFTS

Product of the Birfield Group

HARDY SPICER LIMITED · CHESTER ROAD · ERDINGTON · BIRMINGHAM 24
Telephone: ERDINGTON 2191 (18 lines) Telex No. 33414

800,000
900,000
1,000,000
MINORS!
Congratulations to B.M.C. on the millionth Minor!
Rubery, Owen Motor Division are proud to be associated
with B.M.C. in the production of the Morris Minor
by supplying rear axle cases for this "million-up" model.
RUBERY, OWEN Motor Division
Rubery, Owen & Co. Ltd., P.O. Box 10, Darlaston, Wednesbury, Staffs.
MOTOR RO DIVISION

MORRIS MINOR
1,000,000

One in a million!

The Morris Minor—a car that a million owners think of as one in a million, a car that reflects credit on the British Motor Corporation.

SMITHS are proud to have been associated with B.M.C; proud that a million sets of SMITHS dashboard instruments are giving accurate and reliable service in a million Morris Minors.

SMITHS

a name with a world of meaning

SMITHS INSTRUMENTS
SMITHS CAR HEATERS
SMITHS RADIOMOBILE
K.L.G. SPARKING PLUGS
BLUECOL & SUMMERCOL
PETROFLEX TUBING
SMITHS BATTERIES

SMITHS MOTOR ACCESSORY DIVISION • CRICKLEWOOD, LONDON N.W.2

above: Probably the most famous of the official BMC publicity shots.

THL 434
NOL
ENGINE OIL
THIRTY
DUCKHAM'S
Congratulate
MORRIS
on producing the millionth MINOR
Duckham's oils have been officially recommended by Morris Motors Ltd., for 30 years.
ALEXANDER DUCKHAM & CO. LTD. LONDON, W.6.
PRESSED FELTS LTD.
Suppliers of
UNDERFELTS and INSULATING FELTS
incorporated in the MORRIS Range of Cars
Wish to congratulate
THE BRITISH MOTOR CORPORATION
on the achievement of the
1,000,000th
MORRIS MINOR
MATS CUT AND SHAPED TO TEMPLATES OR DRAWINGS A SPECIALITY
SPRING GARDENS and CALDER MILLS
COLNE–LANCS
TEL: COLNE 1550 (5 lines)

Competition Time – The Quest for the Oldest Morris Minor

As part of the Million milestone celebrations the press was enlisted to promote the idea of finding the earliest post-War Morris Minor in the world. Dealerships all around the globe were alerted to the idea and before long hopeful applicants were writing to Morris Motors Ltd with details of their vehicles.

There were rigorous conditions though. The vehicle had to be the earliest built and to have covered at least 100,000 miles. With such a vehicle being only 12 years old – in an era when high mileage was not the norm – this was indeed a tall order.

Where is the oldest post-War 'Minor'? We want to find it!

To mark the millionth 'Minor', we will exchange a new 'Minor 1000' with the earliest post-War chassis number.

The only stipulation is that the car must have completed 100,000 miles. If you think your 'Minor' qualifies, check that chassis number now and send the details to Morris Motors Ltd, Cowley, Oxford

above: The actual wording of the press release to find the earliest Morris Minor.

Nearly 600 replied in the hope of being successful – but, of course, there could only be one winner.

The search for the oldest production model of the Morris Minor brought Sheffield owner Cyril Swift – a transport driver – to prominence. Out of all the entries received from all over the world he, along with the first production model NWL 576, emerged as the winner. In a blaze of publicity Cyril and his wife received the keys to the Morris Minor Million which had been the main attraction on the stage of the Empire Theatre, Sheffield only a few days before. BMC Deputy Home Sales Director, Tom Sangster along with R.A Bishop,

Release Date: - Not before 1 p.m. Friday 24th March 1961

THE END OF A WORLD-WIDE SEARCH.
FIRST POST-WAR MORRIS MINOR FOUND.

Friday next, the 24th March in Sheffield will mark the culmination of a world-wide search for a motor car; no ordinary motor car but the earliest post war Morris Minor still running.

On the 4th January, Morris Motors Limited, announced the production of the millionth Morris Minor - a unique achievement in the history of the British Motor Industry. At the same time they asked "Where is the oldest post-war Minor?" and offered a new Minor 1000 in exchange for it - the only condition being that the car must have covered 100,000 miles.

The response was, not surprisingly, staggering. Replies were received from all over the world (nearly half-a-million of the cars were exported). There were apparently Minors in places as far apart as Mombasa and Manitoba, Mexico City and Melbourne, Munich and Manchester, Monmouth and Madagascar.

All had covered tremendous mileages and all were "running well and in first class condition".

But the earliest of all, the first off the production line, was found, not inappropriately, in a city of steel - Sheffield. Having started life as a Works Demonstrator it had finally ended up about six years ago in the hands of Cyril Swift a transport driver of 33 Carr Road, Sheffield.

The first Morris Minor, NWL 576, as found in Sheffield in 1961 when it was exchanged for a Minor Million. Having covered over 100,000 miles, an internal factory memo described the car as 'clapped out'.

Director of Publicity, joined the Lord Mayor of Sheffield and George and David Kenning at a special presentation where the special prize of a new Morris Minor Million was handed over. The car was bedecked with every conceivable extra imaginable and at a special buffet luncheon, Mr Swift proudly took ownership of a brand new and somewhat distinctive limited edition car with the registration 5599 WA. A keen motorist and member of the BMC Driver's Club, Mr Swift was keen to accept the new car rather than take the cash alternative of £619. BMC were also keen to take advantage of the publicity, as were Kennings who supplied the accessories for the car which had a retail equivalent of £70. Regrettably, in spite of diligent searches no record exists of this particular vehicle having survived.

Release - Not before 1 p.m. Friday 24th March 1961

PERSONALIZING THE MILLIONTH MINOR

B.M.C. ACCESSORIES ADORN GIVE-AWAY

Mr. Cyril Swift of 33 Carr Road, Sheffield, the winner of the Million Minor replica given by Morris Motors in exchange of the oldest post-war Minor still running, will find may aids to comfort and safer driving in his new car.

Though some may consider it a case of gilding the lily, there is no doubt that the chromium wheel discs and exterior sun visor improve the appearance of the car. Internally, the leopard-skin seat cover gives a dash of gaiety while the Dress Stuart tartan travelling rug cast nonchalantly on the rear seat provides that "Je ne sais quoi" which distinguishes THE CAR from the run-of-the-mill family saloons.

For safe driving, no one can doubt the usefulness of fog and driving lamps as well as wing mirrors and windscreen washers and, though never it is hoped to be used, the presence of a fire extinguisher should delight the most fastidious insurance company.

To complete the personalization, there is an electric cigarette lighter for Mr Swift, for his wife a vanity mirror on the passenger's sun-visor and, for the whole family, plenty of roof for luggage with the fitted continental-type roof rack.

The foregoing is a selection from the very wide range of B.M.C. - approved accessories which are available not only for the Minor but for all cars produced by the Corporation.

163002

Mr Cyril Swift with his new Minor 1,000,000.

Restoration and Glory

When all the excitement died down, attention at the Cowley works turned to 'what to do' with the oldest production Morris Minor in the world. In the end the decision was made to allow BMC apprentices to work on the vehicle with a view to returning it to the road in as new condition. Parts had to be sourced from the dusty storerooms of the extensive Dealer network. Eventually the task was completed and the vehicle was put on public display.

Mr T. A. Sangster, Deputy Director of Home Sales for BMC Ltd, handing over the car keys.

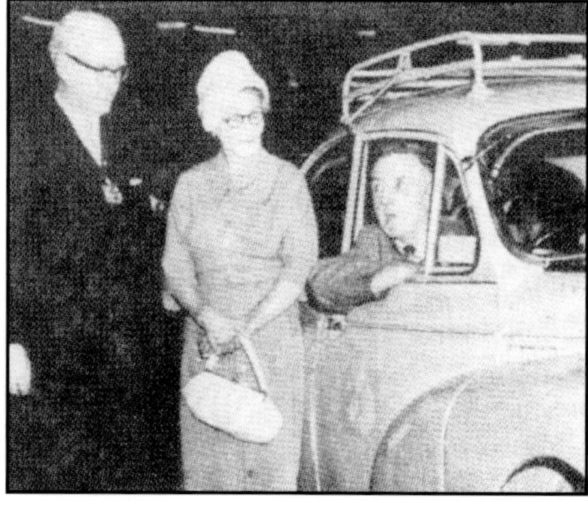

Dream come true! Cyril takes up the driving position while his wife and the Lord Mayor of Sheffield look on.

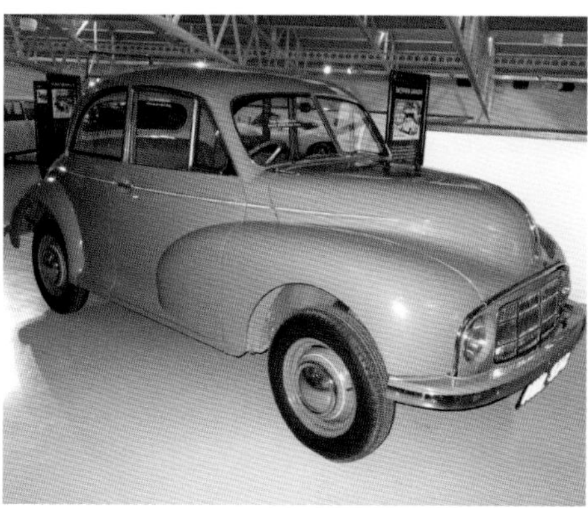

Restored by BMC apprentices, SMM 501 resides in the Heritage Motor Museum at Gaydon.

Publicity

In order to celebrate reaching the historic landmark of one million sales of the Morris Minor worldwide, the BMC Publicity Department decided that the actual 1,000,000th car should be used in a special way. To do this the assistance of the Press was enlisted in a somewhat novel way. At a specially convened Press Party held at Grosvenor House in London on 3 January 1961, Mr J. R. Woodcock, Deputy Chairman of the Nuffield Organisation accompanied by Alec Issigonis handed over the Millionth car to Mr Magnus Williamson the National Chairman of the National Union of Journalists. The intention was that the car would be used in some way to support the Union's Benevolent Fund.

In the event a special competition called the "One in a Million" contest was organised in the National Press. Proceeds from the competition entries were earmarked for use to support the National Union of Journalists Widow and Orphan Fund.

The competition was hastily arranged under the auspices of the Lavenham Press and followed a simple but effective format. In conjunction with all other press information relating to the Minor Million details were embargoed until Wednesday 4 January 1961.

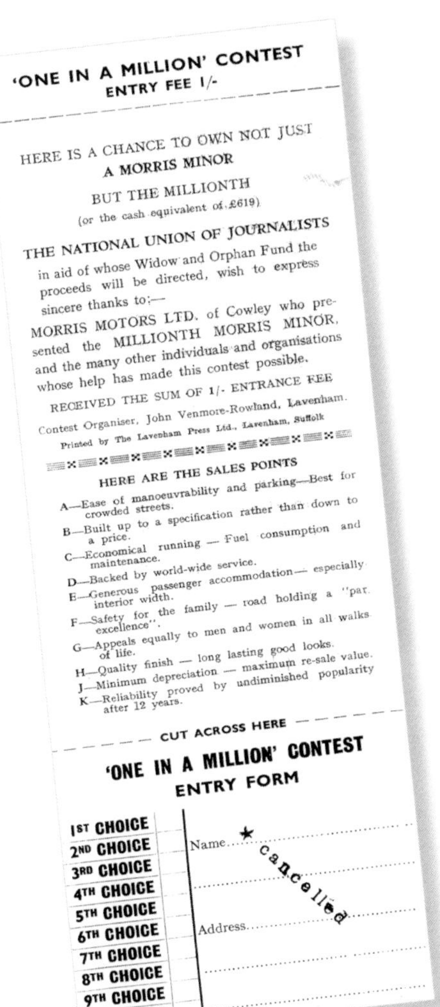

'ONE IN A MILLION' CONTEST
ENTRY FEE 1/-

HERE IS A CHANCE TO OWN NOT JUST
A MORRIS MINOR
BUT THE MILLIONTH
(or the cash equivalent of £619)

THE NATIONAL UNION OF JOURNALISTS in aid of whose Widow and Orphan Fund the proceeds will be directed, wish to express sincere thanks to:—

MORRIS MOTORS LTD. of Cowley who presented the MILLIONTH MORRIS MINOR, and the many other individuals and organisations whose help has made this contest possible.

RECEIVED THE SUM OF 1/- ENTRANCE FEE

Contest Organiser, John Venmore-Rowland, Lavenham.

Printed by The Lavenham Press Ltd., Lavenham, Suffolk

HERE ARE THE SALES POINTS

A—Ease of manoeuvrability and parking—Best for crowded streets.
B—Built up to a specification rather than down to a price.
C—Economical running — Fuel consumption and maintenance.
D—Backed by world-wide service.
E—Generous passenger accommodation— especially interior width.
F—Safety for the family — road holding a "par excellence".
G—Appeals equally to men and women in all walks of life.
H—Quality finish — long lasting good looks.
J—Minimum depreciation — maximum re-sale value.
K—Reliability proved by undiminished popularity after 12 years.

CUT ACROSS HERE

'ONE IN A MILLION' CONTEST
ENTRY FORM

1ST CHOICE		Name.......... ★ cancelled
2ND CHOICE		
3RD CHOICE		....
4TH CHOICE		
5TH CHOICE		
6TH CHOICE		Address..........
7TH CHOICE		
8TH CHOICE		....
9TH CHOICE		
10TH CHOICE		....

above: the official competition entry form for the "One in a Million" contest.

below: The text of J.R. Woodcock's speech which preceded the official handover of the Millionth Car by Alec Issigonis (pictured centre above).

MILLIONTH MINOR PRESS PARTY, GROSVERNOR HOUSE

Tuesday, 3rd January 1961

The following is the text of the speech made by Mr. J.R. Woodcock, Deputy Chairman of the Nuffied Organisation:-

"This is an historic occasion in the British Motor industry and it is my great pleasure to welcome you all -
the President, Secretary and Representatives of the National Union of Journalists, and our wide circle of friends of the Press. The Morris Minor is the first British car ever to achieve a production run of one million. This is an achievement which, to be fully appreciated, has to be viewed in perspective to the complete activites of B.M.C. and its range of products.

When the car was produced as a 2-door saloon in 1948,its list price was £280 but, with the unfortunate fall in the value of the pound sterling, today's price of £416 is equivalent to a price of only £254 twelve years ago. It follows, therefore, that the public is getting more real value for its money than ever before.

Rumours, both weird and wonderful, have appeared in the press during the last four years that the Morris Minor was going to be replaced. But,as you see, the Minor goes on - and indeed why shouldn't it - for, after twelve years, it is still one of Britian's most acceptable small cars. In fact, in B.M.C. it is second only to the production volume to our twins, the Austin Seven and the Morris Mini-Minor.

Because of the enthusiasm which you have always shown for this car, we felt it would be appropriate to mark the occasion by presenting the actual one millionth of this series to the National Union of Journalists to use as they wish in the interests of their Benevolent Fund. Mr. Magnus Williamson, the National President, is with us this evening and, without further ado, I am going to ask Alec Issogonis, who needs no introduction from me, to make the official presentation to him."

The Millionth Car – 1 MHU

(*f*) Manufacturer's :—
Type or Model........MINOR 1000
Chassis, Frame or Car No. } MA2S3. 1000000
Engine No..........503889

(*g*) Rating..........948. CC

(*h*) Seating Capacity..........

(*i*) Unladen Weight

..........tons..........cwt..........lbs.

(*j*) Date of original registration } 1 JUNE 1961

(Nineteen Hundred and SIXTY ONE)

Date Stamp and Initials of Issuing Officer.

29.6.61

It is an offence under the Vehicles (Excise) Act, 1949, to alter any of the above details. (Maximum Penalty £50.)

The actual millionth car has had a chequered but well-documented history. It survives in excellent restored condition. After an extended period of use as a publicity vehicle, first by the manufacturers and then by the National Union of Journalists, the vehicle passed into private ownership in June 1960.

Miss Susan George became the lucky recipient of the car when she was announced as the winner of a televised competition staged in association with the British Red Cross. When registered in June 1961, the vehicle was allocated the distinctive registration 1 MHU.

The car remained in the George family until 1970 when it passed to a new owner in Wales. Clearly they took a dislike to the lilac colour as they decided to change it to a non-standard red. A thorough job was done as virtually all traces of the original colour were hidden.

Some years later the car was involved in an accident. An unexpected encounter with a mail van caused the car to sustain external damage including quite a heavy impact on the off-side rear wing. Even though the damage was localised the car was taken off the road and put into dry storage.

Eventually the car was purchased by Richard Elderfield in the mid 1980's. Once he realised the significance of the car he determined that it should be restored and preserved for posterity. Initially he transferred the car to his home in Warwickshire where it remained in dry storage while he authenticated the provenance of the vehicle and its historical significance. In view of the significance of the vehicle Richard hoped that a similar restoration to that undertaken on the very first car might be undertaken by the MMOC or the British Motor Industry Heritage Trust. In spite of prolonged efforts to secure sponsorship or funding for the project he drew a blank. Meanwhile the car remained in storage.

Eventually the stalemate was broken when Richard took the plunge and enlisted the assistance of a local restorer following a house move to West Sussex. The restoration was sympathetically undertaken and the car was completely restored. In a phased undertaking the bodywork was thoroughly assessed, repairs undertaken where necessary and new panels fitted where the originals were beyond repair. Every trace of the red paint was banished and careful matching of the original lilac paint was undertaken before the final top coats were applied. A complete mechanical overhaul was required due to the fact that the car had been off the road for so long. The original white

leather seats with their contrasting black piping were retained initially and great care was exercised to ensure that all the distinctive Minor Million features were accurately represented. A complete refurbishment of the interior trim followed once the car was returned to the road.

Through the efforts of Richard and Neil Elderfield one of the most significant Morris Minors has not only been saved for posterity but restored to a high standard.
The vehicle was offered for sale at auction during 2010 but failed to meet the reserve price. Speculation that it would complement Richard McKellar's Million in the Morris Minor Garage at Harcourt, Victoria, remains just that... speculation!

Of the seventy or so Minor Millions that are known to have survived, many have been the subject of extensive restoration. At least one, which was allocated to the Bradburn and Wedge dealership in Wolverhampton, England and registered E 330, has covered very few miles and is in remarkable original condition.

above top: the pictures of 1 MHU when first discovered.

1,000,000 restoration completed.

Why Lilac?

Mr Lilac – Jack Field

The question why the Morris Minor Million was painted lilac has always intrigued many people. Unquestionably it was both striking and unusual... even if it was not to everyone's taste.

The answer remained a mystery for many years until a chance encounter made at a Morris Motors Ltd reunion dinner held at the Heritage Motor Centre in 1998. Recollections of the work of the Publicity Department in 1960 led to an interview with Mr. Jack Field. At that time, he was closely involved in securing maximum publicity for the historic landmark of one million Morris Minors being produced. A Morris Minor Saloon, chassis number 881386, was taken off the production line in November 1960 and turned into a prototype Minor Million. Jack Field remembers the occasion well. Along with his colleagues, Jack began investigating the prospect of having a special paint colour for the limited edition series.

The preferred choice was to have gold or silver metallic paint finish. The matter was investigated by the paint technicians, however, the initial results were not encouraging as these finishes could not be guaranteed much beyond six months.

This prompted a review of more distinctive colours which could be offered in conventional paint finish within the existing ICI colour range. Jack had a number of cars painted in vibrant colours including yellow, pink, lime-green, orange and, of course, lilac.

Once ready, Jack invited representatives from BMC management to a specially arranged viewing with the intention of arriving at consensus on which colour to adopt. Unfortunately those present could only agree not to have orange! In an unusual delegation, for such a milestone, management agreed to let Jack Field select the colour! He chose lilac and the rest as they say, 'is history'.

left: ex–RAF pilot Jack Field stands proudly with a lilac Minor Million.

below: Minor Million Register owners led by Philip Smith in 1 MLL.

CONFIDENTIAL UNTIL 4th JANUARY, 1961

Jack Field

Issued by:
The Central Publicity Department
The Nuffield Organization
Cowley, Oxon

The Million Boot Badge

Million Minor Memories – Keith Philpott

In July 1960, at the age of 18, I received a letter of acceptance with a date to start at Oxford during September as a Staff Engineering Apprentice. There were two types of apprenticeships at Cowley. Commercial Apprentices who were selected more for their practical skills and aspirations, and Staff who were seen as Management/Engineering potential, and who might qualify for University places. Fortunately for me the Staff were very much better paid, 12 pounds a week instead of 4. I could afford to live away from home, digs being just over 4 pounds a week, and that situation stayed much the same for the next five years.

It must have been early-on, maybe October 1960, when I was set the task of making the Million boot badges, probably as I had spent my first month in the Steel and General Stores Department.

Stan Judge, one of the three foremen running the apprentice machine-shop at the time, came over to me at my bench one day and explained what was to be done. It was as simple as that. We discussed the idea of modifying two Minor 1000 badges to make the 1,000,000 by scrubbing out the '1' on one of them and spot-marking the space to try to make it look similar to the background of the originals. That was achieved with various degrees of 'success'. There was no question of the job being 'confidential/secret' as far as I can remember anyway. So basically my input was the actual making of the badges. Whether I made all 350 of them I am not entirely sure but I cannot recall working with anyone else on the job. I guess it must have got a little monotonous at times.

I spent eight years at Cowley, five as an apprentice, followed by three endeavouring to become a KD (knocked-down) Field Engineer in KD Engineering Dept., later called Overseas Production Division (OPD).

Phil Smith (Minor Million Registrar) presents Keith Philpot (the boot badge maker) with a special memento in recognition of his involvement in the 1960 Million project.

above: Management Course at Haseley Manor Warwickshire, 2nd from right middle row!

above right: Official 'Works' portrait – Apprentice of the Year 1964.

Morris Minor Million Production Record Trace 1,000,000 – 1,000,050

Chasis No.	RH / LH	Eng.No.	Dealers Name & Address	Dealer Sale	Body Number	Production Date	Dispatch	Registration No.
000	RH	504 066	Publicity Department	–	355 455	22/12/60	20/4/61	I MUH
001	LH	501 841	Export North America No. 73456	–	355 343	13/12/60	14/12/60	NAM 091
002	LH	501 714	Export North America No. 7347	–	355 382	13/12/60	14/12/60	–
003	LH	501 715	Export No. 73458	–	355 304	13/12/60	14/12/60	–
004	LH	501 638	Export No. 73459	–	355 354	13/12/60	14/12/60	–
005	LH	501 634	Export No. 73460	–	355 352	13/12/60	14/12/60	–
006	LH	497 185	Export No. 73462	–	355 368	13/12/60	15/12/60	–
007	LH	497 080	Export No. 73463	–	355 370	13/12/60	14/12/60	–
008	RH	497 213	Myers, Manningham Lane, Bradford	8/4/61	355 365	13/12/60	14/12/60	2251 WY
009	LH	477 126	Export No. 73476	–	355 351	13/12/60	19/12/60	–
010	LH	497 099	Export No. 73477	–	355 321	13-14/12/60	14/12/60	–
011	LH	497 212	Export No. 73478	–	355 373	13/12/60	13/12/60	–
012	LH	496 954	Export No. 73479	–	355 374	13-14/12/60	14/12/60	CC 51366
013	RH	501 856	Sticklands Garages, Gillingham, Dorset	12/1/61	355 375	13/12/60	19/12/60	RFX 166
014	RH	501 853	Caffyns, Meads Road, Eastbourne	17/3/61	355 367	13/12/60	15/12/60	–
015	RH	501 764	T. Nice & Co., St. Marys, Ely, Cambridgeshire	6/1/61	355 366	13/12/60	21/12/60	RCF 682
016	RH	502 529	Stewart & Ardern, Catford, London	8/2/61	355 376	13/12/60	15/12/60	–
017	RH	429 152	Colchester / Bexhill-on-Sea	4/3/61	355 378	13/12/60	22/12/60	–
018	RH	501 657	Brown & Mallalieu, Blackpool	9/2/61	355 379	13-14/12/60	15/12/60	–
019	RH	502 533	Westover Motors, Bournemouth	24/3/61	355 380	13/12/60	19/12/60	–
020	RH	501 855	Roland C. Bellamy Ltd, Grimsby, Lincolnshire	3/2/61	355 377	13-14/12/60	19/12/60	KAB 412
021	RH	489 064	George Ace Ltd, Tenby, Wales	30/12/60	355 382	13/12/60	19/12/60	141 KDE
022	RH	502 532	E. Myres, Manningham Lane, Bradford	7/5/61	355 383	13-14/12/60	15/12/60	–
023	RH	501 801	Wadhams, Waterlooville, Hampshire	11/1/61	355 369	13/12/60	19/12/60	–
024	RH	501 784	Hewens Garages Ltd, Bridge Rd, Maidenhead, Berkshire	10/2/61	355 381	13/12/60	15/12/60	–
025	RH	501 501	J. Cockshoot, Great Ducie St, Manchester	26/4/61	355 358	13/12/60	19/12/60	–
026	RH	501 802	Patrick Shinnie, Aberdeen	12/7/61	355 357	13/12/60	16/12/60	–
027	RH	501 510	Lock & Stagg Ltd, Ipswich, Suffolk	8/2/61	355 361	13-15/12/60	19/12/60	850 HBJ
028	RH	501 511	J. Pepper, Stroke-on-Trent, Staffordshire	15/2/61	355 360	13-15/12/60	22/12/60	–
029	RH	489 193	Stevenage Motor Co., Stevenage, Hertfordshire	10/1/61	355 359	13-15/12/60	21/12/60	5893 NK
030	RH	489 154	Sycamore & Son, Peterborough	28/1/61	355 353	13/12/60	19/12/60	–
031	RH	489 191	T. R. Page, Bexhill-on-Sea	30/1/61	355 384	13/12/60	21/12/60	–
032	RH	501 845	Colmore Depot Ltd, Station St, Birmingham	14/3/61	355 390	12-14/12/60	19/12/60	–
033	RH	502 523	St. Roques Automobile Co., Dundee	21/2/61	355 391	13-21/12/60	21/12/60	–
034	RH	501 667	Wessex Motors, Andover, Hampshire	25/1/61	355 355	13-15/12/60	19/12/60	XMR 350
035	RH	501 735	Thomas Corrie Ltd, Dumfries	28/1/61	355 394	13/12/60	19/12/60	–
036	RH	501 655	Patrick Shinnie, College St, Aberdeen	15/3/61	355 395	13-14/12/60	20/12/60	RRG 350
037	RH	501 736	Stewart & Ardern, Acton, London	17/1/61	355 356	13/12/60	21/12/60	–
038	RH	502 524	Loxham's Morris Services, Corporation St, Preston, Lancashire	13/4/61	355 400	13-23/12/60	5/1/61	–
039	RH	501 844	James Fryer Ltd, Aubrey St, Hereford	11/4/61	355 386	13-14/12/60	16/12/60	XVJ 770
040	RH	501 733	Park Motors Ltd, Portland Place, Halifax	31/3/61	355 350	13/12/60	22/12/60	–
041	RH	501 835	J. Cockshoot, Great Ducie St, Manchester	6/2/61	355 401	13/12/60	19/12/60	–
042	RH	501 679	Haslemere Motor Co., Woodbridge Rd, Guildford	11/1/61	355 404	13-14/12/60	21/12/60	–
043	RH	440 275	Heard Bros, Broad Quay, Bideford, Devon	14/1/61	355 405	13-14/12/60	23/12/60	–
044	RH	501 682	Wycliffe Motors, Stroud, Glos.	13/1/61	355 403	13-15/12/60	29/12/60	–
045	RH	501 623	Bristol Motor Co., Ashton Gate, Bristol	11/4/61	355 372	13-15/12/60	21/12/60	–
046	RH	502 531	J. P Board, Bridgend, Glamorgan	16/2/61	355 409?	13-14/12/60	20/12/60	–
047	RH	501 896	Westfield Autocar Co., Westfield Ave, Edinburgh	8/2/61	355 409?	13/12/60	21/12/60	–
048	RH	501 792	Stewart and Ardern, Ilford, Essex	8/2/61	355 410	13/12/60	21/12/60	–
049	RH	501 848	Stewart and Ardern, Ilford, Essex	15/2/61	355 412	13/12/60	21/12/60	–
050	RH	502 573	Morris Garages Ltd, St. Aldates, Oxford	3/2/61	355 413	13-14/12/60	19/12/60	–

Morris Minor Million Production Record Trace 1,000,051 – 1,000,100

Chasis No.	RH / LH	Eng.No.	Dealers Name & Address	Dealer Sale	Body Number	Production Date	Dispatch	Registration No.
051	RH	502 571	T. Shipside Ltd, Worksop, Nottinghamshire	11/2/61	355 414	13-15/12/60	19/12/60	–
052	RH	502 608	Caffyns Ltd, Meads Rd, Eastbourne	24/2/61	355 385	13-14/12/60	20/12/60	–
053	RH	502 607	Grosvenor Motor Co., Pepper St, Chester	20/3/61	355 402	13-14/12/60	19/12/60	–
054	RH	492141	Derbyshire Motors, Derwent St, Derby	1/3/61	355 399	13/12/60	20/12/60	NFA 289
055	RH	488 912	Kennings Ltd, Sheffield	13/6/61	355 388	13-14/12/60	20/12/60	–
056	RH	501 895	Tenbury Baths Co., Ltd, Oxford St, Kidderminster	6/1/61	355 416	13/12/60	19/12/60	–
057	RH	502 561	Derngate Motor Co., Derngate, Northampton	14/3/61	355 411	13-15/12/60	19/12/60	–
058	RH	501 825	Stewart and Ardern, Croydon	22/12/60	355 417	13/12/60	22/12/60	–
059	RH	502 598	Warwickshire Garages, Stratford-on-Avon, Warwickshire	27/12/61	355 398	13-15/12/60	21/12/60	–
060	RH	502 626	Morris Garages, St. Aldates, Oxford	9/3/61	355 397	13-14/12/60	19/12/60	XJB 17
061	RH	501 888	Gilbot and Son, Norman St, Lincoln	11/2/61	355 418	13-14/12/60	21/12/60	–
062	RH	501 842	Caffyns Ltd, Meads Rd, Eastbourne	–	355 419	13-14/12/60	29/12/60	–
063	RH	490 460	T. Shipside Ltd, Worksop, Nottinghamshire	19/1/61	355 392	13-14/12/60	16/12/60	–
064	RH	502 644	W. H. Alexander, Victoria St, Belfast	1/3/61	355 393	13/12/60	21/12/60	9121 AZ
065	RH	502 643	Caffyns Ltd, Meads Rd, Eastbourne	23/1/61	355 396	13-14/12/60	16/12/60	–
066	RH	502 596	T. Shipside Ltd, Worksop, Nottinghamshire	15/3/61	355 420	13-15/12/60	22/12/60	–
067	RH	488 910	H. A. Hamshaw, Humberstone Gate, Leicester	1/3/61	355 421	13-14/12/60	19/12/60	–
068	RH	502 565	J. Cockshoot, Great Ducie St, Manchester	21/12/60	355 424	13-14/12/60	19/12/60	–
069	RH	502 601	Ruette Braye Motors Ltd, St. Martins, Guernsey, Channel Islands	21/12/60	355 423	13-19/12/60	21/12/60	11000
070	RH	502 568	Westfield Autocar Co., Ltd, Westfield Avenue, Edinburgh	12/4/61	355 427	13-14/12/60	22/12/60	XSF 393
071	RH	501 821	Unknown	–	355 425	13-14/12/60	19/12/60	560 BCG
072	RH	502 503	Loxhams Morris Services, Corporation St, Preston	15/3/61	355 407	13-16/12/60	21/12/60	–
073	RH	501 892	Loxhams Morris Services, Corporation St, Preston	21/1/61	355 408	13-19/12/60	19/12/60	–
074	RH	492 391	Appleyard of Leeds, North St, Leeds	7/3/61	355 389	13-14/12/60	19/12/60	–
075	RH	492 368	Colmore Depot Ltd, Station St, Birmingham	28/2/61	355 429	13/12/60	19/12/60	–
076	RH	492 369	Stewart & Ardern, Acton, London	17/2/61	355 435	13-14/12/60	21/12/60	–
077	RH	56164?	Westfield Autocar Co., Ltd, Westfield Avenue, Edinburgh	18/2/61	355 436	13-14/12/60	21/12/60	DSU 955
078	RH	492 364	Glovers of Ripon, Leeds Rd, Harrogate	6/1/61	355 415	13-14/12/60	21/12/60	–
079	RH	492 312	Woodcote Motor Co., Church St, Epsom, Surrey	13/3/61	355 438	13-14/12/60	22/12/60	–
080	RH	492 356	City Motor Co., City Rd, Cardiff	20/3/61	355 437	13-14/12/60	29/12/60	336 AWO
081	RH	492 234	Slack & Mackle Ltd, Nantwich Rd, Crewe	20/1/61	355 442	13/12/60	21/12/60	–
082	RH	489 340	Appleyards of Leeds, North St, Leeds	23/6/61	355 441	13-14/12/60	15/12/60	–
083	RH	501 480	Charles Buist Ltd, St Marys Place, Newcastle-on-Tyne	30/1/61	355 445	13-21/12/60	28/12/60	–
084	RH	501 823	Dickinson &Adams Ltd, Bridge St, Luton	30/3/61	355 444	13-14/12/60	19/12/60	–
085	RH	502 651	Woodcote Motor Co., Church St, Epsom, Surrey	7/2/61	355 446	13-14/12/60	19/12/60	–
086	RH	502 652	Appleyard of Leeds, North St, Leeds	20/1/61	355 449	13-14/12/60	22/12/60	6936 WX
087	RH	502 653	Brittains Ltd, Preston Rd, Brighton	7/3/61	355 451	13-14/12/60	21/12/60	–
088	RH	502 536	Stewart & Ardern, Acton, London	24/2/61	355 450	13-15/12/60	22/12/60	872 JGW
089	RH	502 712	Wellsteeds Country Garage, Newport, Gwent	14/1/61	355 448	12-14/12/60	15/12/60	–
090	RH	502 659	Colmore Depot Ltd, Station St, Birmingham	19/1/61	355 452	13-14/12/60	19/12/60	–
091	RH	478 819	Fowlers Ltd, Castlehold, Newport, Isle of Wight	4/12/61	355 454	13-14/12/60	22/12/60	VDL 833
092	RH	484 670	Stewart & Ardern, Acton, London	10/3/61	355 440	13-15/12/60	21/12/60	–
093	RH	502 658	Parkside Garage Ltd, Warwick Rd, Coventry	8/3/61	355 422	13-14/12/60	15/12/60	8168 UE
094	RH	492 222	Morris Garages, St. Aldates, Oxford	30/5/61	355 432	13-15/12/60	22/12/60	–
095	RH	502 714	Woodcote Motor Co., Church St, Epsom, Surrey	8/4/61	355 431	13-14/12/60	16/12/60	–
096	RH	502 646	Dickinson &Adams Ltd, Bridge St, Luton	28/2/61	355 430	13-14/12/60	21/12/60	–
097	RH	502 721	Kennings Ltd, Clay Cross, Derbyshire	29/4/61	355 453	13/12/60	15/12/60	–
098	RH	502 716	Appleyard of Leeds, North St, Leeds	16/1/61	355 428	13-14/12/60	22/12/60	–
099	RH	502 720	Barton Motor Co., Hyde Park Corner, Plymouth	12/4/61	355 426	13-14/12/60	19/12/60	–
100	RH	502 723	Braid Bros Ltd, Conway Rd, Colwyn Bay	27/2/61	355 434	13-19/12/60	19/12/60	JJC 290

Morris Minor Million Production Record Trace 1,000,101 – 1,000,150

Chasis No.	RH / LH	Eng.No.	Dealers Name & Address	Dealer Sale	Body Number	Production Date	Dispatch	Registration No.
101	RH	479 895	Macrae & Dick Ltd, Academy St, Inverness	8/5/61	355 406	13-19/12/60	30/12/60	–
102	RH	479 733	C. K. Andrews Ltd, Upland Garage, Swansea	10/5/61	355 456	13-14/12/60	16/12/60	–
103	RH	489 150	Derbyshire Motor Co., Derwent St, Derby	13/6/61	355 457	13-14/12/60	15/12/60	–
104	RH	492 390	W. H. Alexander Ltd, Victoria St, Belfast	2/2/61	355 462	13-14/12/60	16/12/60	–
105	RH	492 108	A & D Fraser Ltd, Springkell Ave, Glasgow	3/3/61	355 467	13-14/12/60	21/12/60	–
106	RH	492 107	Appleyard of Leeds, North St, Leeds	16/1/61	355 479	13-14/12/60	19/12/60	–
107	RH	492 126	J. Pepper Ltd, Stoke on Trent, Staffordshire	4/2/61	355 447	13-14/12/60	19/12/60	–
108	RH	489 238	John C Beadle Ltd, Spital St, Dartford, Kent	20/3/61	355 480	13-15/12/60	20/12/60	–
109	RH	492 125	Reeds Garage Ltd, Broadway, Peterborough	7/2/61	355 477	13-20/12/60	21/12/60	–
110	RH	489 319	T. Shipside Ltd, Worksop, Nottinghamshire	3/5/61	355 481	13-14/12/60	22/12/60	–
111	RH	492 120	Gilbert & Son Ltd, Norman St, Lincoln	10/3/61	355 484	13-14/12/60	21/12/60	–
112	RH	483 379	Derngate Motor Co., Derngate, Northampton	9/1/61	355 485	13-14/12/60	15/12/60	–
113	RH	492 121	T. Shipside Ltd, Worksop, Nottinghamshire	11/2/61	355 486	13-15/12/60	22/12/60	–
114	RH	492 394	D. E Davies Ltd, Barmouth, Gwynedd	20/2/61	355 487	13-14/12/60	23/12/60	EFF 497
115	RH	492 346	Charles Buist Ltd, St Marys Place, Newcastle-on-Tyne	21/3/61	355 478	13-14/12/60	21/12/60	–
116	RH	492 340	Wycliffe Motor Co., Stroud, Glos.	6/1/61	355 488	13-14/12/60	15/12/60	–
117	RH	492 336	Wadhams, Waterlooville, Hampshire	30/1/61	355 489	13-15/12/60	19/12/60	WRV 135
118	RH	492 313	Stewart & Ardern Ltd, Golders Green, London	28/2/61	355 470	13-14/12/60	15/12/60	–
119	RH	492 334	Stewart & Ardern, Acton, London	8/2/61	355 469	13-15/12/60	22/12/60	–
120	RH	492 338	Gales Motor Co., West Hartlepool, Durham	24/3/61	355 465	13-14/12/60	19/12/60	–
121	RH	492 339	Colmore Depot Ltd, Station St, Birmingham	13/2/61	355 461	13-14/12/60	15/12/60	–
122	RH	492 149	Stewart & Ardern, Acton, London	13/2/61	355 471	13-14/12/60	15/12/60	–
Corgi Model Car								
123	RH	482 272	Colmore Depot Ltd, Station St, Birmingham	3/2/61	355 472	13-14/12/60	15/12/60	797 CU
124	RH	501 700	Haslemere Motor Co. Woodbridge Rd, Guildford	30/12/60	355 473	14/12/60	19/12/60	999 SPK
125	RH	501 794	Cleveland Garages Ltd, St. Helier, Jersey	16/12/60	355 468	14/12/60	16/12/60	–
126	RH	502 502	Kennings Ltd, Sheffield	11/1/61	355 463	14/12/60	15/12/60	–
127	RH	502 704	Stewart & Ardern Ltd, Tottenham, London	22/2/61	355 059	14/12/60	15/12/60	9809 MH
128	RH	501 862	Bridge End Foundry Co., Ltd, Station Rd, Cardigan	10/5/61	355 464	14/12/60	22/12/60	–
129	RH	502 599	Kennings Ltd, Sheffield	20/4/61	355 476	14/12/60	15/12/60	–
130	RH	502 727	Kennings Ltd, Sheffield	28/1/61	355 475	14/12/60	15/12/60	–
131	RH	502 778	Regent Garage, The Parade, Leamington Spa	22/2/61	355 493	14/12/60	22/12/60	–
132	RH	502 909	Wheatley Motors Ltd, Yarn Lane, Stockton-on-Tees	8/4/61	355 491	14/12/60	16/12/60	–
133	RH	502 907	Unknown	3/3/61	355 495	14-15/12/60	19/12/60	–
134	RH	502 780	Holland Bros, Wide Bargate, Boston Lincolnshire	10/3/61	355 458	14/12/60	21/12/60	–
135	RH	502 836	Park Motors Ltd, Portland Place, Halifax	13/1/61	355 460	14/12/60	15/12/60	–
136	RH	502 635	J. Cockshoot, Great Ducie St, Manchester	4/1/61	355 497	14-15/12/60	22/12/60	–
137	RH	502 722	Croall, Bryson & Co., Kelso	8/1/61	355 498	14/12/60	21/12/60	–
138	RH	492 198	W. Watson & Co., Bold St, Liverpool	30/3/61	355 499	14-15/12/60	22/12/60	–
139	RH	502 656	Tenbury Baths Co., Ltd, Oxford St, Kidderminster	21/1/61	355 500	14/12/60	15/12/60	–
140	RH	502 832	Stewart and Ardern, Croydon	22/2/61	355 501	14/12/60	15/12/60	–
141	RH	502 800	Wellsteeds Country Garage, Newport, Gwent	13/2/61	355 502	14/12/60	15/12/60	–
142	RH	502 799	Stewart & Ardern Ltd, Tottenham, London	14/2/61	355 503	14-15/12/60	12/12/60	–
143	RH	502 826	Appleyard of Leeds, North St, Leeds	23/1/61	355 504	14-15/12/60	15/12/60	–
144	RH	502 825	Fife Motor Co., Halbeath Rd, Dunfermline	21/1/61	355 505	14-19/12/60	21/12/60	–
145	RH	502 827	Bradburn & Wedge Ltd, Darlington St, Wolverhampton	24/1/61	355 496	13-19/12/60	26/12/60	–
146	RH	502 798	H.T.P. Motors Ltd, Truro, Cornwall	23/3/61	355 508	14-15/12/60	21/12/60	–
147	RH	492 148	J. Cockshoot, Stockport, Cheshire	23/3/61	355 310	14-15/12/60	22/12/60	–
148	RH	492 145	Phil Read Ltd, St Mary Church Rd, Torquay	30/3/61	355 511	14/12/60	22/12/60	–
149	RH	502 636	Bradburn & Wedge Ltd, Darlington St, Wolverhampton	24/1/61	355 512	14/12/60	19/12/60	–
150	RH	479 046	Country Garages Ltd, St Thomas, Scarborough	6/1/61	355 513	14/12/60	21/12/60	–

Minor Minor Million **Production Record Trace 1,000,151 – 1,000,200**

Chasis No.	RH / LH	Eng.No.	Dealers Name & Address	Dealer Sale	Body Number	Production Date	Dispatch	Registration No.
151	RH	502 829	Colmore Depot Ltd, Station St, Birmingham	17/1/61	355 514	14-15/12/60	19/12/60	–
152	RH	502 903	W.H. Johnson & Sons Ltd, St. James St, Kings Lynn, Norfolk	15/4/61	355 474	14-19/12/60	20/12/60	6365 VF
153	RH	502 828	Perth Garage Ltd, York Place, Perth	17/1/61	355 517	14-15/12/60	30/12/60	–
154	RH	502 902	Graham & Roberts Ltd, Botchergate, Cumberland	2/2/61	355 519	14-15/12/60	21/12/60	–
155	RH	502 779	Morris Garages Ltd, St. Aldates, Oxford	22/4/61	355 520	14/12/60	22/12/60	–
156	RH	502 776	Stewart & Ardern, Acton, London	19/1/61	355 483	14-21/12/60	22/12/60	9666 MH
157	RH	502 911	J. Cockshoot, Great Ducie St. Manchester	6/2/61	355 521	14/12/60	20/12/60	–
158	RH	502 910	Haslemere Motor Co., Woodbridge Rd, Guildford	4/1/61	355 522	14-15/12/60	29/12/60	–
159	RH	502 796	Kennings Ltd, Sheffield	12/1/61	355 516	14-15/12/60	22/12/60	–
160	RH	502 906	Kennings Ltd, Sheffield	16/1/61	355 466	14/12/60	20/12/60	–
161	RH	479 755	Victoria Garage Ltd, Victoria Rd, Swindon, Wiltshire	3/2/61	355 490	14-15/12/60	19/12/60	–
162	RH	492 184	W. Watson & Co., Bold St, Liverpool	3/2/61	355 492	14/12/60	19/12/60	956 STF
163	RH	489 318	H.A. Hamshaw, Humberstone Gate, Leicester	1/3/61	355 532	14-15/12/60	15/12/60	416 ARY
164	RH	502 851	A & D Fraser Ltd, Springkell Ave, Glasgow	23/1/61	355 353	14-15/12/60	21/12/60	–
165	RH	502 783	Turvey & Co., Ltd, Holmeside, Sunderland	27/1/61	355 325	14/12/60	15/12/60	–
166	RH	502 850	Kennings Ltd, Sheffield	31/12/60	355 530	14-15/12/60	20/12/60	–
167	RH	502 926	Morris Garages Ltd, St. Aldgates, Oxford	19/1/61	355 545	14-15/12/60	15/12/60	264 KJO
168	RH	502 920	Wycliffe Motor Co., Stroud, Glos.	2/1/61	355 528	14/12/60	16/12/60	–
169	RH	502 547	Westfield Autocar Co., Westfield Ave, Edinburgh	12/1/61	355 523	14/12/60	22/12/60	–
170	RH	479 748	Caffyns, Meads Road, Eastbourne	6/3/61	355 546	14-15/12/60	19/12/60	955 NK
171	RH	479 038	Westfield Autocar Co., Westfield Ave, Edinburgh	26/2/61	355 560	14-15/12/60	28/12/60	–
172	RH	479 734	Hewens Garages Ltd, Bridge Rd, Maidenhead	15/2/61	355 561	14-15/12/60	21/12/60	–
173	RH	502 784	Stewart & Ardern, Acton, London	17/1/61	355 565	14-15/12/60	15/12/60	SJN 575
174	RH	502 749	Stewart & Ardern, Ilford, Essex	31/1/61	355 566	14-15/12/60	15/12/60	5843 PU
175	RH	502 930	Marshalsea Bros. Ltd, Wellington Rd, Taunton	9/3/61	355 563	14-15/12/60	21/12/60	7 KYD
176	RH	489 308	Colmore Depot Ltd, Station St, Birmingham	7/1/61	355 567	14-15/12/60	22/12/60	–
177	RH	492 329	Ware Garages, Market Place, Ware, Hertfordshire	10/2/61	355 568	14-15/12/60	19/12/60	–
178	RH	492 299	W. Watson & Co., Bold St, Liverpool	17/3/61	355 570	14-15/12/60	20/12/60	–
179	RH	492 296	Kennings Ltd, Sheffield	18/1/61	355 571	14-15/12/60	22/12/60	–
180	RH	492 326	A & D Fraser Ltd, Springkell Ave, Glasgow	3/3/61	355 572	14/12/60	22/12/60	–
181	RH	492 294	Hewens Garages Ltd, Bridge Rd, Maidenhead, Berkshire	24/3/61	355 564	14-15/12/60	19/12/60	436 SBH
182	RH	492 325	W. Watson & Co., Bold St, Liverpool	19/6/61	355 573	14-15/12/60	22/12/60	–
183	RH	492 324	Stewart & Ardern, Acton, London	11/1/61	355 574	14-15/12/60	19/12/60	–
184	RH	492 323	McLays Garage Ltd, East High St, Kirkintilloch	30/3/61	355 577	14/12/60	19/12/60	–
185	RH	492 315	Marshalsea Bros. Ltd, Wellington Rd, Taunton	14/4/61	355 578	14-15/12/60	20/12/60	148 LYB
186	RH	492 310	J. Cockshoot, Great Ducie St, Manchester	4/1/61	355 579	14-15/12/60	19/12/60	–
187	RH	492 319	W. Watson & Co., Bold St, Liverpool	24/1/61	355 576	14-18/12/60	20/12/60	–
188	RH	492 309	Wadhams, Waterlooville, Hampshire	10/1/61	355 563	14-15/12/60	20/12/60	–
189	RH	492 283	Duthie & Son Ltd, New Wynd, Montrose, Fife	8/2/61	355 582	14/12/60	23/12/60	–
190	RH	492 169	Stevenage Motor Co., Stevenage, Hertfordshire	23/5/61	355 585	14-15/12/60	21/12/60	–
191	RH	492 168	J.S Horsfall Ltd, Leeds Rd, Nelson, Lancashire	30/9/61	355 587	14-15/12/60	21/12/60	368 TTE
192	RH	492 302	Loxham's Morris Services, Corporation St, Preston, Lancashire	13/2/61	355 586	14-15/12/60	21/12/60	–
193	RH	492 301	P. G. Page Ltd, Crouch St, Colchester	1/3/61	355 575	14-15/12/60	19/12/60	–
194	RH	492 292	Stewart & Ardern, Acton, London	30/1/61	355 533	14-15/12/60	21/12/60	–
195	RH	492 305	Brown & Mallalieu, Blackpool	13/3/61	355 588	14-15/12/60	22/12/60	–
196	RH	492 262	Wray Park Garages Ltd, The Broadway Reigate, Surrey	17/2/61	355 591	14-19/12/60	28/12/60	TPN 675
197	RH	492 260	Wadhams, Waterlooville, Hampshire	15/3/61	355 584	14-15/12/60	21/12/60	543 BBP
198	RH	492 257	Appleyard of Leeds, North St, Leeds	13/2/61	355 590	13-14/12/60	19/12/60	–
199	RH	492 202	Appleyard of Leeds, North St, Leeds	10/5/61	355 581	14-15/12/60	19/12/60	–
200	RH	489 306	E. W. Jackson & Son, Frenchgate, Doncaster, Yorkshire	9/3/61	355 593	14-15/12/60	21/12/60	–

Morris Minor Million Production Record Trace 1,000,201 – 1,000,250

Chasis No.	RH / LH	Eng.No.	Dealers Name & Address	Dealer Sale	Body Number	Production Date	Dispatch	Registration No.
201	RH	492 139	Kennings Ltd, Sheffield	15/3/61	355 592	14-15/12/60	19/12/60	–
202	RH	492 136	Forsselius Ltd, Blossom St, York	25/1/61	355 589	14-15/12/60	20/12/60	–
203	RH	502 947	Parkside Garage Ltd, Warwick Rd, Coventry	1/2/61	355 562	13-14/12/60	19/12/60	9234 HP
204	RH	502 887	A & D Fraser Ltd, Fullarton St, Ayr	16/2/61	355 569	14-15/12/60	20/12/60	–
205	RH	503 621	Charles Buist Ltd, St Marys Place, Newcastle-on-Tyne	23/1/61	355 573	15-19/12/60	21/12/60	–
206	RH	503 501	Page, Colchester / Bexhill-on-Sea	22/2/61	355 676	15-29/12/60	3/1/61	–
207	RH	502 999	Taylor Garages Ltd, Town Quay, Falmouth, Cornwall	17/5/61	355 665	15/12/60	21/12/60	–
208	RH	502 873	Haslemere Motor Co., Woodbridge Rd, Guildford	10/2/61	355 677	15-16/12/60	21/12/60	790 TPB
209	RH	502 872	Kennings Ltd, Sheffield	16/2/61	355 678	15-19/12/60	23/12/60	MEP 515
210	RH	503 623	Barton Motor Co., Hyde Park Corner, Plymouth, Devon	27/1/61	355 664	15-16/12/60	20/12/60	–
211	RH	502 950	Charles Buist Ltd, St Marys Place, Newcastle-on-Tyne	8/2/61	355 671	15-20/12/60	20/12/60	–
212	RH	503 622	Wray Park Garages Ltd, The Broadway, Reigate, Surrey	28/2/61	355 683	15-20/12/60	28/12/60	–
213	RH	503 610	Robertson & Porter Ltd, Country Garage, Dingwall	28/2/61	355 685	15-20/12/60	19/12/60	–
214	RH	503 636	Greens Garage Ltd, Stockton Rd, Thirsk, North Yorkshire	22/3/61	355 682	15-16/12/60	22/12/60	–
215	RH	503 629	Bristol Motor Co., Ashton Gate, Bristol	7/4/61	355 684	15/12/60	20/12/60	–
216	RH	489 119	Haslemere Motor Co., Woodbridge Rd, Guildford	22/2//61	355 524	15-16/12/60	21/12/60	–
217	RH	489 398	Kennings Ltd, Sheffield	15/3/61	355 669	15-20/12/60	29/12/60	–
218	RH	440 058	Caffyns, Meads Road, Eastbourne	30/3/61	355 689	15-19/12/60	23/12/60	580 NKO
219	RH	489 127	Stradlings Ltd, Northbrook St, Newbury, Berkshire	17/2/61	355 680	15-16/12/60	22/12/60	–
220	RH	489 118	Turvey & Co., Ltd, Holmeside, Sunderland	21/1/61	355 675	15-19/12/60	21/12/60	–
221	RH	489 117	Wessex Motors, Andover, Hampshire	28/4/61	355 666	15/12/60	19/12/60	269 BHO
222	RH	502 936	Stewart & Ardern, Acton, London	30/1/61	355 667	15-19/12/60	21/12/60	–
223	RH	502 804	W. H. Johnson & Sons Ltd, St. James St, Kings Lynn, Norfolk	21/1/61	355 670	15-19/12/60	20/12/60	–
224	RH	502 856	Eastern Garages Ltd, Market Rd, Chelmsford, Essex	27/1/61	355 668	15/12/60	2/1/61	–
225	RH	503 633	Wadhams, Waterlooville, Hampshire	25/1/61	355 686	15-16/12/60	21/12/60	286 TR (1 MILL)
226	RH	502 993	W. Watson & Co., Bold St, Liverpool	20/2/61	355 681	15/12/60	20/12/60	–
227	RH	503 632	Stewart & Ardern	3/1/61	355 531	15-19/12/60	22/12/60	379 UVX
228	RH	501 897	City Motor Co., City Rd, Cardiff	19/1/61	355 509	15-19/12/60	2/1/61	–
229	RH	492 509	W. W. Webber Ltd, London Rd, Basingstoke, Hampshire	1/2/61	355 690	15/12/60	19/12/60	–
230	RH	493 966	Kennings Ltd, Sheffield	11/3/61	355 674	15-20/12/60	20/12/60	–
231	RH	493 964	W. H. Alexander, Victoria St, Belfast	27/1/61	355 691	15-16/12/60	21/12/60	–
232	RH	493 936	Bristol Motor Co., Ashton Gate, Bristol	16/2/61	355 694	15-19/12/60	29/12/60	464 LHT
233	RH	493 959	W. H. Alexander, Victoria St, Belfast	22/2/61	355 693	15-16/12/60	21/12/60	–
234	RH	493 958	J & W Tait Ltd, Broad St, Kirkwall, Orkney	24/3/61	355 439	15-19/12/60	22/12/60	–
235	RH	493 972	Bath Garages Ltd, James St, West Bath	24/2/61	355 687	15-19/12/60	26/12/60	–
236	RH	493 969	Lock & Stagg Ltd, Friars Rd, Ipswich	11/2/61	355 695	15-19/12/60	19/12/60	–
237	RH	492 208	A & D Fraser Ltd, Springkell Ave, Glasgow	17/4/61	355 688	15-16/12/60	20/12/60	–
238	RH	492 565	A & D Fraser Ltd, Springkell Ave, Glasgow	25/1/61	355 696	15/12/60	16/12/60	–
239	RH	492 254	W. Watson & Co., Bold St, Liverpool	2/3/61	355 697	15/12/60	19/12/60	–
240	RH	492 562	Athol Garage Ltd. Hill St, Douglas, Isle of Man	25/2/61	355 698	15/12/60	20/12/60	–
241	RH	492 561	W. Watson & Co., Bold St, Liverpool	7/2/61	355 672	15-19/12/60	19/12/60	TWM 888
242	RH	492 560	Kennings Ltd, Sheffield	3/1/61	355 679	15-20/12/60	19/12/60	–
243	RH	492 597	King & Harper Ltd, Bridge St, Cambridge	20/1/61	355 705	15-16/12/60	20/12/60	–
244	RH	492 596	T. Shipside Ltd, Worksop, Nottinghamshire	9/5/61	355 699	15-16/12/60	20/12/60	–
245	RH	493 901	J. Cockshoot, Great Ducie St. Manchester	31/1/61	355 706	15-19/12/60	21/12/60	–
246	RH	492 226	W. Gillespie & Son, Love St, Paisley	25/2/61	355 708	15-20/12/60	22/12/60	–
247	RH	492 194	Haslemere Motor Co., Woodbridge Rd, Guildford	18/5/61	355 701	15-19/12/60	21/12/60	–
248	RH	492 580	Stewart & Ardern, Acton, London	22/2/61	355 704	15-16/12/60	19/12/60	9687 MH
249	RH	492 566	Simpsons Ltd, Rawlinson St, Barrow-in-Furness	24/2/61	355 710	15-21/12/60	22/12/60	GEO 470
250	RH	492 441	Miller & Co., Ltd, Bayhead St, Stornoway	28/3/61	355 711	15-28/12/60	2/1/61	–

Morris Minor Million Production Record Trace 1,000,251 – 1,000,300

Chasis No.	RH / LH	Eng.No.	Dealers Name & Address	Dealer Sale	Body Number	Production Date	Dispatch	Registration No.
251	RH	493 933	John C Beadle Ltd, Spital St, Dartford, Kent	27/2/61	355 707	15-20/12/60	21/12/60	236 NKL
252	RH	493 718	Brittains Ltd, Preston Rd, Brighton	3/5/61	355 712	15-20/12/60	21/12/60	752 BPO
253	RH	493 914	Whellers Motors Ltd, Hendford, Yeovil, Somerset	10/1/61	355 713	15-20/12/60	21/12/60	673 KYC
254	RH	492 912	Kennings Ltd, Sheffield	16/6/61	355 714	15-21/12/60	28/12/60	–
255	RH	493 916	Not Known	–	355 703	15-21/12/60	29/12/60	–
256	RH	493 910	Castle Garage Ltd, Mill St, Ludlow, Shropshire	4/2/61	355 700	15-23/12/60	29/12/60	WNT 567
257	RH	492 586	Bradburn & Wedge Ltd, Darlington St, Wolverhampton	24/1/61	355 709	15-20/12/60	30/12/60	E330
258	RH	492 577	Not Known	–	355 714	15-20/12/60	22/12/60	–
259	RH	492 574	Neil Beaton Ltd, Portree, Isle of Skye	17/7/61	355 702	15-23/12/60	2/1/61	–
260	RH	492 572	W. Watson, Birkenhead, Merseyside	2/3/61	355 719	15-20/12/60	22/12/60	–
261	RH	492 567	Not Known	28/1/61	355 721	15-20/12/60	21/12/60	–
262	RH	492 569	Stewart & Ardern, Acton, London	22/2/61	355 725	15-20/12/60	21/12/60	–
263	RH	492 588	Caffyns, Meads Road, Eastbourne	29/3/61	355 443	15-20/12/60	22/12/60	–
264	RH	492 585	McLays Garage Ltd, East High St, Kirkintilloch	15/2/61	355 716	15-20/12/60	30/12/60	–
265	RH	478 683	T. Shipside Ltd, Worksop, Nottinghamshire	19/2/61	355 433	15-20/12/60	30/12/60	–
266	RH	478 998	Stewart & Ardern, Catford, London	6/2/61	355 720	15-20/12/60	21/12/60	–
267	RH	478 893	W. H. Johnson & Sons Ltd, St. James St, Kings Lynn, Norfolk	20/2/61	355 726	15-20/12/60	21/12/60	–
268	RH	477 125	Haslemere Motor Co., Woodbridge Rd, Guildford	9/2/61	355 717	15-20/12/60	21/12/60	–
269	RH	479 057	Colmore Depot Ltd, Station St, Birmingham	4/2/61	355 727	15-20/12/60	22/12/60	–
270	RH	479 037	Thomsons Motor Garage, Commercial Rd, Lerwick, Shetland	1/3/61	355 722	15-20/12/60	2/1/61	–
271	RH	478 884	Grosvenor Motor Co., Pepper St, Chester	20/3/61	355 729	15-28/12/60	2/1/61	–
272	RH	479 944	Stewart & Ardern	19/1/61	355 721	15-20/12/60	22/12/60	–
273	RH	492 507	Hewens Garages Ltd, Bridge Rd, Maidenhead, Berkshire	10/4/61	355 731	15-20/12/60	22/12/60	–
274	RH	492 504	P. S. Nicholson, High St, Elgin, Morayshire	21/6/61	355 732	15-29/12/60	3/1/60	–
275	RH	492 514	E. Sycamore & Son, Whytefield Rd, Ramsey, Huntingdon	7/2/61	355 370	15-21/12/60	23/12/60	–
276	RH	493 945	Western Garage Ltd, Wolborough St, Newton Abbot, Devon	20/3/61	355 718	15-20/12/60	23/12/60	–
277	RH	492 503	H. T. Price Ltd, Builth Motors, Builth Wells, Brecon	4/4/61	355 728	20-21/12/60	30/12/60	–
278	RH	492 177	Kennings Ltd, Sheffield	18/2/61	355 733	20/12/60	2/1/61	–
279	RH	478 884	Not Known	2/1/61	355 723	20-28/12/60	16/3/61	–
280	RH	503 725	Kennings Ltd, Sheffield	16/1/61	355 797	20-21/12/60	28/12/60	3358 VF
281	RH	503 763	Stewart & Ardern, Acton, London	7/3/61	355 796	20/12/60	22/12/60	–
282	RH	503 821	J. Cockshoot, Great Ducie St, Manchester	2/3/61	355 800	20/12/60	23/12/60	–
283	RH	503 706	Wessex Motors, Andover, Hampshire	9/2/61	355 984	20-21/12/60	29/12/60	–
284	RH	503 736	J. Cockshoot, Great Ducie St, Manchester	11/1/61	355 799	20-21/12/60	23/12/60	–
285	RH	503 695	Westover Motors, Bournemouth	31/1/61	355 790	20-21/12/60	23/12/60	–
286	RH	503 663	Bradburn & Wedge Ltd, Darlington St, Wolverhampton	–	355 802	20-21/12/60	29/12/60	–
287	RH	503 802	Lowndes Garages Ltd, Priory St, Carmarthen	28/1/61	355 804	20/12/60	21/12/60	MEJ 326
288	RH	504 123	Westfield Autocar Co., Westfield Ave, Edinburgh	21/1/61	355 782	20/12/60	28/12/60	–
289	RH	504 134	Stewart & Ardern, Golders Green, London	24/4/61	355 803	20/12/60	22/12/60	–
290	RH	504 007	Charles Buist Ltd, St Marys Place, Newcastle-on-Tyne	5/4/61	355 780	20-21/12/60	29/12/60	–
291	RH	504 133	T. Nice & Co., St. Marys, Ely, Cambridgeshire	8/3/61	355 692	20/12/60	21/12/60	MEB 93
292	RH	503 526	Stewart & Ardern	7/2/61	355 781	20/12/60	22/12/60	–
293	RH	504 121	Stewart & Ardern, Acton, London	24/2/61	355 779	20/12/60	22/12/60	9968 MH
294	RH	503 880	Kennings Ltd, Sheffield	21/4/61	355 771	20-21/12/60	23/12/60	–
295	RH	503 899	H. T. P. Motors Ltd, Truro, Cornwall	11/7/61	355 769	20/12/60	2/1/61	–
296	RH	504 002	W. Watson & Co., Bold St, Liverpool	11/5/61	355 580	20/12/60	22/12/60	–
297	RH	503 825	Kennings Ltd, Sheffield	1/2/61	355 774	20-21/12/60	23/12/60	–
298	RH	504 124	Wycliffe Motor Co., Stroud, Glos.	6/1/61	355 783	20-22/12/60	29/12/60	–
299	RH	492 146	Eastern Automobiles, London Rd, Chelmsford, Essex	7/3/61	355 770	20-29/12/60	30/12/60	–
300	RH	492 230	Grosvenor Motor Co., Pepper St, Chester	4/3/61	355 786	20/12/60	22/12/60	–

Morris Minor Million Production Record Trace 1,000,301 – 1,000,350

Chasis No.	RH / LH	Eng.No.	Dealers Name & Address	Dealer Sale	Body Number	Production Date	Dispatch	Registration No.
301	RH	503 661	Adam Purves & Son, Market St, Galashiels	28/2/61	355 777	20-22/12/60	30/12/60	LS 8338
302	RH	503 598	Barton Motor Co., Hyde Park Corner, Plymouth	6/1/61	355 787	20-22/12/60	23/12/60	880 KYD
303	RH	503 817	City Motor Co., City Rd, Cardiff	4/3/61	355 792	20/12/60	29/12/60	
304	RH	503 819	Charles Buist Ltd, St Marys Place, Newcastle-on-Tyne	19/1/61	355 795	20/12/60	22/12/60	–
305	RH	503 747	Bradburn & Wedge Ltd, Darlington St, Wolverhampton	24/1/61	355 785	20-21/12/60	29/12/60	–
306	RH	504 004	Not Known	–	355 794	20-21/12/60	22/12/60	–
307	RH	503 732	Barton Motor Co., Hyde Park Corner, Plymouth	24/1/61	355 789	20-21/12/60	29/12/60	299 GUO
308	RH	503 662	Wellsteeds Country Garage, Newport, Gwent	7/1/61	355 772	20-28/12/60	2/1/61	–
309	RH	503 527	Parkside Garage Ltd, Warwick Rd, Coventry	23/3/61	355 776	20/12/60	22/12/60	–
310	RH	440 101	W. Watson, Birkenhead, Merseyside	17/3/61	355 791	20-21/12/60	22/12/60	–
311	RH	494 038	Colmore Depot Ltd, Station St, Birmingham	28/2/61	355 785	21/12/60	22/12/60	–
312	RH	494 037	A & D Fraser Ltd, Springkell Ave, Glasgow	24/1/61	355 793	21/12/60	22/12/60	–
313	RH	494 036	Stewart & Ardern	23/1/61	355 775	21/12/60	22/12/60	–
314	RH	494 034	Bristol Motor Co., Ashton Gate, Bristol	19/4/61	355 853	21-22/12/60	28/12/60	–
315	RH	494 089	C. K. Andrews Ltd, Upland Garage, Swansea	8/7/61	355 851	20-21/12/60	22/12/60	–
316	RH	494 087	W. H. Alexander, Victoria St, Belfast	21/2/61	355 801	21-22/12/60	23/12/60	–
317	RH	494 085	Brittians Ltd, Preston Rd, Brighton	12/7/61	355 849	21-22/12/60	29/12/60	612 CPO
318	RH	494 083	Stewart & Ardern	21/1/61	355 847	21/12/60	22/12/60	7290 MV
319	RH	492 443	Westover Garage, Bournemouth	4/4/61	355 848	21/12/60	28/12/60	RJT 630
320	RH	492 462	James Fryer Ltd, Aubrey St, Hereford	7/3/61	355 854	21-22/12/60	29/12/60	–
321	RH	492 454	W. H. Alexander, Victoria St, Belfast	1/3/61	355 852	21-22/12/60	28/12/60	–
322	RH	504 169	Bath Garages Ltd, James St, West Bath	28/3/61	355 857	21-22/12/60	6/1/61	LGL 815
323	RH	504 213	Kennings Ltd, Clay Cross, Chesterfield, Derbyshire	17/2/61	355 846	21/12/60	23/12/60	–
324	RH	504 120	Stewart & Ardern	24/1/61	355 855?	21-22/12/60	22/12/60	–
325	RH	504 007	Automobile Palace Ltd, Temple St, Llandrindod Wells	3/2/61	355 855?	21-22/12/60	29/12/60	–
326	RH	504 212	Barton Motor Co., Hyde Park Corner, Plymouth	30/3/61	355 856	21/12/60	28/12/60	–
327	RH	503 733	W. H. Alexander, Victoria St, Belfast	19/5/61	355 850	20-22/12/60	28/12/60	–
328	RH	489 260	Lowndes Garages Ltd, Priory St, Carmarthen	7/3/61	355 773	20-21/12/60	29/12/60	MEJ 496
329	RH	489 259	Wessex Motors, Andover, Hampshire	4/4/61	355 778	20-22/12/60	29/12/60	XWV 703
330	RH	484 680	James McHarrie Ltd, Gountry Garage, Stranraer	1/4/61	354 171	22-25/11/60	21/12/61	EOS 444
Originally Chassis No. 881386								
331	LH	497 868	North America Export No. 73495	–	355 538	14/12/60	15/12/60	–
332	LH	497 270	North America Export No. 73496	–	355 494	14-15/12/60	15/12/60	–
333	LH	497 259	North America Export No. 73497	–	355 540	14-15/12/60	15/12/60	–
334	LH	497 256	North America Export No. 73498	–	355 541	14-15/12/60	15/12/60	–
335	LH	497 863	North America Export No. 73499	–	355 529	14/12/60	15/12/60	–
336	LH	497 862	North America Export No. 73500	–	355 515	14/12/60	15/12/60	–
337	LH	497 861	North America Export No. 73501	–	355 543	14-15/12/60	15/12/60	–
338	LH	497 864	North America Export No. 73502	–	355 542	14-15/12/60	15/12/60	–
339	LH	497 857	North America Export No. 73503	–	355 482	14-15/12/60	15/12/60	–
340	LH	497 865	North America Export No. 73504	–	355 544	14/12/60	15/12/60	–
341	LH	497 858	North America Export No. 73505	–	355 507	14-15/12/60	15/12/60	–
342	LH	497 866	North America Export No. 73506	–	355 537	14-15/12/60	15/12/60	–
343	LH	497 959	North America Export No. 73507	–	355 526	14-21/12/60	23/12/60	–
344	LH	497 129	North America Export No. 73508	–	355 536	14-15/12/60	15/12/60	–
345	LH	497 246	North America Export No. 73509	–	355 518	14-15/12/60	15/12/60	–
346	LH	495 949	North America Export No. 73510	–	355 534	14-15/12/60	15/12/60	–
347	LH	497 126	North America Export No. 73511	–	355 539	14-15/12/60	15/12/60	–
348	LH	497 202	North America Export No. 73512	–	355 506	14-19/12/60	20/12/60	–
349	LH	497 870	North America Export No. 73513	–	355 527	14-20/12/60	20/12/60	CF 9647

MMOC Minor Million Register

The Minor Million Register was formed as part of the Morris Minor Owners Club (UK) in the late 1970's. The aim of the Register is to bring together owners with a common interest in the Minor Million vehicles.

The register has about 70 on record but there must still be more out there. If you know of an owner or spot a lilac wonder hidden somewhere then Phil Smith (Minor Million Register) would be delighted to hear from you... so keep your eyes peeled for glimpses of lilac!

minormillion@mac.com

WRV 135

264 KJQ

790 TPB

Concours

Aiming For Concours

Right from the outset, the intention was to complete the restoration of the Million to Concours standard. Meticulous attention to detail at every stage meant that this objective was achievable, even if at times there was the temptation to over-elaborate in the finish applied to some components. In spite of Richard's extreme enthusiasm, the process was helped by the fact that both Bill and Richard, apart from being accomplished home based restorers, are experienced judges, having judged Concours vehicles at local, regional, and National Morris Minor events in Australia.

Not every aspiring Concours competitor will be so fortunate. In this concluding section of "One in a Million", some information, advice and guidance is offered about preparing and presenting a vehicle for entry to Concours competition. A summary of both the British and Australian judging systems has been included, along with some generic advice which, if followed, should provide entrants with a head start in being successful in Concours competition.

For the purposes of continuity, in this final section the word Concours will be used, even though in Australia and in other parts of the world the term 'Concourse' has been adopted. Whether it's 'Concours' or 'Concourse' the term is essentially an abbreviation of the French phrase Concours d' Elegance which referred to the presentation of vehicles in the most elegant and perfect way.

In the 21st century Classic Car scene in Britain, this has been interpreted to mean that vehicles should be presented as they would have appeared when they left the vehicle production line as a new vehicle.

Elsewhere, as in Australia, while this holds true for certain categories, the scope of the categories accepted for judging has been expanded to reflect developments since the vehicles were first built. Consequently categories exist for uprated and modified vehicles.

Morris Minor Owners Club Ltd Concours – UK Judging Guidelines and Information

Concours competition has been an integral part of the Rally Scene within the Morris Minor Owners Club in the UK for many years. It is seen as something to aspire to for members wishing to present their vehicles in a manner, which reflects the original specification and standard of build when the vehicle left the factory. Unlike the Australian system there are no distinctions made between original and restored vehicles in terms of individual classes or categories.

As a great deal of time and effort is required in preparing and showing a vehicle to these exacting standards, it is important that there is a high, yet consistent standard of judging. It is essential that this is seen to be fair and professional in all aspects of its operation. To this end a Chief Judge is appointed with the express responsibility of overseeing the organisation and conduct of the judging. It is his/her responsibility to implement the agreed rules in a fair and unbiased way, within a rigorous system, where clear guidelines are presented and agreed to by all competitors. An intrinsic part of this is the acceptance, that within the rules set out, the ruling of the Chief Judge is final in the event of any dispute arising.

Within the Morris Minor Owners Club, the system of organising Concours has developed considerably since its inception. There are now some clearly established categories.

In 2010 these were as follows:

Concours Categories

Concours Status	Mark Band
Concours	650 – 799
Masters Class	800 – 919
Grand Masters	920 – 1000

Any vehicle can be entered in Concours regardless of its previous judging history. Vehicles achieving above the entry level of 650 marks will be invited to continue to compete in Concours events.

Owners of vehicles failing to achieve the entry level requirements will be advised on areas for improvement and invited to resubmit their vehicle at a future time.

Grand Masters Status

Grand Masters is the ultimate achievement within the MMOC Concours. It is generally accepted that vehicles achieving this accolade are probably better than when they left the factory. Owners opting for this category are striving for perfection.

Entry to Grand Masters is normally restricted to those vehicles that have achieved Masters Class status already (800 – 919 marks) and which have a realistic chance of securing 920+ marks on a regular basis. Normally vehicles in this category are judged on a set number of occasions during one rally season, one of which must be the annual National Rally.

Within the MMOC guidelines there are a number of penalties and restrictions which have been adopted as custom and practice over the years. These include three main areas.

1. **Transportation of vehicles by trailer**

   The transportation of a vehicle to, and/or from any MMOC event at which it is to be judged is prohibited. If it is known prior to judging that a vehicle has been trailered, the Chief Judge will advise the entrant that the vehicle is not eligible for judging. If after the results have been announced, it is discovered that a vehicle was transported by trailer on any part of its journey to or from the event, both the persons involved and the vehicle will be subject to a one year ban from competition.

2. **Lifting of vehicles**

   No vehicles should be raised from the ground in the Concours Display area or any other designated judging areas. Primarily this ruling relates to health and safety, as most of the judging tends to take place on grassed areas where the ground is uneven.

3. **Restrictions on Converted Saloons**

   While converted saloons are accepted into all categories of Concours, except Grand Masters, the vehicles are subject to an automatic 50-point penalty, which is deducted at the end of the judging process. The conversion must have been completed as per factory specification for a Tourer or Convertible model.

Judging Arrangements

Arrangements for judging are subject to strict regulation so as to ensure fairness amongst entrants, and to assist the judges in organising an appropriate schedule, in order to complete the judging in the limited time available.

All vehicles entered must be insured, have a current MOT certificate and display a valid tax disc. Specialised judging mark sheets have been developed over time and are reviewed on an annual basis. Regardless of which style of sheet is used there are four fixed judging categories. These are Engine Bay, Interior, Underside and Exterior.

Originality Checklist

An originality checklist has been devised to complement the Judging mark sheet. This itemises where bonus marks can be awarded for particular original features. It also itemises specific penalties that are applied for non-original features including modifications and upgrades and over embellishment of parts.

In the interest of fairness and in the event of a vehicle achieving marks that are close to the threshold between categories, it may be appropriate for a second opinion to be sought from an experienced judge within the team. Adjustments must not exceed 3% of the total marks allocated. Although it may seem to the outsider to be a little over the top, provisions are made for circumstances where there may be a need for a tie-break decision. Would be Concours competitors may be interested in the procedures adopted in such circumstances.

Checks may be made on one or more of the following.

- Oil level.
- Cleanliness of oil.
- Engine tick-over.
- Accuracy of recommended tyre pressures.
- Cleanliness of the inside of one hub cap.

Australian Judging Categories

The Australian Concours judging system has developed over time and reflects the wider diversity of Morris Minor usage 'down under'.

Essentially there are five main categories and as the following information reveals, while the 'as they left the factory' ruling applies in some categories, it does not apply to all. All vehicles entered in the Australian Concours classes must be in roadworthy condition and have the requisite club registration plates and appropriate road worthiness certificate. Entrants must comply with this regulation or face possible disqualification from being judged.

1. Original

A vehicle that has not been altered since coming off the production line, except for normal routine maintenance and the replacement of parts due to normal usage.

Allowed:

- Rust repairs to body and panels
- Normal mechanical maintenance
- Club registration number plates
- 1000 rims on Series II vehicles
- In-line fuel systems and other modifications for unleaded fuel
- Not in everyday use

Disallowed:

- Complete respray
- Complete seat/interior re-trim
- Seat covers, floor mats
- Major repairs to body/panels
- Chrome work in the engine bay

2. Restored

A vehicle that has been restored as closely as possible to that of its original specification, using original or reproduction parts and materials.

Allowed:

- Complete respray (original colour/s only)
- Complete interior re-trim (as above)
- Major repairs to body and panels
- Club registration number plates
- 1000 rims on Series II vehicles
- In-line fuel systems and other modifications for unleaded fuel
- Not in everyday use

Disallowed:

- Non-original components/presentation
- Chrome work in the engine bay

NOTE: If a vehicle was restored and then have been in everyday use for a period exceeding two years, entrant may choose to enter in Maintained Class.

3. Maintained

A vehicle in Original or Restored condition which must be in everyday use.

Allowed:

Additional safety features required by relevant Motor Transport bodies

- Seat belts
- Flashing turn indicators
- Mud flaps
- Radio in keeping with the period of the vehicle
- 1000 rims on Series II vehicles
- Brake booster (VH 44)
- In-line fuel systems and other modifications for unleaded fuel

Disallowed:

- Vehicles restored within two years (four years in the case of the bi-annual National Rally).
- Club registration number plates
- Chrome work in the engine bay

4. Modified A (Morris/BMC/Leyland sourced)

This category is for vehicles with the motor, transmission and rear-end sourced from BMC, with bolt-on modifications to the running gear.

Allowed:

Any motor sourced from either Morris, BMC or Leyland and fitted without any modifications or cuts to the bodywork.

Any transmission sourced from either Morris, BMC, or Leyland.

- Wide wheels retaining MM centres
- Larger Morris drum brakes
- Brake boosters
- Twin carburettors
- Extractors
- Bolt on tail lights
- Sports steering wheel
- Additional gauges (max. of 3 – oil, temp, amp or vacuum.) Original gauges must remain.

Disallowed:

- Any motor or transmission other than Morris, BMC, or Leyland
- Changes to upholstery
- Non standard paint
- Any item specified in Modified B
- Any item specified in Custom Class

NOTE: Vehicles entered in modified classes are allowed mechanical and interior modifications to improve performance, safety and comfort, but exterior body work is to remain unaltered.

Modified B

A vehicle with Morris, BMC, Leyland or any other engine and transmission, requiring no major body cuts/alterations to install motor or transmission.

Allowed:

- Disc brakes
- Telescopic shock absorbers
- Any type of wheels (must fit under body)
- Any differential (original spring mounts must be used)
- Any seats (front and rear trim to match)
- Metallic paint

Disallowed:

Any item specified in custom class.

Vehicles entered in modified classes are allowed mechanical and interior modifications to improve performance, safety and comfort, but exterior body work is to remain unaltered.

5. Custom A and B Classification Classes

Anything goes in these categories. Cars may even resemble spaceships! Typical departures from original include:

- Non standard seats or trim
- Recessed aerial
- Bubble windows
- Chrome work in engine bay
- Spoiler (front)
- Changes of front guards (low light to high light or vice versa)
- Recessed number plates
- Recessed lights
- Louvres/flutes

Vehicle Preparation and Presentation

Anyone serious about competing in Concours would be well advised to acquaint themselves with the judging rules and procedures. Most organisations have a set of guidelines, and a list of members who are willing to give impartial advice and guidance. Whatever category the vehicle is being entered into there are two guiding principles. Ensure that the vehicle complies with the regulations in terms of originality or modification and always make sure that the vehicle is presented in the best possible manner. The following guidance is offered to prospective Concours competitors. For ease of reference, extracts have been taken from a sample judging sheet and comments have been added to explain what the expectations are in terms of the standards expected in preparing and presenting the vehicle.

Interior

SECTION ONE *INTERIOR CONDITION*		MARK	-	+	TOTAL	AMEND
1. Condition of carpets and underfelt.	30			XX		
2. Condition of upholstery, stitching and wear / seat belts.	40					
3. Condition, interior trim, seat frames, pedal rubbers, door panels / headlining.	30					
4. Interior fitments, dash panel gauges, glove box, parcel tray, control knobs, gear lever, steering wheel column, hand brake, heater.	50			XX		
5. Load carrying area, tools, spare wheel, handbook and any other literature.	60					
6. Overall cleanliness of interior.	**40**	➤➤➤	➤➤➤	➤➤➤		
				TOTAL		

Interior fitments as outlined on the judging schedule shown are all subject to close inspection in Concours judging. For most entrants the most difficult decision is whether to replace the original interior, with new seat covers, door cards, carpets etc. Fortunately most parts are available new, albeit at a price. Some people feel that by doing so, part of the original character of the vehicle is lost forever. The balance can be redressed in some judging scenarios if an originality checklist is used. The additional marks added for originality can counterbalance any deductions which might be made for wear and tear.

The headlining is another area which needs careful thought. Condition, fit, and general appearance are all important considerations. The headlining saga outlined on pages 48-52 is worthy of consideration before embarking on replacing a headlining. A less than perfect fit is likely to result in a deduction of marks.

Attention to detail in the interior section is particularly important. Judges tend to look at how clean everything is.
Items such as the windows, the driving mirror, instrument glasses and interior light lenses must be spotless.
The same goes for seats, door cards, and carpets.

Areas not immediately visible, such as the carpet underfelt, the parcel shelf and glove box interiors all tend to be inspected.
The same goes for seat belts, if they have been fitted. Checks are usually made to see if the edges are frayed and if the mounting points are secure.

The fit and condition of door seals are also included in the checklist, as is the condition of pedal rubbers and the rubber heel-pad on the carpet. Other considerations include the general condition of all painted items such as the dash board, the gear lever and the hand brake. All should be painted in the appropriate colour and be free of scratches, chips and any evidence of paint fade or overspray. The steering wheel should be properly centred and be free of cracks and blemishes. The steering column should be painted in the appropriate colour and, where it meets the carpeted area at its base, be free of oil which can cause unsightly staining. Reference to the judging sheet *(above)* shows that in the UK, the boot loading area is included in the interior judging section.

Apart from the general condition of the wooden boot floors, or covered floor area in the case of Traveller models, the inner wings and the spare wheel storage area, it is expected that the original type tool kit with the accompanying tool roll will be presented for examination. The content of the kit, as well as its condition and the way it is presented will all be given consideration when marks are being awarded. Many entrants choose to add additional information such as the original handbook or workshop manual. Some even include the original bill of sale or a Heritage certificate to authenticate the history of the vehicle.

Paint and General Exterior

SECTION TWO *PAINT AND GENERAL EXTERIOR*		MARK	-	+	TOTAL	AMEND
1. Alignment / fitting of all panels, wings, doors, bonnet, traveller wood chopped convertible and hood (erect for judging).	60			XX		
2. Condition of bumper valances and paintwork under wings.	50			XX		
3. Chrome plating, brightwork, fit and finish.	30			XX		
4. Windows, frames, screen, rubbers, wiper arms and blades (washers).	40			XX		
5. Standard of exterior paint work, wing piping, traveller wood or hood.	30			XX		
6. Overall cleanliness of exterior.	**40**	➤➤➤➤➤➤➤➤➤				
				TOTAL		

First appearances count for a lot. Time spent making sure the exterior of the vehicle is scrupulously clean and well polished will be reflected not only in the paintwork, but in the allocation of higher marks. Paintwork should have a high lustre and be free of residues of polish. Ideally there should be no obvious polishing marks in the paint itself, or any signs of overspray, sinkage or blemishes caused by scratches, dents or reactions to other substances.

Wing piping should be present, and be an appropriate colour match, as per the original specification. Using silicone filler as a replacement for wing piping will normally be penalised. Body panels should be free of any dents or damage and there should be no ripples evident in the flat panels or any sign of bubbling, due to rust, on the bottom edges.

The alignment of all panels is an important consideration. Gaps between adjacent panels such as doors and guards/wings, and between panels and the body, such as the bonnet and boot lid, and the body should be evenly spaced allowing the correct profile to be maintained. The condition of the front and rear valances, where fitted, should be carefully checked. These panels tend to be quite flimsy and can be easily damaged. During the documented restoration great care was taken with the alignment of the front valance to make sure it sat flush with the bottom edge of the front wings. Often alignment is poor and this detracts from the overall appearance of the front of the vehicle. Making sure the rubber spacers are properly located can help alleviate this problem.

An area which is often overlooked is the condition of the paintwork on the underside of the front and rear guards/wings.

Judges are advised to check carefully for signs of road grime and to see whether the paint colour and quality is similar to the rest of the exterior. Underseal is a definite 'No-no' in the case of top Concours cars. In the UK, this was a dealer added option. Consequently it does not form part of the 'as it left the factory' specification.

Other exterior items requiring attention are all the chrome plated components. Given that all Morris Minors are at least forty years old, much of the chrome work is likely to have been replaced with new old stock (NOS) or reproduction items. However, fit as well as appearance is taken into consideration when judging occurs.

Care must also be taken to remove any excess polish which may have accumulated on badges and edges of escutcheon plates.

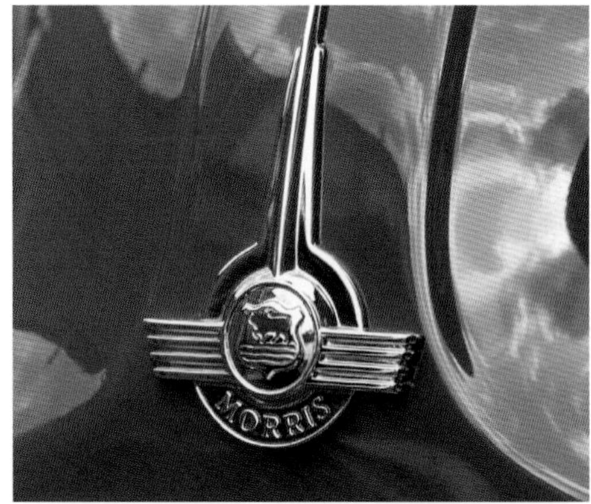

Engine Bay

SECTION THREE ENGINE BAY		MARK	-	+	TOTAL	AMEND
1. Condition of bulkhead, inner wings, tie plates and underside of bonnet.	30			XX		
2. Exhaust, manifold, front shock absorbers, radiator, hoses and clips.	40			XX		
3. Engine ancillaries, carburettor, distributor, dynamo, aircleaner & fuel pump.	60			XX		
4. Engine block, head rocker cover, sump, plug leads and caps (tick over).	50			XX		
5. Wiring harness, battery, battery terminals, regulator & fuse holder.	30					
6. Overall cleanliness of engine bay.	**40**	➤➤➤➤➤➤➤➤➤➤				
				TOTAL		

Of all the sections considered for judging the engine bay is perhaps the most intricate. With so many different components to contend with, and the potential for fuel leakage, it is also one of the most difficult areas to keep clean and present well.
The expectation at Concours level is that the paintwork on the bulkhead/firewall, inner wings, tie plates and the underside of the bonnet will be of a similar standard and lustre to the rest of the vehicle. The engine/motor should be painted in the correct colour and be spotlessly clean and free of any oil residue.

Components fitted should be appropriate for the age and original specification of the vehicle. Exceptions to this rule apply in some of the Australian categories, but generally speaking the aim should be to fit original type components to vehicles being entered in original and restored categories. It is particularly important in this section to avoid the over restoration of individual components and the chroming of certain items such as the rocker cover or the carburettor.
The tendency to over polish is also frowned upon for judging purposes. Components susceptible to this treatment include shock absorbers, aluminium bodied coils and radiator and oil filler caps.

Electrical components are scrutinised in order to examine the overall condition of the wiring harness, all associated connections and the condition of any additional wiring which may have been added. Marks tend to be deducted if the wiring harness is dirty or frayed, if the electrical connectors to individual components are dirty, or non standard connectors have been installed.

The overall condition of the battery tray, the method by which the battery has been secured and the type of battery fitted are all examined and appraised. Many Concours competitors go to great lengths to fit the larger style rubber cased batteries which were originally fitted to Morris Minors in the 1950's and 1960's.

Checks are also made for any sign of leaks, either from the carburettor, the engine or the radiator and the condition and alignment of all hoses, clips, nuts, bolts and screws are checked. Marks are deducted if damaged, excessively worn or dirty fastenings have been used.

At most outdoor Morris Minor Concours events in the UK, the functioning of the electrical components is tested. The operation of the lights, indicators and the horn are checked, as is the operation of the engine, which is checked for the rate of tick over.

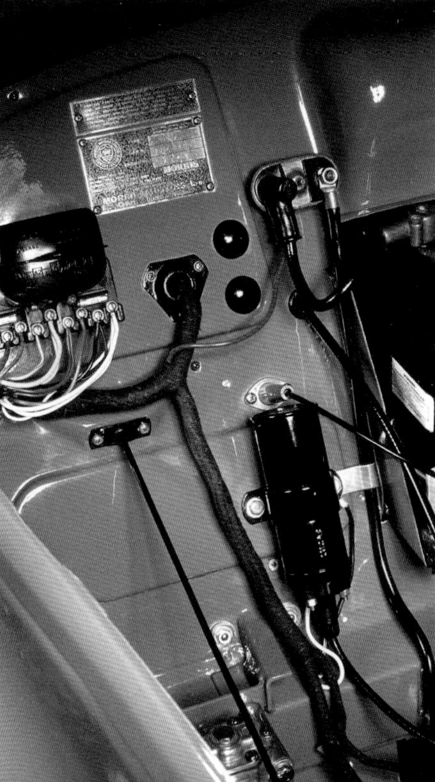

Chassis Underside

SECTION FOUR *CHASSIS UNDERSIDE*		MARK	-	+	TOTAL	AMEND
1. Tyres, wheels, wheel discs.	30			XX		
2. Complete underside, restoration technique (welding / painting), brake pipes, fuel pipes & fuel tank.	40					
3. Front suspension, rear axle, springs, shock absorbers, prop-shaft, gearbox.	60			XX		
4. Originality of vehicle taking into account over restoration, excess chrome, crackle finishes, consistency of polishing, and over polishing etc.	40			XX		
5. Road tax, number plates, lights, horn & flashers etc. (check working)	30					
6. Overall cleanliness of chassis underside.	**40**	➤➤➤➤➤➤➤➤➤➤				
				TOTAL		

The underside of the vehicle is perhaps the most overlooked area as far as presenting Concours vehicles is concerned. Expectations in this section are just as rigorous as they are for the rest of the vehicle. Perhaps for reasons relating to the ease of access to the underside of the vehicle, many entrants fall short in presenting the underside to the standard expected. The methods adopted in painting the Morris Minor bodyshell at the factory ensured that the underside was painted the same colour as the rest of the vehicle. This is the standard ruling for Concours judging, though some relaxation of the regulations has emerged since the advent of stone chipping. This application which provides additional protection for the whole of the underside, including the underside of wings/guards, is gaining acceptance, provided the finish applied, is the same body colour as the rest of the vehicle.

The underside will be examined for evidence of structural repairs and to see how well any welding has been done. Distortion of panels and failure to grind back areas which have been subject to repair will incur penalties. The key areas judges tend to examine are the central crossmember, particularly the jacking points at either side, spring hanger mounting points and the front chassis rails which have a tendency to be damaged through the incorrect jacking up of the vehicle or being badly repaired at some time in the past.

Checks will also be made on all the suspension components as part of this section. It is becoming commonplace for a lot of the components including rear springs, front suspension legs, prop/tail shaft, tie bars as well as the back axle and differential to be powder coated in black. This has the advantage of allowing easier cleaning, as well as providing longer term rust proofing. The correct silver colouring of the torsion bars will also be subject to scrutiny. Attention is paid to the condition of suspension rubbers, brake pipes and fuel lines as well as the appearance and condition of the fuel tank and all associated fittings. The use of metal retaining clips to secure the brake pipes to the rear axle will also be checked as will the fitting of bleed nipple covers and the correct application of locking nuts on the U bolts. In the event of plastic tie wraps being used to secure the brake pipes marks will be deducted. Some relaxation of the 'as it left the factory' criteria has occurred in relation to the exhaust system. The use of stainless steel systems has become accepted practice.

Road wheels and tyres are an important consideration too. Wheels should have an even profile, be free of dented edges and have a good quality paint finish in the correct colour for the age of the vehicle. Wheels should be painted to the same standard inside and out, and have a good finish applied to the recessed area of the wheel. Tyres should be roadworthy and free of any signs of perishing on the side wall, or flat spots on the tread pattern. The same brand of tyre must be fitted all round including the spare tyre. It is usual in competition for the tyres to be painted with tyre-wall black or polished with black shoe polish. The tread must be free of mud or stones and the hub caps must be free of rust and be polished brightly.

For those with an eye for detail, wheels can be carefully fitted so that the valves are all in the same relative position. For those then wishing to add the perfect finish, the hub caps can be aligned so that the M motif, if present, matches perfectly on each side.

That may be taking things a touch too far, as it is unlikely that as Morris Minors rolled off the assembly lines in assembly plants around the world, that the workers took such care when fitting the wheels and hub caps. However, to do so might just make your Morris Minor "One in a Million".

The money shot!

Morris Minor Owners Club – The world's largest car club

Based in the UK and with a membership of 12,500, the Morris Minor Owners Club is a highly regarded source of knowledge and information. For a very modest annual subscription, members can take advantage of cheaper insurance and travel, technical advice, discounted spares and a calendar of events organised by an active network of over 60 branches.

Minor Matters the Club publication is a professionally produced, full-colour magazine with supplements for junior members and classified advertisements.

Other active Morris Minor Clubs exist throughout the world. In Australia there are in excess of 20 Morris Minor Car Clubs. Richard and Ray strongly recommend joining your local Morris Minor Car Club in order to enjoy all that the Club scene has to offer.

Parts and Suppliers

Richard and Bill highly recommend the companies below and would like to thank them for supplying the quality parts and services that brought 1,000,086 back to life.

UK Suppliers

Spares

Bull Motif Spares
Reardene Workshops, Cleeve Road
Middle Littleton, Worcestershire WR11 8JR
info@bullmotif.com
www.bullmotif.com

Charles Ware's Morris Minor Centre
20 Clothier Road, Brislington
Bristol BS4 5PS
morris.minor@ukonline.co.uk
www.morrisminor.org.uk

Morris Minor Owners Club
gostling@mmoc.org.uk
www.mmoc.org.uk

Morris Minor Centre (Birmingham) Ltd
993 Wolverhampton Road, Oldbury
West Midlands B69 4JR
info@morrisminor.co.uk
www.morrisminor.co.uk

Woodies – S T Foreman
Unit 25 Eastmead Industrial Estate
Lavant, Chichester West Sussex PO18 0DB
forwoodies@aol.com
www.morriswoodwork.co.uk

Upholstery

Newton Commercial
sales@newtoncomm.co.uk
www.newtoncomm.co.uk

Australian Suppliers

Paint

Perrows Automotive Paints
47 Breen Street, Bendigo
Victoria 3550
www.perrows.com.au

Paint Protection

Toughseal Australasia
5 George Street, Spotswood
Victoria 3015
info@toughseal.com.au
www.toughseal.com.au

Rubber Components

Scott's Old Auto Rubber
18a Haughton Road, Oakleigh
Victoria 3166
scott@scottsoldautorubber.com.au
www.scottsoldautorubber.com.au

Sales Brochures & Collectables

QMC – Quality Motoring Collectables
26 Splitrock Road, Beaconsfield Upper
Victoria 3803
kate@qualitymotoringcollectables.com.au
www.qualitymotoringcollectables.com.au

Spares

Morris Minor Australia
Thorpe – 56 Alex Avenue
Moorabbin Victoria 3189
+61 3 9555 1793

Upholstery

C & N Vehicle Trimming Pty Ltd
5 Douglas Street Sunshine North
Victoria 3020
+61 3 9331 0722

Tyres

Antique Tyre Supplies
134 McEwan Road, West Heidelberg
Victoria 3081
info@antiquetyres.com.au
www.antiquetyres.com.au

Wheel Repairs

Ajax Motor Wheels
Cnr Exley Drive & Ewar Street
Moorabbin Victoria 3189
+61 3 9555 7737

Copyright Permissions

Poem

Our Country
by Dorothea MacKellar
(first published 1908)
pippa@curtisbrown.com.au

BMC publicity brochures & technical drawings

Heritage Motor Centre
Banbury Road
Gaydon, Warwick CV35 0BJ
www.heritage-motor-centre.co.uk

Jack Field image

Practical Classics
www.practicalclassics.co.uk

1,000,000 (1MHU) Photographs

Richard & Neil Elderfield

THE PARTS LISTED IN THE FOLLOWING PAGES ARE APPLICABLE ONLY TO THE MINOR 1,000,000 2-DOOR SALOON. ALL OTHER COMPONENTS CAN BE FOUND IN THE MAIN BODY OF THE LIST, PAGES A.1 TO T.5 INCLUSIVE.

Photography Phil Smith

Illustrations by Better World Ltd.
Published by Better World Ltd.

GICAL TOUR OF CHINA

INTERMEDIATE LEVEL CURRICULUM

Sampler Pack

t for Sale or Distribution ~

BetterChinese

…词表，中、英、汉语拼音三种文稿，方便学习。
…实例演示为主，并配有实用性练习。
…国文字、语句、文化三部分，总体上语言与文化并重，既提高学生的中文水平，又增
…化知识。

…四册，每册9集，一共36集故事。每册有配套的练习册、光盘和Audio CD，还
…etterChinese.com 的支持。

…**f China** follows three American families who visit Beijing for the first time to …nese culture and language. This series consists of four volumes, each with nine …tal of 36 lessons. There are accompanying Workbook, CD-ROM, and Audio CD … Online lessons and exercises are available at www.BetterChinese.com.

…lents in a non-native Chinese speaking environment, the features of Magical Tour of

…uage fluency to meet guidelines of the Advanced Placement (AP) test.
…onal Standard's 5C (communication, cultures, connections, comparisons,
…s) principles of teaching foreign languages.
…ry topics with emphasis on authenticity of content.
…of multimedia materials to build communicative

…, spiral-up approach to reinforce learning.
…, full-colored comic book lesson format
…e learning appeal.
… cultural insights, including the
…ritten characters and popular
…ich enable students to achieve
… in Chinese language and culture.

…世界　华夏文化
…绰约　采撷精品

…, 2010

…L TOUR OF CHINA **Sampler Pack** 奇妙中国游 样书